Children and Youth in Adoption, Orphanages, and Foster Care

Children and Youth in Adoption, Orphanages, and Foster Care

A Historical Handbook and Guide

EDITED BY LORI ASKELAND

Children and Youth: History and Culture
Miriam Forman-Brunell, Series Editor

GREENWOOD PRESS
Westport, Connecticut • London

362.730973
C536

Library of Congress Cataloging-in-Publication Data

Children and youth in adoption, orphanages, and foster care : a historical handbook and guide / edited by Lori Askeland.
      p.   cm.—(Children and youth: history and culture, ISSN 1546–6752)
    Includes bibliographical references and index.
    ISBN 0–313–33183–9 (alk. paper)
    1. Adoption—United States—History. 2. Adoption—United States—History—
Sources. 3. Orphanages—United States—History. 4. Orphanages—United States—
History—Sources. 5. Foster children—United States—History. 6. Foster
children—United States—History—Sources. 7. Child welfare—United States—History.
8. Child welfare—United States—History—Sources. I. Askeland, Lori. II. Series:
Children and youth (Westport, Conn.)
  HV875.55.C45   2006
  362.73'0973—dc22   2005022189

British Library Cataloguing in Publication Data is available.

Library of Congress Catalog Card Number: 2005022189
ISBN: 0–313–33183–9
ISSN: 1546–6752

First published in 2006

Greenwood Press, 88 Post Road West, Westport, CT 06881
An imprint of Greenwood Publishing Group, Inc.
www.greenwood.com

Printed in the United States of America

The paper used in this book complies with the
Permanent Paper Standard issued by the National
Information Standards Organization (Z39.48–1984).

10 9 8 7 6 5 4 3 2 1

Copyright Acknowledgments

The editor and publisher gratefully acknowledge permission for use of the following material:

Adoptions from the Heart. "Future Contract Agreement, New York." Copyright 2005. All rights reserved. Used by permission.

Bastard Nation: The Adoptee Rights Organization. "Mission Statement" and excerpts from "The Basic Bastard." Excerpted from the Bastard Nation website, http://www.bastards .org/. Copyright 2005. All rights reserved. Used by permission.

Buchwald, Arthur. From *Leaving Home: A Memoir*. Originally published by G. P. Putnam, now part of the Penguin Group. Copyright 1992. All Rights Reserved. Used by permission.

The Child Welfare League of America (CWLA). "Minimum Safeguards in Adoption." Approved by Vote of the Board of Directors of the Child Welfare League of America, November 5, 1938. Copyright 1938, CWLA Press. All rights reserved. This material appears by special permission of the publisher. Neither this publication nor any part thereof may be reproduced or transmitted in any form or by any means, electronic or mechanical, including photocopying, microfilming, and recording, or by any information storage and retrieval system, without permission in writing from the publisher. Child Welfare League of America, Washington, DC (http://www.cwla.org).

National Association of Black Social Workers. "Statement on Transracial Adoption." Copyright 1972. All rights reserved. Used by permission.

National Council for Adoption (NCFA). "Mission," "Agenda," "Concerned about Privacy?" ("Why Privacy?"), and "Correct Adoption Terminology," from the NCFA website, http://www.ncfa-usa.org/. Copyright 2004. All rights reserved. Used by permission.

Paton, Jean. Excerpt and drawing from *The Adopted Break Silence: The Experiences and Views of Forty Adults Who Were Once Adopted Children*. Philadelphia: Life History Study Center. Copyright 1954. All rights reserved. Used by permission.

Permanent Bureau of the Hague Conference on Private and International Law. "Convention of 29 May 1993 on Protection of Children and Co-operation in Respect of Intercountry Adoption," *Collection of Conventions, 1951–2003*. Antwerp, Belgium: Maklu Uitgevers N.V. Copyright 2003. All rights reserved. Used by permission.

Reed, Helen Doss. Excerpt from "All God's Children," chapter 12 of *The Family That Nobody Wanted*. Boston: Little, Brown. Copyright 1954. All rights reserved. Used by permission.

Contents

Series Foreword

Pocahontas, a legendary figure in American history, was just a preadolescent when she challenged two cultures at odds to cooperate instead of to compete. While Pocahontas forged peace, many more now forgotten Native American, Anglo-American, African American, and other children contributed to their families' survival, communities' development, and America's history in just as legitimate, though perhaps less legendary ways. Contracts and correspondence from colonial Chesapeake reveal that even seventeenth-century toddlers labored. But the historical agency of the vast majority of children and adolescents has been undervalued and overlooked in dominant historical narratives. Instead, generations of Americans have credited fathers and other hoary leaders for their actions and achievements, all the while disregarding pivotal boyhood experiences that shaped skills and ideals. Reflecting these androcentric, Eurocentric, and age-based biases that have framed the nation's history, American history texts have reinforced the historical invisibility of girls and boys for centuries. For students searching libraries for scholarly sources and primary documents about children and adolescents in various historical contexts, this near absence of information in master narratives has vexed their research.

The absence of children in standard history books has not only obscured children's history but also the work of scholars who have been investigating youth's histories and interrogating their cultures since the turn of the last century. A new curiosity about children in times past was generated by the progressive era agenda which sought to educate, acculturate, and elevate American children through child study and child welfare. In *Child Life in Colonial Days* (1899), "amateur historian" Alice Morse Earl drew upon archival sources and material culture in order to examine the social history of Puritan girls and boys. Children were also included in Arthur W. Calhoun's *A Social History of the American Family* (1917) and in Edmund S. Morgan's *The Puritan Family: Religion and Domestic Relations in Seventeenth Century New England* (1944), but few other professional historians within the male-dominated profession considered children worthy of study. Those children who made appearances in historical accounts were typically the privileged daughters and sons of white men of means and might.

In the 1960s, larger social, cultural, and political transformations refocused scholarly attention. The influence of sixties' youth culture and second wave feminism and renewed interest in the agency of "ordinary people," youth in particular, laid the foundation for a "new" social history. The confluence of a renewed interest in youth and the development of new methodological approaches led French demographer and social historian Philippe Ariès to study a nation's youngest population. Challenging a dominant assumption that childhood was transhistorical in *Centuries of Childhood: A Social History of Family Life* (1962), Ariès argued that over time, changing cultures and societies redefined notions of childhood and transformed children's experiences. Ariès work on European children was soon followed by Bernard Wishy's *The Child and the Republic: The Dawn of American Child Nurture* (1968), which explored the changing nature of child rearing advice in the United States.

Despite important inroads made by these and other scholars (e.g., Robert Bremner), the history of childhood became embedded within historical sub fields during the 1970s. The history of childhood was briefly associated with psychohistory due to the controversial work of Lloyd deMause who founded *The History of Childhood Quarterly*. It was largely historians of the family (e.g., John Demos, Philip Greven Jr.) and those in the history of education (who refocused attention away from the school and onto the student) who broke new ground. Essays appeared in scholarly journals in the 1970s but were not reprinted until the following decade when *Growing Up in America: Children in Historical Perspective* (1985) brought new visibility to the "vitality and scope of this emerging field" (preface). That important collection edited by historians Joseph M. Hawes and N. Ray Hiner, along with their *American Childhood: A Research Guide and Historical Handbook* (1985), served to promote research among an up-and-coming generation of historians whose work would be included in another path breaking anthology. By placing children at the center of historical inquiry, privileging gender as a critical factor in childhood socialization, and expanding social history to include cultural history, historians in *Small Worlds: Children and Adolescents in America, 1850–1950* (1992) demonstrated that the relationships between childhood and adulthood and kids and culture were historically significant. By privileging previously overlooked and disregarded historical sources, "reading" material culture artifacts as historical texts, and applying gender, race, and class analyses to an age-based one, these historians continued to the mapping of childhood's terrain. Creatively and methodically, they traced childhood ideals and children's experiences within cultures and over centuries.

In the early to mid 1990s, those in the fields of psychology and education initiated a scholarly debate about the dangers that popular culture posed to the healthy development of female adolescents in contemporary America. Those scholars influenced by a different scholarly trajectory—cultural studies and feminist theory—saw agency instead, illuminating the many ways in which girls and female adolescents (as other youth) resist, contest, subvert, and reappropriate dominant cultural forms. Moreover, scholars such as Kimberly Roberts brought to light the discursive nature of the contemporary "girl crisis" debate just as others have uncovered numerous other discourses that create, reflect, and reinforce the cultural norms of girlhood, boyhood, female and male adolescence. Trained in fields other than history (e.g., American Studies, communications studies, English, Rhetoric and Composition), the latest generation of scholars has blurred the boundaries and forged new fields. Informed by the work of cultural studies scholar Angela McRobbie, "girl's culture" aimed to balance the boy-centered biases of the older "youth studies." Nevertheless, such late twentieth-century anthologies as *The Children's Culture Reader* (1998), *Delinquents & Debutantes: Twentieth-Century American Girls' Cultures* (1998) and *Generations of Youth: Youth Cultures and History in Twentieth-Century America* (1998) reflect a new multi- and inter-disciplinarity in the study of children and youth which utilizes textual and representational analyses (as opposed to social history) to study the subcultures that children and youth have constructed within larger historical contexts. By developing new methods of inquiry and widening subjects of study, scholars have been able to examine "lived experiences" and "subjectivities," though most of the recent work focuses on teenagers in the twentieth century.

Today, there is an abundance of scholarly works (e.g., monographs, anthologies, and encyclopedias), book series on children (e.g., The Girls' History & Culture Series), national, regional, and local conferences, major academic journals, and in 2000, The Society for the History of Children and Youth, was finally founded by two of the field's pioneers, Joseph M. Hawes and N. Ray Hiner. That professional organization draws together the many college and university professors who teach courses on the history of children and youth, girlhood and female adolescence regularly offered in schools of education, departments of history, psychology, political science, sociology, and in programs on Women's Studies, Media/Communications Studies, and American Studies. But the history of children and adolescents has an even broader audience as media attention on bad boys and mean girls (e.g., "Queenbees") generates new questions and a search for answers in historical antecedents.

To meet the research needs of students of all ages, this accessibly written work—as the others in the series—surveys and synthesizes a century of scholarship on children and adolescents of different classes, races, genders, regions, religions, sexualities, and abilities. Some topics in the series have a gendered, racial, or regional focus while others (e.g., sickness and health, work and play, etc.) utilize a larger multicultural perspective. Whichever their focus, each and every book is organized into three equal parts to provide researchers with immediate access to historical overviews, primary source documents, and scholarly sources. Part I consists of synthetic essays written by experts in the field whose surveys are chronological and contextual. Part II provides access to hard-to-find primary source documents, in part or whole. Explanatory head notes illuminate themes, generate further understanding, and expedite inquiry. Part III is an extensive up-to-date bibliography of cited sources as well as those critical for further research.

The goal of the Children and Youth: History and Culture reference book series is not simply a utilitarian one but also to ultimately situate girls and boys of all ages more centrally in dominant historical narratives.

Miriam Forman-Brunell, Series Editor
University of Missouri, Kansas City

Acknowledgments

For research assistance, I would like to thank the librarians at Thomas Library, Wittenberg University—especially Kathy Schultz, Karen Balliet, Ken Irwin, Alisa Mizikar, Sandy Grube, and Suzanne Smailes. I am grateful to each of the contributors to this volume and several other researchers for their help and advice, especially Wayne Carp and Ellen Herman. My friends Grant Balfour and Maureen Fry thoughtfully read early chapters of this work. Federico Cataife provided much-needed help with transcriptions, sometimes at the last moment. For financial support, I would like to thank the Wittenberg University Faculty Research Fund Board, and the generous sabbatical program at Wittenberg, without which this project could not have been completed.

This book's existence is due in large part to my own knitted-together family. My nieces and adopted daughters, Gwen and Alex, two brave, beautiful young women, who survived foster care both in Great Britain and in the United States, turned my world—and my research interests—upside down. Denise, my sister, brought them into the world. She and Jan, the girls' birth father, trusted their care to my life partner, Frank, and me; I am humbled by that gift. George and Sandra Tompkins, foster parents par excellence, are, quite simply, heroes. Lyn Phillips, a wondrous social worker and friend, inspired in me a deep regard for her immensely challenging profession. Nina WenChen Zhao came into our lives as an exchange student from China during this last year and a half; she has made me see family-making even more globally. And my own dad and mom, Koreen and Karen Askeland, have continued to parent my sisters and me with a wisdom and humility that I hope to emulate. This extended, complex family made this work both possible and real to me.

I dedicate this book to all of my family, but most especially to my faithful companion, Frank Doden, who has provided constant love, practical support, and daily laughs.

Introduction

This book provides a historical and multicultural overview of the major issues in adoption and various forms of foster care in the United States from the precolonial days to the early twenty-first century. It is the first book to provide a comprehensive historical account of adoption, orphanages, and both voluntary and subsidized foster care as cultural institutions. In it, we examine the various social, legal, political, cultural, and economic forces that have contributed to the numbers and public perceptions of displaced children during various periods of U.S. history.

Above all, we have striven in this book to present a balanced view of the complex motivations and circumstances of all those whose lives are touched by adoption, orphanhood, and fostering. This includes the experiences of parents who have felt compelled to find other caregivers for their children, the motivations of the adoptive and fostering parents who have chosen to take them in, and the "child savers," social workers, orphanage administrators, and adoption agents who have attempted to mediate this process. But, most importantly, this book also focuses on how children themselves have responded to their familial status—to the sometimes traumatic, sometimes healing, sometimes bittersweet changes that temporary care and adoption can entail.

This book is divided into three parts. The initial section consists of six original essays. The first, by Lori Askeland, focuses on the existence of a variety of modes of child care—including kinship care provided by extended families, indentureships, and informal adoption—in European, African American, and Native American communities before the mid-1800s, during which time the orphanage also first arose in the United States. During the 1850s, adoption began to be modernized and prototypes of the modern foster care system arose, with a new legal focus on the "best interests" of children rather than the legal rights of adults. That shift to the modern era is addressed by Marilyn Holt in Chapter 2, which traces the connections between the so-called "orphan trains," adoption reform, and the beginnings of a formal foster care system, which slowly spelled the end of the large orphanages of the nineteenth and early twentieth centuries. In Chapter 3, Dianne Creagh examines the orphanage's evolution, and the increasing role of the federal government and the rise of a scientific approach to adoption and fostering during the Great Depression through the 1960s. Creagh's chapter thus ends with a brief discussion of how the civil rights movements after World War II began to spotlight the unequal power relations and the stigmas often associated with both adoption and fostering, as women, birth parents, adoptees, and traditionally subordinated ethnic groups—especially Native Americans and African Americans—began to make formal demands for increased rights, including the right to know and preserve one's own history.

These widespread movements helped to reshape the American family during the contemporary period, as fewer families were headed by a married, heterosexual couple. This period, dating from around 1970 to the present, is covered in two chapters. As Martha Satz and Lori Askeland explain in Chapter 4, the numbers and demographics of the children available for domestic adoption dramatically changed during this period, as did perceptions of transracial families and adoption by same-sex couples, which resulted in a variety of new laws and the creation of new forms of adoption, especially "open adoption," which nonetheless bears some resemblance to earlier forms of adoption. In Chapter 5, Elizabeth Bartholet discusses the politics and controversies surrounding international adoption. Bartholet suggests that while several international and domestic laws have helped legitimize international adoption, political controversies about the domination of wealthy "receiving" countries over poorer, "sending" countries leave the fate of international adoption in some doubt. What should be beyond dispute, she concludes, is the continued obligation to fight for the "best interests" of poor children, worldwide.

Chapter 6, by Claudia Nelson, discusses the "orphan" and other displaced children as they have appeared in a variety of American storytelling traditions, and particularly in literature addressed to children during the print-based era. This final overview highlights the fact that throughout human history, children have been cared for by persons who were not their birth parents, whether temporarily or throughout their childhoods. An estimated 5 million living Americans, children and adults, are adoptees, while an additional 500,000 live in foster care at any given time. Indeed, many more people, of all ages, have been adopted by stepparents or cared for by relatives or kin for extended periods.

It is clear even from these children's stories, in fact, that social rules governing family formation and ideas about "orphans" have changed over time, and vary from culture to culture, sometimes dramatically. Yet the rules and beliefs reiterated in these stories help to determine whether adopted and fostered children are viewed as "outside" the "normal" family or as valued members of the "American family." In short, the stories we tell about fostering and adoption matter; for, although many adoptive and fostering relationships are warm, loving, and successful, most cultural, social, and legal institutions in the United States continue to take the "biological" family as the norm for all families. Thus, many children and adults whose lives have been shaped by adoption and foster care still sustain mixed feelings related to their experience, and some even feel stigmatized by it.

This mixture of shame and stigma resulted in a unique culture of secrecy about infancy adoption during much of the twentieth century, which has itself presented a serious challenge for historians, who depend on documentation to tell any story of the past. Thus, Part II offers primary documents that have been specially selected to highlight the issues discussed in each of the first six essays, and roughly corresponding with each. Italicized headnotes provide context and, when useful, direct the reader to other relevant chapters where the issues they address are also raised.

Since this text is intended as a starting point for students and researchers interested in exploring the intertwining histories of adoption and foster care in the United States, Part III consists of an extensive list of secondary works—including both print and electronic sources—which has been divided into several themes discussed in parts I and II.

As our expansive list of sources reveals, the changing shape of the American family during the past decades has recently brought a spotlight to the continual existence of families brought together by kinship care, fostering, and adoption. But many important questions still remain to be explored. It is our hope that our readers will help carry forward a better understanding of the role of children in history and our current society, and, more specifically, all those whose lives have been touched by adoption, orphanages, and foster care.

Lori Askeland
Wittenberg University

I Essays

1 Informal Adoption, Apprentices, and Indentured Children in the Colonial Era and the New Republic, 1605–1850

Lori Askeland

> Sometimes I feel like a motherless child/A long way from home.
> —African American spiritual

Virtually all human cultures in recorded history have told, sung, and dramatized stories of children being abandoned or orphaned. And, as in real life, the loss of their parents usually requires the children of myth and legend to adapt to new families, often to entirely new environments. Collectively, these stories hint that the practice of adults taking in "other people's children"—whether accomplished through informal agreements or through complex rituals or legal procedures—has always been a factor in human social existence. However, the legal and cultural institutions designed to help or, in some cases, hinder this process have varied quite widely across cultures. In the United States, today, we have developed formal social and legal institutions to care for displaced children, such as foster care, group homes, and legal adoption. But these contemporary institutions did not always exist. This chapter will focus on the ways that the earliest Americans, until about 1850, dealt with children in need of care outside their biological families. It will first discuss the approaches to adoption and fostering developed by some of the native peoples in the United States. Second, it will outline the child-rearing practices developed by the Europeans who have primarily controlled the legal institutions of this country. Finally, it will delineate African American practices of informal adoption and fictive kinship, which are rooted both in African traditions and in the struggle to survive under the long shadow cast by the institution of slavery.

Despite the diversity of these three major traditions, for most of this early history we will see that, while each society no doubt valued children, they all developed adoptive and foster care services mainly in order to respond to adult and group needs for continuity, lineage, and/or labor, rather than gearing them to children's needs for nurturance. Children's needs became a primary focus of adoption and fostering practices in the United States only when the "best interests of the child" doctrine was slowly established over the course of the nineteenth and twentieth centuries.

NATIVE AMERICAN TRADITIONS: DIVERSE FAMILY STRUCTURES AND "MOURNING WARS"

The complex kinship networks of most indigenous American peoples are distinct in key ways from traditional European models. Furthermore, at the time of the first European contact, hundreds of different groups inhabited a dozen or so distinct indigenous cultural areas of the North American continent. These peoples were, in many ways, nearly as distinct from one another as they were from the Europeans who began aggressive efforts to colonize the region in the sixteenth and seventeenth centuries. However, many scholars agree that there are some remarkably consistent features of indigenous child-rearing practices, some of which connect to our more contemporary understanding of adoption and foster care. More importantly, a few tribes had specific rituals and procedures for adopting outsiders into an existing kin network. This section will provide a general overview of native child-rearing practices, followed by a specific discussion of the Iroquois practice of "adoption," or "re-quickening," which was used to replace deceased members of the group.

Up to the time of the European contact, most native groups were small and insular, built on face-to-face contact with a small number of people who all shared the same belief system and worldview. Thus, while in some communities the mother would be primarily responsible for the raising of infants of both sexes and, more especially, girls as they passed into adulthood, it was also common for certain members of the extended family to take over many key aspects of childrearing (Pettitt 1946; Szasz 1988; Bentz 1996). Indeed, some scholars note that all reputable elders of these communities typically played some role in a child's rearing (Pettitt 1946; Szasz 1988). Although virtually all native communities were organized more for subsistence than surplus trade, the shape of the families and the roles other adults might play in the rearing of children were often connected to the economic basis of their society. In nomadic hunting-and-gathering societies, for instance, grandparents often were the primary caregivers, while the parents worked outside the home settlement (Bentz 1996).

In fact, it was comparatively rare for married couples to share a dwelling place alone with their children—this seems only to have been the practice for communities in the North and West of what is now the United States (Miller 1996). The agricultural Pueblo and Iroquois nations were organized on matrilinear lines, and in both cases maternal uncles had responsibilities to, and usually formed a strong bond with, the sons of their sisters (Snow 1994; Bentz 1996). Iroquois men, for example, often did not live with their wives and children, who lived in the maternal longhouse with many other related families (Richter 1992).

One Iroquois nation, the Seneca, have a tale translated as "The Origin of Stories," that opens in a way familiar to readers of Western fairy tales, but which also reveals something of the structure and values of Senecan society, particularly as they relate to orphaned or displaced children:

> There once was a boy who had no home. His parents were dead and his uncles would not care for him. In order to live, this boy, whose name was Gaqka, or Crow, made a bower of branches for an abiding place and hunted birds and squirrels for food. He had almost no clothing but was very ragged and dirty. When the people from the village saw him they called him Filth-Covered-One, and laughed as they passed by, holding their noses. (Parker 1923/1989)

As might be expected, the orphaned Gaqka ultimately overcomes his lowly position after a long journey full of adventure and adversity, and brings his people great blessings. Thus, both the uncles' neglect of their duty and the rejection of the orphaned boy by the rest of the group is criticized in this story as inconsistent with Senecan values.

However, despite the fact that most tribal people viewed the world in family terms, and valued community-wide roles in the rearing of children, adoption was not merely an informal or automatic occurrence. Family and clan lineages were often followed very closely and taken very seriously. The Iroquois—whose organizational and governing structure is often cited as a key model for the U.S. Constitution—also traditionally practiced a complex system of adoption which deserves special mention here. The "Great Law of Peace" (*Kaianerekowa*), which served as a constitution for the six separate nations of the Iroquois Confederacy, contains specific provisions for the adoption of individuals, groups, or even an entire nation. There were varying levels of adoption for individuals or groups—family adoption, adoption into a clan or a new lineage, or adoption into the Confederacy (Strong 2002).

Among the Iroquois, adoption was used for a variety of purposes: to legitimize as full tribal members persons whose fathers (rather than their mothers) were members of the matrilinear nations of the League; to keep alive or replace deceased persons or even entire clans that had depopulated or become rapidly extinct; to provide a home for a member of a clan who was unwanted by his or her home clan; and/or to keep special knowledge alive in a clan by cross-adopting a specialist or shaman into another clan for purposes of training other members. Outsiders could also be honorarily "adopted" as a diplomatic gesture, but this did not imply adoption into a specific family, clan, or the Confederacy as a whole (Mann 2000). In virtually all cases, the needs of the community for continuity and lineage were of primary importance.

All these adoptions were accomplished through specific rituals. The most dramatic of these rituals applied to persons taken as captives in wars, which were sometimes fought for the specific purpose of taking in new members to replace, or "re-quicken," deceased members of the community (Richter 1992; Mann 2000; Strong 2002). Most of these so-called "mourning wars" were waged on neighboring Indian peoples. European Americans typically only became targets for raids as they moved farther and farther into the region, bringing deadly diseases, such as smallpox, which accelerated the decline of all native populations in the area (Richter 1992). One of the most famous of these European American captives, Mary Jemison, or Dickewamis (1742–1833), was kidnapped when she was about fifteen years old, during the French and Indian Wars of the 1750s. In her best-selling book-length narrative of her life story, as told to a white interviewer, Jemison described her subsequent adoption, which was accompanied by a mourning ritual, as serving to replace a dead brother for two grieving sisters, who thereafter raised her as a member of the family. As she explained in her narrative:

> During my adoption, I sat motionless, nearly terrified to death at the appearance and actions of the company, expecting every moment to feel their vengeance, and suffer death on the spot. I was, however, happily disappointed, when at the close of the ceremony the company retired, and my sisters went about employing every means for my consolation and comfort. (Seaver 1824/1994)

Jemison would grow up within the tribe and, despite opportunities to leave, chose to commit her life to them, giving birth to several children and dying in old age on the Buffalo Creek Reservation.

While such native traditions are quite distinct from the practice of adoption in the Anglo-American world and had little direct impact on the legal history of adoption as it developed in the new Republic, they still provide a more complex view of the way native peoples and tribal communities have understood family formation—and the formation of even broader social groups. In particular, as anthropologists Judith Modell and John Terrell, and sociologist Katarina Wegar, have explained, paying at least brief attention to different cultural traditions can highlight the social construction of things that feel "natural" to us still today, including how we define terms like "family." In particular, the importance of adoption in many native groups points up the relatively unusual European tradition of giving absolute primacy to blood connections as foundational to kinship (Wegar 1997).

EUROPEAN ROOTS: POOR LAWS, APPRENTICESHIPS, INDENTURESHIPS, AND ORPHANAGES

On the other side of the Atlantic Ocean, there is written evidence of some form of legal adoption existing at least since around 2285 B.C. when it first appears in the Babylonian "Code of Hammurabi." Adoption seems to have been long practiced in various parts of the Mediterranean world, Asia, Africa, and the Middle East. Typically, as with the Iroquois practice described above, it was instigated not in order to best serve the needs of the individual children, but to serve broader, and generally adult-centered, social and/or religious needs for kinship and continuity (Goody 1969; Presser 1971–1972; Zainaldin 1979; Carp 1998). Yet, at the same time, the same Babylonian Code, as well as passages in the Torah and the Christian Bible along with other foundational documents of Western culture from both Greek and Roman cultures, required generosity to the poor, and particularly to orphaned children; often such kindness was viewed as a central, moral act (Trattner 1999).

Perhaps strangely, then, with the rise of both Christianity and feudalism in Western Europe, biological relationships were privileged almost universally, and legal adoptive relationships were strongly discouraged. Apparently, this resistance was rooted in the dual goals of maintaining relatively simple inheritance lines and restricting sexual relations to marriage (Goody 1983; Modell 1994; Carp 1998). The common law tradition in England, on which most domestic law in the United States is now based, did not recognize any adoptive relationships; in fact, adoption was not legalized in England until 1926.

On the other hand, however, children from virtually all levels of most European societies were transferred to different households for extended periods of time through apprenticeships, various forms of indentureships, and other quasi-adoptive relationships (Grossberg 1985; Youcha 1995; Carp 1998). Unlike today, these early European adults much preferred older children for these quasi-adoptive or fostering relationships, as infants could do no work. The nature and focus of a child's apprenticeship was determined largely by his or her family's financial situation and by gender. The wealthiest boys, from merchant and professional families, were typically apprenticed, for a fee, to professionals and fine craftsmen—lawyers, doctors, silversmiths—to learn an exclusive trade during their teenaged years. Boys from the middling classes were sent to work and learn a trade—often thus relieving the economic burden on their birth family as well as providing vocational training. Girls in all classes were often legally and voluntarily transferred to another family as domestic servants. Noting that often there seemed to be no economic necessity involved, Edmund Morgan speculates that Puritan parents mainly feared "spoiling" their children, and so voluntarily placed their children with another family for work, skills, and discipline (Morgan 1943; Youcha 1995).

Apprenticeships and indentures were limited in time, with an ending date specified in the written contract, and did not extend into the child's adulthood. Yet, particularly in colonial America, it was not uncommon for property-owning adults to practice "testamentary" adoption—whereby they would use their legal wills to recognize as heirs young relatives, godchildren, or children placed out as servants in their home. Sometimes children so recognized would even change their legal name to highlight their relationship to the adult (Kawashima 1981–1982; Carp 1998).

When English or colonial American parents died impoverished, abandoned their families, or otherwise proved incapable of providing support for their children, their offspring might become dependent upon the charity of their birthplace, if grandparents or other legal kin were not available. Important laws were enacted in England during the late 1500s that laid out the responsibilities of tax-supported churches and/or local governments to these children and other impoverished people. These "Elizabethan Poor Laws," as they are known, were imported to most of the Anglo-American colonies. They simultaneously imposed strict limits on the movements of poor people and required local governments to collect taxes to support almshouses. These same officials were empowered to place poor children who were about seven years of age or older into apprenticeships or indentureships (Folks 1902/1978; Kelso 1969; Grossberg 1985; Katz 1996; Hasci 1997; Brundage 1998; Carp 1998). Sometimes this meant that the children were placed in almshouses, which housed poor people of all ages and both genders—usually in cramped, unclean, and crowded conditions (see especially Katz 1996).

But, perhaps more typically in the early American colonies, poor and orphaned children experienced "early America's version of foster care" (Youcha 1995). These children would be transferred by the local authorities "involuntarily" (meaning with very little input from either their parents or themselves) to local farmers, householders, or heads of businesses—whomever would take them. Indeed, on their arrival to the colonies south of New England, more than half of all colonists were initially involuntarily indentured servants, separated from their families of origin, and were mostly male teenagers, between the ages of fourteen and nineteen. Life was very difficult for these young persons; many died before their indentures were complete. Some, in fact, were apparently "spirited"—kidnapped—from English streets and shipped to Virginia (Mason 1994; Ashby 1997). One indentured boy, Richard Frethorne, listed in a letter all the men from their Virginia plantation who had died—either from starvation or battles with the native people. He begged his parents to send him food, and pleaded that they pay his master the indenture price and bring him back to England: "I entreat you not to forget me, but by any means redeem me . . . if you love or respect me as your child, release me from the bondage and save my life" (Frethorne 1623/2006).

Even in New England, where most young persons arrived as part of an intact family, destitute children were sometimes auctioned off to whomever would take the least money for their upkeep (Folks 1902/1978; Kelso 1969; Demos 1970; Trattner 1999), while others were sold into apprenticeships, with the proceeds of the sale going to the overseers (Youcha 1995). Perhaps because the family was the basic social institution in this challenging New World context, "early Euro-Americans showed little preference for the primacy of biological kinship," by comparison to their European counterparts and even many of their own descendents, who would later embrace the traditional English and European prejudice against adoption (Carp 1998).

The English legal code was especially resistant to recognizing the legitimacy of children born out of wedlock. Such a child was labeled a "bastard," or, more formally, "filius nullius," that is, the child of no one. In England, and the early colonies, not even the subsequent marriage of his or her parents could change his status (Grossberg 1985; Mason 1994). Under the civil law tradition, which was established in a few states (mostly former Spanish and French colonies like Texas and Louisiana), these "illegitimate" children could be legitimized by the marriage of their parents and they could even be granted a legal status, if not inheritance rights, in private legal proceedings. Legal historian Michael Grossberg notes that this civil law formality represented "the first procedures available to create nonmatrimonial but legally binding family ties," prior to the establishment of legalized adoption (Grossberg 1985). Once again, the American colonies were often less resistant to establishing quasi-adoptive legal procedures than were their English counterparts. Although these procedures undoubtedly lessened the stigma against illegitimate children, something of the social and legal prejudice against these children has persisted to the present day in the United States.

Orphanages first started appearing in the American colonies well before the Revolutionary War, but they were relatively few in number until the 1830s, when several were constructed in response to the poverty and the breakup of kinship networks resulting from large-scale immigration and urbanization. Cholera and yellow fever epidemics, in particular, spurred many localities to construct orphanages. More broadly, the sentimentalization of the child in the literature of this period and the growing perception of childhood as a time of innocence led to a critique of child abuse and neglect in almshouses (Hasci 1997; Carp 1998b). Most orphanages were strictly segregated by race, and constructed by groups affiliated with Protestant, Catholic, and Jewish religious groups. The latter two groups often felt a need to protect children of their religious background from the dominance of evangelical Protestant-based care (Hasci 1997). Although orphanages were severely criticized during the latter half of the nineteenth century, they remained the most important form of temporary or permanent care for dependent children in the United States until well into the twentieth century (Youcha 1995; Hasci 1997; Carp 1998b).

MAINTAINING AND ADAPTING AFRICAN KINSHIP TRADITIONS IN THE SHADOW OF SLAVERY

Some widely publicized studies in the twentieth century, despite sometimes being well intentioned toward black Americans, too readily characterized the African American family as utterly disorganized and dysfunctional as a consequence of the several hundred years of kidnapping from Africa and enslavement in the Americas (see especially Moynihan 1965). Recent scholarship has, however, returned to the insight of W.E.B. Du Bois, who, at the beginning of the last century asserted that there remains "a distinct nexus between Africa and America which, though broken and perverted, ought not to be neglected by the careful student" (Du Bois 1909/1970). A much more complex portrait of black family structures has thus emerged, which identifies key strengths of black families in the face of the challenges of slavery, poverty, and the enduring legacy of racism. In contrast to many Euro-American families, black families have long emphasized the active participation of a broad, extended family structure that frequently includes "fictive" kin—unrelated adults who perform important support roles in a family and are regarded as kin. Within this structure, informal adoption and foster care have long been widely practiced, and these practices are now believed to have some roots in African traditions.

It should be emphasized that not all African Americans were enslaved in early America. Some very early Africans, though captured into slavery, arrived here legally defined as indentured servants, like the "involuntarily" indentured servants of the poor, described above. Some lived in "free" regions (i.e., areas without legalized slavery) for many generations. Others were able at some point to purchase their own freedom and that of many family members. A very few owned slaves themselves. Yet all lived in the shadow of slavery, eventually. Free blacks in all parts of the country typically experienced prejudice from white society in the form of social exclusion, discrimination in jobs, legal restrictions, and even the threat of being captured and kidnapped back into slavery (Woodson 1925; Curry 1981; Berry and Blassingame 1982; Penningroth 2003).

Hence, although this section of this chapter will emphasize the survival skills of black families, slavery as a legal system posed a serious threat to African kinship systems. In Afrocentric scholarship, the transatlantic slave trade is sometimes referred to as the "Maafa," a Kiswahili word meaning "great disaster" (Ani 1994; Boyd-Franklin 2003). Beyond the stigma implied by either illegitimacy or involuntary indentureship, children born into the status of slaves were at the mercy of a system that began by kidnapping children and adults from their African homes and then systematically attempted to strip them of their cultural heritage. Even further, those who profited from this system sought to deny the very humanity of enslaved persons throughout their entire life course—and that of their biological descendents as well. In a country where the family was seen as the basic social unit—responsible for providing to its members food, shelter, clothing, social status, and economic possibilities—enslaved persons' family connections were denied any legal status (Frazier 1939/2001; Blassingame 1972; Genovese 1974; Gutman 1976; Boyd-Franklin 2003). Not only was there no legal means for enslaved people to marry, but children could be separated from their parents and kin and sold off to another family, at will, by their masters. It should be noted, however, that the best evidence suggests that most African Americans managed to emerge from slavery in intact, if legally unrecognized, two-parent families (Genovese 1974; Gutman 1976).

The legal reality faced by enslaved children was nevertheless harsh and impossible to predict: the "masters" to whom free children might be apprenticed—craftsmen or heads of households—did not "own" the children, as slaveholders did. Free masters gained through that title only the right to receive the financial benefits of the children's labor and their obedience until they completed the term of their indentureship or reached adulthood. These adults could be legally sanctioned—and sometimes were—for failing to live up to their responsibilities to properly educate, feed, and clothe their apprentices and refrain from physically injuring them. Not so with slaveholders: their legal, economic, and socially reinforced power over their slaves, young and old, was virtually absolute (Mason 1994; Boyd-Franklin 2003). And, as Andrew Billingsley and Jeanne M. Giovannoni note, "the very existence of slavery meant that child welfare institutions could develop in this country without concern" for most black children, which "ensured an inherently racist child welfare system." Hence, not only were most white-run orphanages before and long after the Civil War strictly segregated, but only a very few were devoted exclusively to black children (Billingsley and Giovannoni 1972).

Given these challenges, the survival of African kinship patterns in the black American community and the adaptation of family structures to this hostile environment is an extraordinary human accomplishment. Many scholars begin by singling out the traditional emphasis on an extended family network, rather than an isolated nuclear family, which characterizes kinship systems in both West Africa and in the black American family (Herskovits 1938–1939; Aschenbrenner 1975; Sudarkasa 1980; Hill 1999). As with the Iroquois society described above, marriage was important in most African societies (sometimes including polygamous unions). But married partners almost always resided in a family compound. Thus, while marriages might sometimes fail, the extended family remained the key locus of stability for children and adults (Foster 1983; Sudarkasa 1988; Hill 1999; Boyd-Franklin 2003). Some scholars specifically tie this focus on the broader family unit to an underlying belief typical of many African cultures that any individual person is only comprehensible in relation to the collective group: "I am because we are; and because we are, therefore I am" (Mbiti 1969; Boyd-Franklin 2003).

Slavery in West Africa, in fact, was defined as an absence of kin. To be enslaved was to be rendered "orphaned," regardless of the actual status of one's parents or other kin, and then grafted to the lineage of the master's family, with no hope of protection from one's blood relatives. (This differs from American slavery, which defined slaves as property whose purpose was commodity production.) Now, this form of slavery could be extremely harsh—slaves were expected to work for their masters' families and the status of slave was always stigmatized to some degree in West African cultures. However, it also inscribed a pattern of flexible kinship rules, and normalized adoptive or quasi-adoptive practices in African families—flexible kinship patterns that many black people carried with them into the new world (Wright 1993; Penningroth 2003).

In North America, slavery contributed to a high mortality rate and low life expectancy for many African Americans, along with grueling workloads and the continual threat of family members being sold to other owners. This threat was particularly keen between 1810 and 1850 when the internal slave trade moved thousands of African Americans from the older, eastern plantations surrounding the Chesapeake to the Deep South (Penningroth 2003). Thus, many antebellum African American children were raised in large part by adults who were not their parents. Elderly women on large plantations, too old for field work, often were placed in charge of large numbers of enslaved children. Frederick Douglass, particularly in his second slave narrative, *My Bondage and My Freedom*, and Harriet Jacobs both describe being raised by their grandmothers when young. Many ex-slaves who composed narratives of their lives describe being protected by relatives—aunts, especially—when slightly older (Douglass 1855; Jacobs 1861/1987; Blassingame 1972).

In addition to blood relatives, however, perhaps the most notable aspect of the African American family tradition for our purposes is the widespread inclusion of "fictive" or para-kin in the family network (Hill 1999; Boyd-Franklin 2003; Penningroth 2003). In order to survive or eventually escape slavery, most African Americans depended on their kin for emotional, spiritual, and material support in the form of labor, loans, or other forms of property. If separated from their families by death or the slave trade, older black children and young adults usually had to negotiate their way into a new family, by offering, for example, to contribute extra labor to the household in exchange for family benefits like food and protection. Such created kin relationships were not automatic or guaranteed, but, once established, they were often valued equally to blood or marital relationships (Penningroth 2003). Separated from his family, a Georgia slave named Charles Ball found himself forced to live with a new slave family. After weeks of mourning, he finally "proposed" to the adult couple in the slave quarters: "that whilst I should remain a member of the family I would . . . bring all my earnings into the family stock, provided I might be treated as one of its members" (quoted in Penningroth 2003).

This flexible family structure, rooted in African traditions, was key to the survival of many African Americans in the crucible of American slavery and its aftermath. Widening this circle, after the Civil War, a variety of organizations emerged within the black community to care for abandoned and orphaned children. The founder of the Reed Home and School (1884) in Georgia described the following scene, witnessed while she was a student in the 1880s, which "most inclined [her] heart and made [her] more determined than ever to before" to serve her people:

> One cold, icy morning I was crossing the bridge and heard a pitiful scream below. I looked down and there stood a poor little boy of about nine or ten years old, with the lash being applied to his back. There was no one to say a word of comfort to this dear little fellow. It pressed my heart and caused me to weep bitterly. . . . I at once pleaded with the Lord and asked him for strength . . . that I might go out and save one boy from the chain gang. (quoted in Billingsley and Giovannoni 1972)

While many white reformers sought to save (white) society from the "danger" of loose, undisciplined black children, this African American woman sought to protect these children from the horrors of growing up in a deeply racist society—horrors which included unjust incarceration, exploitative labor practices, and even lynching. The hundreds of small and large institutions created by reformers like these helped to "amass and utilize the strength within the Black community" (Billingsley and Giovannoni 1972), in order to support these most vulnerable young persons, who, like all children, embodied the future of their people.

CONCLUSION

The idea of arranging child custody to serve "the best interests of the child," evoked by the African American reformer quoted above, entered into the American legal world only in 1809, and then did not become prevalent as a legal doctrine until mid-century (Grossberg 1985). All three of the cultures discussed in this chapter mainly rooted their adoptive and fostering practices in adult needs for labor and continuity, rather than children's need for nurturing. Yet the European-derived legal traditions imported to the United States strongly resisted formalizing such relationships or making them permanent. Massachusetts would finally pass a groundbreaking adoption law in 1851, which streamlined the adoption process and made it much more readily available as a legal option. Although this law was important in many ways, it was nevertheless building on many centuries of informal and quasi-adoptive relationships in families from a variety of cultural backgrounds.

REFERENCES

Ani, Marimba. 1994. *Yurugu: An African-Centered Critique of European Cultural Thought and Behavior*. Trenton, NJ: Africa World Press.

Aschenbrenner, Joyce. 1975. *Lifelines: Black Families in Chicago*. New York: Holt, Rinehart and Winston.

Ashby, LeRoy. 1997. *Endangered Children: Dependency, Neglect, and Abuse in American History*. New York: Twayne.

Bentz, Marilyn G. 1996. "Child Rearing." In *Encyclopedia of North American Indians*, ed. Frederick E. Hoxie, 115–18. Boston: Houghton Mifflin. Full-text at college.hmco.com/history/readerscomp/naind/html/na_007000_childrearing.htm.

Berry, Mary Frances, and John Blassingame. 1982. *Long Memory: The Black Experience in America*. New York: Oxford University Press.

Billingsley, Andrew, and Jeanne M. Giovannoni. 1972. *Children of the Storm: Black Children and American Child Welfare*. New York: Harcourt Brace Jovanovich.

Blassingame, John. 1972. *The Slave Community: Plantation Life in the Antebellum South*. New York: Oxford University Press.

Boyd-Franklin, Nancy. 2003. *Black Families in Therapy: Understanding the African American Experience*. 2nd ed. New York: Guilford Press.

Brundage, Anthony. 1998. "Private Charity and the 1834 Poor Law." In *With Us Always: A History of Private Charity and Public Welfare*, ed. Donald T. Critchlow and Charles H. Parker, 99–119. Lanham, MD: Rowman and Littlefield.

Carp, E. Wayne. 1998. *Family Matters: Secrecy and Disclosure in the History of Adoption*. Cambridge, MA: Harvard University Press.

———. 1998b. "Orphanages vs. Adoption: The Triumph of Biological Kinship, 1800–1933." In *With Us Always: A History of Private Charity and Public Welfare*, ed. Donald T. Critchlow and Charles H. Parker, 123–44. Lanham, MD: Rowman and Littlefield.

Curry, Leonard P. 1981. *The Free Black in Urban America, 1800–1856*. Chicago: University of Chicago Press.

Demos, John. 1970. *A Little Commonwealth: Family Life in Plymouth Colony*. New York: Oxford University Press.

Douglass, Frederick. 1855. *My Bondage and My Freedom*. E-text at docsouth.unc.edu/neh/douglass55/menu.html.

Du Bois, W.E.B. 1909/1970. *The Negro American Family*. Cambridge, MA: MIT Press.

Folks, Homer. 1902/1978. *The Care of Destitute, Neglected and Delinquent Children.* Washington, DC: National Association of Social Workers.

Frazier, E. Franklin. 1939/2001. *The Negro Family in the United States.* Notre Dame, IN: University of Notre Dame Press.

Frethorne, Richard. 1623/2006. "From Richard Frethorne, to His Parents (Virginia, 1623)." In *The Heath Anthology of American Literature,* 5th ed., vol. A, ed. Paul Lauter et al., 270–75. Boston: Houghton Mifflin.

Genovese, Edward D. 1974. *Roll, Jordan, Roll: The World the Slaves Made.* New York: Pantheon.

Goody, Jack. 1969. "Adoption in Cross-Cultural Perspective." *Comparative Studies in Society and History* 11, no. 1: 55–78.

———. 1983. *The Development of Family and Marriage in Europe.* Cambridge: Cambridge University Press.

Grossberg, Michael. 1985. *Governing the Hearth: Law and the Family in Nineteenth-Century America.* Chapel Hill: University of North Carolina Press.

Gutman, Herbert. 1976. *The Black Family in Slavery and Freedom, 1750–1925.* New York: Pantheon.

Hasci, Timothy A. 1997. *Second Home: Orphan Asylums and Poor Families in America.* Cambridge, MA: Harvard University Press.

Herskovits, Melville J. 1938–1939. "The Ancestry of the American Negro." *American Scholar* 8, no. 1: 84–94.

Hill, Robert B. 1999. *The Strengths of African American Families: Twenty-Five Years Later.* Rev. ed. Lanham, MD: University Press of America.

Jacobs, Harriet A. 1861/1987. *Incidents in the Life of a Slave Girl, Written by Herself,* ed. Lydia Maria Child. Edited by Jean Fagan Yellin. Cambridge, MA: Harvard University Press.

Katz, Michael. 1996. *In the Shadow of the Poorhouse: A Social History of Welfare in America.* 2nd ed. New York: Basic Books.

Kawashima, Yasuhide. 1981–1982. "Adoption in Early America." *Journal of Family Law* 20: 677–96.

Kelso, Robert W. 1969. *The History of Public Poor Relief in Massachusetts, 1620–1920.* Montclair, NJ: Patterson Smith.

Mann, Barbara A. 2000. "Adoption." In *Encyclopedia of the Haudenosaunee (Iroquois Confederacy),* ed. Bruce Elliott Johanson and Barbara Alice Mann, 3–7. Westport, CT: Greenwood Press.

Mason, Mary Ann. 1994. *From Father's Property to Children's Rights: The History of Child Custody in America.* New York: Columbia University Press.

Mbiti, John S. 1969. *African Religions and Philosophy.* New York: Praeger.

Miller, Jay. 1996. "Families." In *Encyclopedia of North American Indians,* ed. Frederick E. Hoxie, 192–97. Boston: Houghton Mifflin. Full-text at college.hmco.com/history/readerscomp/naind/html/na_011700_families.htm.

Modell, Judith. 1994. *Kinship with Strangers: Adoption and Interpretations of Kinship in American Culture.* Berkeley: University of California Press.

Morgan, Edmund S. 1943. *The Puritan Family.* New York: Harper and Row.

Moynihan, Daniel P. 1965. *The Negro Family: A Case for National Action.* Washington, DC: U.S. Government Printing Office.

Parker, Arthur C. 1923/1989. *Seneca Myths and Folk Tales.* Lincoln: University of Nebraska Press.

Penningroth, Dylan C. 2003. *The Claims of Kinfolk: African American Property and Community in the Nineteenth-Century South.* Chapel Hill: University of North Carolina Press.

Pettitt, George A. 1946. *Primitive Education in North America.* Berkeley: University of California Press.

Presser, Stephen B. 1971–1972. "The Historical Background of the American Law of Adoption." *Journal of Family Law* 11: 443–516.

Richter, Daniel K. 1992. *The Ordeal of the Longhouse: The Peoples of the Iroquois League in the Era of European Colonization.* Chapel Hill: University of North Carolina Press.

Seaver, James E. 1824/1994. *A Narrative of the Life of Mrs. Mary Jemison.* Edited by June Namias. Norman: University of Oklahoma Press.

Snow, Dean R. 1994. *The Iroquois.* Oxford: Blackwell.

Strong, Pauline Turner. 2002. "Transforming Outsiders: Captivity, Adoption, and Slavery Reconsidered." In *A Companion to American Indian History,* ed. Phillip J. Deloria and Neal Salisbury, 339–56. Malden, MA: Blackwell.

Sudarkasa, Niara. 1980. "African and Afro-American Family Structure: A Comparison." *Black Scholar* 11, no. 1: 37–60.

Szasz, Margaret Connell. 1988. *Indian Education in the American Colonies, 1607–1783.* Albuquerque: University of New Mexico Press.

Terrell, John E., and Judith Modell. 1994. "Anthropology and Adoption." *American Anthropologist* 96, no. 1: 155–61.

Trattner, Walter I. 1999. *From Poor Law to Welfare State: A Social History of Welfare in America.* 6th ed. New York: Free Press.

Wegar, Katarina. 1997. *Adoption, Identity, and Kinship: The Debate over Sealed Birth Records.* New Haven, CT: Yale University Press.

Woodson, Carter G. 1925. *Free Negro Heads of Families in the United States in 1830.* Washington, DC: The Association for the Study of Negro Life and History.

Wright, Marcia. 1993. *Strategies of Slaves and Women: Life-Stories from East/Central Africa.* New York: L. Barber Press.

Youcha, Geraldine. 1995. *Minding the Children: Child Care in America from Colonial Times to the Present.* New York: Scribner.

Zainaldin, Jamil S. 1979. "The Emergence of a Modern American Family Law: Child Custody, Adoption and the Courts." *Northwestern University Law Review* 73, no. 6: 1038–89.

2 Adoption Reform, Orphan Trains, and Child-Saving, 1851–1929

Marilyn Irvin Holt

In the late 1840s, a few men in Boston and New York shared the idea of transporting poor, urban children to rural homes. The children, they argued, would have a chance to grow up in an environment that would allow them to become productive members of society. By the early 1850s, Charles Loring Brace and the New York Children's Aid Society had a workable program in place. Other agencies followed with their own, and the practice of transporting and placing children became known as the orphan trains.

This type of long-distance placement was new in America, without understood rules to guide its implementation. Agencies borrowed from social traditions and rules of guardianship established under English Common Law. They relied heavily on their understanding of a social contract existing between the placing agency and receiving family, and there was a strong sense that Christian charity played a vital role. Nevertheless, agencies were well aware of the law, as it applied to guardianship, and conscious of the new, emerging laws related to legal adoption.

Nineteenth-century standards for child placement offered several options. Placing agencies used what was available, without demanding that one be the norm. Ultimately, this rather laissez-faire approach brought criticism from the social welfare community and from state governments. This criticism, as well as the shortcomings found in orphan train placements, provided a context for clarifying foster care and adoption. Although its practitioners never intended it, the orphan trains influenced public policy, state statute, and social definitions of foster care and adoption in American society.

CHILD RELOCATION

In 1854, Charles Loring Brace reported that during the previous year the New York Children's Aid Society (CAS) had sent 164 boys and 43 girls "to homes in the country, or to places where they could earn an honest living" (*Annual Reports* 1854/1971). CAS, under Brace's direction, sponsored a number of in-city programs for the poor, but Brace was also an advocate of child relocation. He was not the only person to do so, nor was he the first to experiment with removing youngsters some distance from urban centers. John Earl Williams of Boston's Children's Mission to the Children of the Destitute began a modest in-state placement program in 1850 (*First Annual Report of the Children's Mission* 1850), but it was Brace who gave the concept definition and created a relocation model that was emulated by other agencies. Among the most active were the Children's Mission, New England Home for Little Wanderers (Boston), New York Foundling Hospital, and New York Juvenile Asylum.

The argument for child relocation was couched in terms of child rescue and Christian charity. Children placed in entirely new surroundings would be physically and spiritually saved from the worst that city life handed out to the poor and abandoned. More practically, the number of children requiring aid and intervention had reached staggering proportions by the mid-1850s, with no end in sight. Immigration and economic depressions constantly added to the numbers, and as a singular event, the Civil War exacerbated the problem when war widows, orphans, and dependent children joined the ranks of the needy. In the immediate postwar environment, Boston estimated 6,000 vagrant children; New York officials believed that there were as many as 30,000 in that city (Abbott 1927; Bremner 1980). Left to their own devices, Brace and others argued, the children of the poor would become a generation of criminals and anarchists who, by their sheer numbers, could wreak havoc on the social order. "These boys and girls . . . if unreclaimed, poison society all around them" (*Children's Aid Society of New York* 1893). Intervention could redirect the positive traits of self-reliance and generosity among peers that Brace believed these children possessed, and over the years CAS emphasized the point with examples of those whose lives had been changed. "Once a New York pauper," wrote one boy, "[I am] now a Western farmer" (Brace 1872). For Brace, institutionalization was not the answer. Instead, he saw the opportunity to marry urban problems with those of rural areas that complained about the lack of workers to adequately build up the country. Urban youngsters could find a new, wholesome life in the homes of agrarian society, which out of charity or the need for farm labor would welcome the opportunity to open their homes. This relocation plan, the transportation of youngsters to rural areas, became known as the orphan trains. During its almost eighty years of operation, this program removed and placed at least 200,000 children and teenagers (Holt 1992).

CAS led the way, and other agencies followed. There were some variations in whom the agencies chose to place and how. The New York Foundling Hospital, for example, matched child and receiving family before its groups of children ever left New York, and since the Catholic charity's charges were usually between the ages of two and six, they were not advertised as potential farm laborers and housekeepers. Nevertheless, practical details of the Foundling Hospital's operation, as well as those of other agencies, resembled those tried and proven by CAS. Children and adolescents were gathered off streets and out of orphanages and reformatories. Some were turned over by destitute parents or unwed mothers. Despite the orphan train label, the majority of those placed out had at least one living parent. Typically, groups of children, often containing family clusters of brothers and sisters, were sent out with one or more representatives of the placing agency. For its part, the agency had a planned destination in mind since it had already contacted local communities through newspaper stories, personal visits, and correspondence with civic and religious leaders. Railroads sometimes gave reduced rates, and individual conductors and ticket agents were known to be sympathetic and helpful to traveling parties. Upon reaching their destination, the children were placed with families who asked for them, who were approved by the local arrangements committee or parish priest, and who agreed to meet the placing agency's expectations for child care and education. Once in their new homes, the children's experiences ranged across the spectrum, from loving families that offered every opportunity to abusive households. While one girl was "just tickled to have parents," another youngster ran away from his harsh circumstances, growing up "in the fields and homes of people who would feed and shelter him for a day's work" (Holt 1992).

There were no firm guidelines for who could or could not take a child. Placing agencies assumed that local committees, clergy, and the communities at large would weed out anyone who was morally intemperate or who engaged in disreputable enterprises such as saloon-keeping or prostitution. Agencies expected "good homes where influences are of the best" ("Placing-Out Agent" 1988), and there were no criteria that demanded only two-parent households be allowed to apply for a child. Those asking for a child were not required to explain their motives. Certainly, many households were looking for a worker, but others acted on the spur of the moment. "I just liked his [boy's] personality," said one woman. There were also families looking for a child to rear as their own. Thrilled with the toddler provided through the Foundling Hospital, one man proclaimed, "Beats the stork. . . . We asked for a boy of 18 months with brown hair and blue eyes and the bill was filled to the last specification" (Holt 1992).

Agencies' conditions for placement and parental responsibilities, or the lack of them, provide a context in which to examine the relationship between foster care, adoption, and the orphan trains. They also lay a foundation for exploring the contentious dialogue that emerged in the late nineteenth and early twentieth centuries when child-welfare advocates, many trained in the emerging fields of sociology and social work, applied their standards and found much to criticize in how the orphan trains had, and were, going about the business of placing children and establishing lines of guardianship.

NINETEENTH-CENTURY PLACEMENT OPTIONS

As discussed in the first chapter of this volume, historically, American society has accepted a number of methods for rearing children outside their own homes and for naming the adult or entity responsible for minors. These methodologies coexisted, and they were applied as individual situations demanded.

1. In colonial America and well into the nineteenth century, children of all social classes lived in the homes of nonrelatives when they were indentured to learn a trade. The indenture contract was legally binding on both parties, stating the responsibilities of the "employer" and the indentured. In another application, indenture was used by institutions to place children in homes and to deplete the institution's population, but in these cases, youngsters were more likely to learn farming or housekeeping, rather than trades such as woodworking or surveying.

2. Institutions were the acknowledged guardians of their wards. Whether these places chose to indenture children, place them into foster care or adoptive homes, or house them within the institution, they were entities that acted in place of parents.

3. Among the middle and upper classes, it was common for courts, using English Common Law, to appoint a guardian for minor children who had lost both parents or their father. (State laws varied on the rights of widowed women to act as guardian for their children.) The court-appointed guardian might or might not be related, but until the child reached the age of majority, the guardian decided where the child lived, how any inheritance might be spent, and what type of education was offered.

4. Either foregoing courts or disagreeing with them, individuals could establish guardianship through private laws; as one example, a widowed woman in Illinois replaced her children's court-appointed guardians by petitioning the state legislature for a private law that gave her guardianship (Illinois General Assembly, 1837).

5. Last, but not least, of the possibilities for assuming guardianship was adoption, which in the mid-nineteenth century when the orphan trains began, was not, as a rule, a legal proceeding but a socially understood contract. It implied that the child would be treated as a member of the family, could take that family's name, and inherit.

Those involved in orphan train placements understood these options, and they were aware that Massachusetts, in 1851, had expanded traditional English Common Law to establish adoption as a legal proceeding and binding contract. The Massachusetts law required court approval, consent of the child's guardian or parent, and evidence that the adoptive family was capable of raising the child. It was not a social contract in the traditional sense, but a legally binding agreement. States followed Massachusetts's lead, but there was no cohesive, national mandate to do so. When, for example, a CAS agent informed Brace that Illinois placements in 1856 included a girl who was "adopted as their own" by a well-to-do family, it went without saying that this was not a court-approved adoption. Illinois had no adoption law until 1867 (*Annual Reports* 1856/1971; Nims 1928).

With the exception of the New York Juvenile Asylum, which demanded that its placements be indentured, most placing agencies did not have one standard for establishing a line of guardianship and adult accountability. The New York Foundling Hospital, which operated an in-city foster care program along with orphan train placements, did not demand a specific form. Some receiving families indentured but, more often than not, adopted either through social agreement or legal proceedings. The New England Home for Little Wanderers made it clear that placements were to be treated as sons and daughters, and by 1890 strongly encouraged adoption through the courts. The Children's Mission, which placed a range of ages, expressed a preference for indenture or adoption, but demanded neither. Generally, agencies allowed families to consider their options and decide for themselves. This made it easier to place children since some families would have refused children and teenagers if they came with legal contracts attached. And, on a practical note, this open-ended strategy did not tie agencies to policies based on individual state laws. So, it made no difference that some states enacted adoption laws during the nineteenth century and others did not. In fact, states' diverse response to accepting and applying adoption law left social workers in the 1920s grappling with "the extent to which the procedure [was] resorted to" and trying to decide adoption's merits "as a method of social treatment" (Nims 1927; Holt 1992).

For its part, CAS believed that those taking children should decide, although it strongly opposed indenture. Adults had to promise to abide by a basic agreement with CAS. The society agreed to remove a child if the receiving family was dissatisfied, and it reserved the right to remove a child if CAS representatives later found the new home to be unsatisfactory. "Unsatisfactory" was broadly interpreted. The home itself might have had the right kind of environment, but family dynamics could be problematic. There was discord when husbands and wives differed over whether a child should have been taken in the first place, and placed-out children did not always blend easily into sibling relationships with a couple's biological children. When agents found problems, the placing agency exercised its right to guardianship, and in one recorded instance, CAS argued its right to guardianship when it contested a 1903 court-approved adoption in Nebraska. In that case, the adoption was set aside, the society retained guardianship, but the judge refused to remove the child from her home as CAS wanted (Kidder 2001). Those who took children agreed to provide proper care, religious instruction, and schooling; there was no mention or expectation of financial compensation to offset the cost of food, clothing, medical care, or education. They were expected to periodically report, by correspondence, on children's well-being and "progress." (The placed-out were also encouraged to correspond with Brace or with the CAS agent that had made the placement.)

CAS stated its terms of placement on cards handed out to receiving families. During the first years, the society's focus on youngsters taken as "little laborers" was reflected in its terms. Clearly, CAS had different expectations based on the age of the boy being placed. Boys fifteen and older were to work for room and board until reaching eighteen when they were "at liberty to make their own arrangements." Boys between twelve and fifteen also worked for room and board until they were eighteen, but their "employer" was required to see that they attended school. Youngsters under twelve were supposed to stay until they reached eighteen, but they were to have a place in the family and be "treated . . . as one of their own children in matters of schooling, clothing and training" (CAS placement card). That CAS failed to specifically mention girls was not an oversight. The agency focused on boys because Brace believed they were easier to place as laborers and because he suspected that street girls, unlike boys, were more difficult to rehabilitate; between 1853 and 1893, girls accounted for only 39 percent of CAS placements (Holt 1992).

By the end of the 1800s, the basic language of CAS terms remained in place, but it also began to reflect changing times and attitudes. This was partly a response to increased outside criticism, but it also reflected the lessons learned from instances in which youngsters ran away or were transferred without CAS knowledge to another family or to an institution. CAS, as well as other agencies, also recognized that while it had focused on youngsters as laborers, another segment of the population did not want workers. Childless couples, as well as those who had lost a child through death, sought young children. Aware of her situation, a placed-out girl later wrote: "My [new] mother had twin girls that were stillborn, and I guess I was supposed to make up for them" (*Minneapolis Star and Tribune* 1986). Those wanting children under the age of five or six typically asked for girls, believing that they were easier than boys to rear (Zelizer 1985). When CAS placed both boys and girls under the age of fourteen, it strongly stressed long-term residence in the homes that took them, and it began to mention adoption as a form of guardianship. "If not adopted," read one announcement, "[children] must be retained as members of the family until they are 18 years of age, and they must be sent to school regularly" (*Elk County Citizen* 1899). By the early 1900s, the society tried to be more exact in states with adoption laws. A 1916 announcement, for example, stated that legal adoption was not required but those families wishing to exercise that option "can not adopt the little person for at least a year" (*Wilson County Citizen* 1919). Whether families abided by CAS wishes is unclear.

Generally, CAS trusted local committees to screen placement families and for those families to be honorably motivated. CAS was not alone. Other placing agencies relied on the good intentions of placement homes and their sense of obligation to the children. Other agencies also faced problems of removing and then relocating children more than once, and they sometimes found that children had been transferred without their approval. As one example, a receiving family in Kansas decided that the child it had accepted from the Foundling Hospital was "difficult" and placed her in an orphanage (Holt 1992).

NEW PERSPECTIVES AND METHODOLOGIES

In the late nineteenth century there was a noticeable shift in philosophies and methodologies. Child-welfare agencies, rooted in religious charity, more often found themselves at odds with secular agencies and regulators steeped in social work training and methodologies. Social work and sociology were becoming recognized fields of study by the late 1890s. By 1923, sixteen university programs were allied with the recently organized Association of Training Schools for Professional Social Work. Academically trained social workers adopted the Progressive Era's approach to solving social ills, using population studies and scientific inquiry and problem-solving. There was no room for charity as a missionary effort. The new professionals ascended while religious-based agencies grappled with either falling into step or being dismissed as antiquated. Worse was the prospect of being shut down or severely curtailed in their work by state and/or city departments responsible for monitoring all charitable agencies within a jurisdiction. These departments and boards, which propagated in the late 1800s, were increasingly staffed by trained professionals who had the power to evaluate the activities of private charitable organizations, to demand reports, and to call their practices into question. It was a bitter pill for organizations that had operated on the precept that nothing needed to be known about their work but its well-intentioned, religious foundation.

In this changing environment, orphan train practitioners began to shift their emphasis from transporting children to concentrating on other forms of child care, including in-city foster care or programs that kept children at home while their parents received help to keep the family together. Organizations devoted to child rescue, even those not engaged in child transportation, were influenced by the new professionals. A case in point was the New York Society for the Prevention of Cruelty to Children (NYSPCC), organized in 1874 and modeled after the American Society for the Prevention of Cruelty to Animals (1866). Established after the sensational case of Mary Ellen, a girl severely abused by her guardians, NYSPCC opened a shelter, investigated boarding and foster homes, and campaigned against baby farms where infants were more likely to die than receive care. During the Progressive Era, however, NYSPCC reflected national trends. Its emphasis shifted from crusader tactics to scientific study of abuse, including environmental factors such as poverty, and its methodology emphasized family rehabilitation (Gordon 1988; Pleck 1987). Orphan train agencies, such as the New England Home for Little Wanderers which began to hire professional social workers in the early 1900s, generally took the same direction. In doing so, these agencies began to abandon orphan train placements altogether. When the orphan train era came to a close, all orphan train agencies except CAS had quit the practice.

The appearance of trained social workers in the field of charitable good works signaled a reevaluation of the orphan trains. At the same time, a number of different voices began to question and criticize the practice. By the end of the 1800s, complaints came from reformers, charitable organizations, state boards of charities, and state governments. The dialogue informed and clarified the weaknesses of orphan train placements. In turn, it heightened awareness of adoption procedures and contributed to changing or enhancing existing laws. As child-care advocates and reformers learned from placement agencies' experiences, they also began to define adoption and foster care as two similar, but separate, forms of child placement. Social adoption was replaced with codified adoption laws that transferred guardianship to adoptive parents. Foster care, on the other hand, was regulated by policies that kept guardianship in the hands of placing agencies.

ORPHAN TRAINS RECONSIDERED

With the Progressive Era, foster care and adoption became distinct avenues for providing home care, and while the orphan trains can be said to be an antecedent of modern-day foster care, it can also be argued that child relocation was tied to the development of adoption procedures. Both were informed by the practice. Among the most common criticisms aimed at the orphan trains, as well as the CAS as the primary practitioner, were:

1. Failure to investigate homes before placement or make follow-up home visits to assure children's safety and well-being. The accusations were partly true, but agencies did not make placements without first relying on local committees and clergy to vet receiving families and then make follow-up visitations. There is ample evidence that children were removed when

agents felt homes were unsatisfactory. Some children, however, were moved several times before there was a workable match between child and family, and CAS sometimes failed to visit homes in which teenagers were placed, calculating that they could look after themselves. CAS reliance on correspondence from placing families and the children was also a point of contention, since letters could easily hide the true nature of home life.

2. Failure to keep track of those who were placed out. CAS was most vulnerable to this accusation, but other agencies were just as culpable.

3. Placement of children without parental consent. While agencies argued that parents relinquished guardianship either by placing their children with an institution or voluntarily turning over children to a placing agency, critics argued that many parents, often illiterate and/or foreign-born, had not understood the long-term implications or the distance away from "home." Nor had they realized that the agencies felt it best to cut all ties between a child and biological relatives.

4. Religious prejudice. Protestants and Catholics accused each other of trying to convert children through placement, but neither side was faultless. Jewish and Protestant children were placed in Catholic homes; Catholic children were placed with Protestants. None of the participating charities made concerted attempts to place children according to religious heritage or, for that matter, cultural background.

5. Foisting incorrigible, diseased, mentally or physically handicapped children on unsuspecting communities and families. There were instances in which children with a disability or behavioral problem were placed, but agencies never intended to engage in the kind of activity of which they were accused. In fact, a CAS agent bemoaned his failed attempt to place-out an eight-year-old boy with "diseased eyes and other defects." Evidently, the agent was acting on his own for he acknowledged that "it was not 'policy,' as the learned say, to bring such a boy with others . . . , and the law, too, is against it" (Kidder 2001).

States that had once welcomed orphan train placements began to grumble. Increased populations and urbanization meant that they had their own poor and dependent to care for and place. States resented being a "dumping ground for dependents from other states" (Butler 1923), and in-state agencies argued that their resources should not be expended on out-of-state "pauper children" who might be abandoned by both the placing agencies and receiving families. The Kansas Children's Service League, for example, called the care and supervision required of it and other in-state organizations "financial burdens . . . which we could not bear" (Richmond 1994).

Complaints turned into legislation aimed at the orphan trains. In 1895, Michigan required agencies to place a bond with county probate judges for each child resettled. Almost ten years earlier, Minnesota wanted to impose an age limit—no child above the age of twelve was to be transported. The restriction would curtail the arrival of teenage boys who were increasingly viewed as troublesome placements, but it acknowledged the apparent cultural preference for younger children. By the late 1890s, Minnesota's board of corrections and charities brought enough pressure to bear that CAS changed its mode of operation. Rather than take children into a town for placement, it left youngsters with an in-state charity that then found placement homes. Minnesota authorities were not placated. By the beginning of the twentieth century, a number of states including Indiana, Illinois, Missouri, Minnesota, and Nebraska had addressed a number of home placement issues. Among them were placement of "mentally defective" children, placement of children with certain diseases or physical handicaps, and legislation that instructed courts to demand proof of guardianship from an institution prior to formal adoption (White 1893; *Annotated Code of Nebraska* 1901; Holt 1992). Kansas, which passed its first adoption law in 1864, passed one of the most restrictive laws against child transportation in 1901. Among its stipulations was a requirement that placing organizations pay a guaranty bond of $5,000 to the state. The 1901 statute was reinforced with a 1903 law that forbade adoption of children sent by out-of-state agencies unless all requirements governing adoption had been met, including a guarantee that the child was healthy in mind and body and not of "vicious character" (Swanson 1923).

By 1924, twenty-eight states had laws regulating the "importation of dependent children" (U.S. Children's Bureau, No. 139, 1924). At the same time, state laws began to contain "religious protection" clauses that demanded children be placed in adoptive homes of like faith, "as far as practicable" (*Cobbey's Annotated Statutes* 1905). The language of state laws trying to stop child relocation did not always address adoption directly, but as the Kansas law of 1903 and directives for religious protection suggest, the thought that went into curbing child relocation sometimes extended to state guidelines for adoption. The same could be said of foster care which emerged from the orphan train debates as a recognized form of child placement with guidelines that sometimes echoed the same concerns voiced for adoptive homes.

CONCLUSION

Weaknesses in the placing-out practices of orphan train agencies were instructive tools for reformers and child-care advocates. While they might agree with orphan train advocates when they reasoned that home life was preferable to institutionalization, they argued that placements took study, not the quick dispersal of children as seen in orphan train policies. In 1926, for example, a commentator noted the "need of studying the personality of each child if a good placement is to be made" (Verry 1926), and adoption laws such as Minnesota's 1917 statute began to mandate that some oversight agency, usually a state board of charity, decide if a child was "a proper subject for adoption" and if the adoptive home was "suitable" for the child (U.S. Children's Bureau, No. 148, 1925). The fact that orphan train agencies admitted to sometimes trying multiple placements before one was successful indicated hasty methods that focused on finding a family rather than making a good match between child and family. Social work philosophy of the early twentieth century argued that agencies had to consider personality and personal relationships within a family. It was just as important to accept the probability that not all children were candidates for long-term, permanent placement, nor did a simple willingness to take a child prove that a receiving family was emotionally or financially able to provide a good adoptive home.

Adoption law and its procedures varied from state to state and evolved over time. Guidelines became more detailed. The language became more precise. It was not until the Progressive Era, for example, that reformers and child-care advocates made clear distinctions between foster care and adoptive homes (Bellingham 1984). Other aspects of child placement and adult guardianship changed too. Private laws went by the wayside. Indenture fell into disrepute as reformers called for a "more intelligent" approach to child placement and criticized states that retained indenture laws (Deardorff 1926). Over time, with demands for change and state laws that eliminated some forms of guardianship, the courts actually reduced the choices one had for establishing and maintaining guardian status.

Adoption, as Brace and his contemporaries understood it in the 1850s, had two meanings. There was adoption in the social context, unencumbered by court proceedings, and there was the less-available, less-tried legal process. Those who championed the orphan trains had never intended to alter or reform adoption in either form; nor did they set out to clearly separate foster care from adoption placements. Nonetheless, the issue of child relocation was influential. State pressure to control or terminate the interstate transport and placement of dependent children sometimes directly influenced the wording of state adoption laws, and shortcomings in orphan train home placements served as instructive examples for reformers. By 1930, when the orphan trains were no longer active, adoption as a legal proceeding with state guidelines had superceded the old social contract. Foster care was no longer portrayed as an expression of religious charity. It too required guidelines grounded in methodology, (see in Chapter 3 of this volume). No doubt changes would have occurred without the orphan trains and the debates that surrounded the practice, but it can be argued that the orphan trains had an impact. However unwittingly, the well-meaning practice of transporting children to new homes via the orphan trains played a role in the evolution of foster care and adoption as specific types of home placement. The orphan trains informed and shaped social ideologies, reformist discussions, and public policy.

REFERENCES

Abbott, Edith. 1927. "The Civil War and the Crime Wave of 1865–70." *Social Service Review* 1 (June): 219.

Annotated Code of Nebraska, 1901. Beatrice, NE: J. E. Cobbey.

Annual Reports of the Children's Aid Society, nos. 1–10, Feb. 1854–Feb. 1863. 1971. New York: Arno Press and the New York Times.

Bellingham, Bruce William. 1984. " 'Little Wanderers': A Socio-Historical Study of the Nineteenth Century Origins of Child Fostering and Adoption Reform, Based on Early Records of the New York Children's Aid Society." Ph.D. diss., University of Pennsylvania.

Brace, Charles Loring. 1872. *The Dangerous Classes of New York and Twenty Years' Work Among Them.* New York: Wynkoop.

Brace, Emma, ed. 1894. *The Life of Charles Loring Brace, Chiefly Told in His Own Letters.* New York: Scribner's.

Bremner, Robert H. 1980. *The Public Good: Philanthropy and Welfare in the Civil War Era.* New York: Alfred A. Knopf.

Butler, Amos W. 1923. "The Indiana Plan for Supervision." In *Public Welfare in the UnitedStates: The Annals,* ed. Howard W. Odum, 122–24. Philadelphia: American Academy of Political and Social Services.

Children's Aid Society. Placement Card. Orphan Train Heritage Society of America, Concordia, KS.

The Children's Aid Society of New York: Its History, Plan and Results. 1893. New York: Wynkoop and Hallenbeck.

Cobbey's Annotated Statutes of Nebraska, Supplement of 1905. Beatrice, NE: J. E. Cobbey.

Deardorff, Neva R. 1926. "Bound Out." *Survey* 56, no. 8: 459.

Elk County Citizen. July 13, 1899. Newspaper Microfilm. Kansas State Historical Society, Topeka, KS.

First Annual Report of the Children's Mission to the Children of the Destitute. 1850. Boston: Benjamin H. Greene.

Gordon, Linda. 1988. *Heroes of Their Own Lives: The Politics and History of Family Violence, Boston, 1880–1960.* New York: Viking.

Holt, Marilyn Irvin. 1992. *The Orphan Trains: Placing Out in America.* Lincoln: University of Nebraska Press.

Illinois General Assembly, Private Laws, 1837. Elizabeth Collins, Petitioner. Illinois State Archives, Springfield, IL.

Kidder, Clark. 2001. *Orphan Trains and Their Precious Cargo: The Life's Work of Rev. H. D. Clarke.* Bowie, MD: Heritage Books.

Minneapolis Star and Tribune, September 17, 1986.

Nims, Elinor. 1927. "Experiments in Adoption Legislation." *Social Service Review* 1 (June): 241–48.

———. 1928. *The Illinois Adoption Law and its Administration.* Chicago: University of Chicago Press.

"Placing-out Agent Clara Comstock." 1988. *Crossroads* (Newsletter of the Orphan Train Heritage Society of America) 4: 4.

Pleck, Elizabeth Hafkin. 1987. *Domestic Tyranny: The Making of Social Policy Against Family Violence from Colonial Times to the Present.* New York: Oxford University Press.

Richmond, Robert W. 1994. *A Century of Caring: The Kansas Children's Service League, 1893–1993.* Topeka: Kansas Children's Service League.

Swanson, Nina. 1923. "The Development of Public Protection of Children in Kansas." *Collections of the Kansas State Historical Society* 15: 250–65.

U.S. Children's Bureau Publication no. 139. 1924. *Laws Relating to Interstate Placement of Dependent Children.* Washington, DC: U.S. Government Printing Office.

U.S. Children's Bureau Publication no. 148. 1925. *Adoption Laws in the United States: A Summary of the Development of Adoption Legislation and Significant Features of Adoption Statutes, with the Text of Selected Laws.* Washington, DC: U.S. Government Printing Office.

Verry, Ethel. 1926. "Eighty Years Ago." *Survey* 56, no. 6: 384–85.

Vogt, Martha Nelson, and Christina Vogt. 1983. *Searching for Home: Three Families from the Orphan Trains.* Grand Rapids, MI: Triumph Press.

White, Francis H. 1893. "Placing Out New York Children in the West." *The Charities Review: A Journal of Practical Sociology* 2: 216–25.

Wilson County Citizen. June 2, 1919. Orphan Trains of Kansas File. Kansas Collection, University of Kansas, Lawrence, KS.

Zelizer, Viviana A. 1985. *Pricing the Priceless Child: The Changing Social Value of Children.* New York: Basic Books.

3 Science, Social Work, and Bureaucracy: Cautious Developments in Adoption and Foster Care, 1930–1969

Dianne Creagh

The 1920s marked the beginning of the end for zealous urban welfare work on behalf of dependent children. The righteous indignation over the plight of abandoned and abused youth that had erected grand orphanages and carried out vast rescue and relocation schemes withered from a flame to a flicker. The years that followed, from Roosevelt's New Deal to Johnson's Great Society, were relatively staid in terms of tenacious innovation. Compared to activists in the late 1800s and early 1900s, adoption and foster care administrators of the mid-twentieth century cultivated an atmosphere of studied objectivity, painstaking adherence to scientific principles, and above all, caution.

Nevertheless, these were groundbreaking decades in which significant developments transformed adoption and foster care into the multifaceted systems we know today. The transformation was driven by a diverse collection of increasingly specialized policymakers and reformers who segmented those seeking adoption and foster care services into distinct populations along social, economic, and ethnic lines. Therefore, this chapter explores this important period thematically rather than chronologically so the reader can better grasp how particular interest groups shaped adoption and foster care in often contrary ways.

The first two sections discuss how foster care and adoption gradually eclipsed orphanages, the dominant mode of sheltering and caring for dependent children in the nineteenth century, as social workers and child development experts imposed new standards and practices on voluntary organizations. The next four themes focus on the forces driving the emergent white adoption market in a more bureaucratized direction, while simultaneously homogenizing adoptive families. The final three sections detail the momentous contrary developments that truly distinguished adoption in the mid-twentieth century from previous decades: the growth in international adoption across racial lines which openly rejected the "as if begotten" model of adoptive kinship, and the simultaneous increase in confidentiality surrounding most other adoption procedures that frustrated adoptees' efforts to trace their biological origins—a frustration that would eventually lead some to publicly denounce legalized secrecy in adoption by the end of the period.

The four decades surveyed here may have lacked some of the passion and boldness of earlier times, but they deserve careful consideration for the historic shifts in ideology, policy, and practice that redirected dependent child care down unexplored pathways, toward an uncertain future.

ORPHANAGES AND ORPHAN TRAINS

By the 1920s, time-honored solutions to child dependency were dissolving as new sensibilities emerged regarding the nature of poverty and dependent children. In 1929, the last of the New York Children's Aid Society orphan trains deposited their cargos in western communities before finally succumbing to mounting obstacles, including laws barring the interstate traffic of children, a growing tendency among professional social workers to keep troubled families together, and mandatory education statutes that discouraged the use of dependent children as indentured labor (Holt 1992; see also Chapter 2 in this volume). Enthusiasm for charitable orphanages had also steadily declined among child-welfare advocates. Boarding children in private homes or, better still, enabling mothers to keep their children with the help of state-funded mothers' pensions was the new strategy of choice (Mink 1995; Cauthen and Amenta 1996). During the 1920s, many institutions emptied their beds and released their wards into foster care or suburban cottage systems, amending their missions to institutionalize only those with physical and emotional challenges.

Distress caused by the Great Depression, however, temporarily revived the demand for institutional services. At the height of the economic crisis, hundreds of thousands of homeless children were set adrift to search for work and shelter. Destitute youth who remained at home remained vulnerable to the demoralizing effects of poverty that drove their parents to illness, alcoholism, desertion, and death. Many ended up as dependent cases, some orphaned or abandoned, but most committed by destitute family members who hoped to reclaim them at some future date. Journalist and humorist Art Buchwald recalled the years after his mother was committed to a mental institution as a nomadic, unpredictable time. He and his sisters were shuffled from one institution to another, while their father struggled to pay their boarding fees with his meager income. "As I changed shelters, I became convinced that I would always be on the move," he wrote in his autobiography, *Leaving Home*. "I adjusted to the shifts, first with tears, but, as I grew older, with a smile. I never let on how frightening the moves were to me." Buchwald recalled never being certain to whom he really belonged. No matter how kind the matrons of the orphanages and foster homes were, he "felt like an intruder using one of their bedrooms" (Buchwald 1993).

By the mid-1930s the orphanage population had swelled to 144,000, the highest capacity ever (Berebitsky 2000). In order to stretch their already meager resources, they crowded two or three residents into each bed, cut services, dug into their own capital funds, and begged contributions for food and fuel. When the crisis abated, however, orphanages found themselves worse off financially than before the Depression. Some picked up where they had left off in the 1920s, redirecting their work to serve children deemed ineligible for foster care. Others emptied their beds and closed their doors for good.

SUBSIDIZED FOSTER CARE

As institutions groaned under the weight of overcapacity during the 1930s, the growing system of paid foster care experienced a similar strain. Many parents used both foster homes and orphanages to shelter and feed their children until the family could be reunited. Since most dependent children were not available for adoption, they failed to attract applicants with free homes who were seeking sons and daughters to call their own. Over time, subsidized foster care eclipsed the free foster system, forcing agencies to provide stipends to foster parents under increasingly harsh financial conditions. Compounding the problem was the difficulty caseworkers faced in finding qualified applicants who could provide a stable, healthy environment. One Jewish orphanage launched an earnest, if ultimately ineffectual, radio campaign to recruit new foster parents, imploring listeners to respond to their call for "new homes" and "good homes," because "One family home is likely to serve one child or family of children and befriend it for many years" (Boretz 1938). The rising tide of needy children forced agencies to make exceptions for less-qualified applicants, and overload foster parents already on the payroll.

The ongoing challenges of caring for children made homeless by family stress demanded a federal initiative that could keep families from dissolving in the first place. Mothers' pensions, a collection of unevenly distributed and meagerly funded state programs that benefited only a select few white widows, were a Progressive Era innovation that had proved utterly inadequate. Aid to Dependent Children (ADC), Title IV of Roosevelt's 1935 Social Security Act, expanded the definition of dependency to include children who had lost a parent's care due to death, absence from the home, or prolonged incapacity (Cauthen and Amenta 1996). Although it was far from adequate to meet the needs of all who might benefit, especially foster children living away from home, ADC did serve to reduce child dependency by providing just enough funds to keep many parents from having to relinquish their children. In 1933, 59 out of every 10,000 children in the United States lived in foster care, an all-time high. Gradually, the number fell to 38 per 10,000 by 1960 (Ashby 1997).

In 1962, just as the ever-shrinking system was suddenly flooded anew with children displaced by a revived interest in detecting and preventing child abuse, further amendments extended ADC's scope to cover foster care costs for children who became wards of the state. By the mid-1970s, the number of children in foster care had ballooned once more to an all-time high of 75 out of every 10,000, leading to new congressional initiatives in the early 1980s to expedite the adoption of children languishing in unstable foster arrangements (Ashby 1997).

MATERNITY HOMES AND PROFESSIONAL CASEWORK WITH UNWED MOTHERS

Interest in infant adoption also grew during the Depression. Since the late nineteenth century, significant improvements in pediatric medicine, nutrition, and prevention of epidemics in infant hospitals had dramatically increased the number of dependent babies surviving to childhood. And significant shifts in social work practices with unwed mothers channeled these infants directly into the adoption market.

Up until the late 1920s, the evangelical women who staffed maternity homes pressed unwed mothers to keep their offspring in order to redeem themselves and avoid future indiscretions. In the early 1910s, professionals in the emerging field of social work were seeking new domains of influence. Turning their gaze on the perceived crisis of illegitimacy, they launched an attack against what they termed the sentimental, antiquated approach of religious reformers that treated unwed mothers as innocent victims of seduction and abandonment. Social workers saw these same women as neurotic, delinquent, ignorant, and unfit to raise their own children. They began scrutinizing maternity home operations and advocating for trained caseworkers to be brought on staff. Once in charge, social workers counseled clients to sign relinquishment agreements, freeing up thousands of healthy, white infants for adoption (Kunzel 1993).

Awaiting these babies were thousands of middle-class, childless couples eager to open their homes to the newborn of a perfect stranger. A Minnesota study published in 1933 revealed that most adoptive parents of the early twentieth century lived in the city rather than the country and rejected working-age children in favor of babies they could raise as their own. (Leahy 1933). Typically middle-aged and financially secure, they viewed adoption not as an act of charity or a means of acquiring household help, but as a path to personal fulfillment through parenting. For this purpose infants were ideal—particularly girls, who were often perceived as more malleable and innocent—allowing couples to raise a child who had known no other parents and match their adoptive family to the biological model. The *New York Times* reported in 1935 that adoption agencies were having difficulty placing older children. One "nice 10-year-old boy" was repeatedly rejected by prospective parents who complained he was "too old," without ever seeing him ("Adoption Sought" 1935).

This new demand for infants coincided with the rise of the "companionate" family, the end result of the marked transformation in the family's social role over the course of the nineteenth century from performing "economic, educational, and welfare functions" to providing emotional and psychological contentment for its members (Mintz and Kellogg 1988). The ability of childless couples to meet the new expectations of domestic bliss depended heavily on the availability of adoptable infants, which in turn depended on the willingness of unhappily pregnant young women to relinquish their offspring.

After World War II, social workers moved with increasing authority toward a revised diagnosis of unwed mothers as "disturbed" but "curable" (Solinger 1992). Relinquishment now offered the maternity home client an unprecedented opportunity to transform herself and reemerge into respectable society, childless and unscathed. Through the mother's transformation, her baby, too, could be cleansed of stigma and made into a highly marketable commodity.

Since states denied women easy access to birth control and abortion, it is little wonder that most residents complied with the maternity home's adoption mandate. Social workers counseled the mother to consider the advantages her child would receive in its new home, which the worker promised to select with extreme care. One unmarried mother noted the way her social worker expressed approval of adoption with body language: "It's not what Mrs. K. says exactly, it's just that her face lights up when I talk about adoption the way it doesn't when I talk about keeping Beth" (Kunzel 1993). It was also not uncommon for agencies to withhold financial assistance from uncooperative mothers, while offering those interested in adoption free room and board. Yet casework was not a one-way street. Many birthmothers collaborated with social workers in streamlining the process. Nevertheless, some caseworkers and even public officials took extreme measures to separate reluctant women from their babies, using deceitful and illegal means. One unwed mother in Georgia reported that a juvenile detention officer, in cahoots with a pro-adoption juvenile court judge, "informed me that my baby had been born dead" and advised her to sign a paper "authorizing the burial of the child." Later she was "shocked" to receive adoption documents in the mail from California since she had been "under the impression that the child was deceased" (Solinger 1992).

"ILLEGITIMACY" IN BLACK FAMILIES

In contrast to the highly marketable white child, black illegitimate infants were considered to be an encumbrance upon society, an attitude that "exacerbated racism and racial antagonism in the postwar era" (Solinger 1992). The same psychiatric theory that advocated investing considerable time and resources in saving white mothers from stigma rejected black mothers as sexually deviant, beyond rehabilitation. Some adoption policymakers dismissed the idea of providing services to pregnant black women on the grounds that black culture condoned unwed motherhood. Referring to the resourceful black tradition of kinship care in the face of exclusion from mainstream welfare programs, they offered the circular argument that since "Negroes always care for their own children," there was "very little need for foster care for dependent Negro children" (Solinger 1992). A minority of the professional social work set did welcome pregnant black women who were interested in relinquishment and reform, and set out to place their babies in black adoptive families. Despite studies claiming a significant number of black couples were willing to adopt, however, most maternity homes still refused to admit black clients, claiming there were no black applicants that measured up to their standards of propriety and affluence. The result was a pervasive neglect of black dependent children by the adoption community. In 1951, they constituted only 4 percent of all U.S. adoptions (Melosh 2002).

The Urban League temporarily revived the tradition of zealous child advocacy in the 1950s by confronting widespread racial discrimination in adoption work. The campaign met with skepticism from white agencies that were reluctant to relax their prohibitions against adoptive mothers working outside of the home, a bias that disqualified most black women from consideration. The number of black children placed in same-race families remained miniscule. Estimates for 1960 revealed that only 5 percent of adoptable nonwhite babies ended up in permanent homes, whereas workers placed-out a full 70 percent of white babies (Solinger 1992).

Meanwhile, the shortage of white babies was becoming more acute due to the emergence of oral contraceptives and the growing number of sexually liberated unwed mothers who rejected relinquishment. Agencies began offering black children instead. From the mid-1960s through the early 1970s, estimates placed the number of such adoptions at around 15,000 (Berebitsky 2000). In 1972, however, the National Association of Black Social Workers, informed by ideals of black pride and separatism, condemned the practice. It called for adoption workers to prioritize same-race placements and implement more flexible standards for black parent applicants (Melosh 2002). Advocates for Native American children likewise charged that the discriminatory tradition of separating Indian children from their families and placing them in government boarding schools and white homes amounted to cultural genocide (Garner 1993; Melosh 2002, 175–76; see also Chapter 4 in this volume).

ADOPTION BECOMES MAINSTREAM

In the 1930s, as interest in adoption grew, so did the frustration of would-be adoptive parents. Applicants faced the bewildering prospect of being unable to find adoptable children among the hundreds of thousands temporarily committed to state and private agencies by their own parents. Couples were further frustrated by the cool reception they received from professional social workers who presumed them unfit until extensive interviews, background checks, and invasive home studies proved otherwise. From would-be parents everywhere letters of complaint and yearning poured in to President and Mrs. Roosevelt. One desperate California woman pleaded with the First Lady, "Please oh Please can't you help me get a baby I grieve every time I see a baby, my heart aches to have one." She and her husband had "tried every way to get a child" but were told it would take at least two years due to the high demand. "I just don't know how I can go on much longer without a child," she confided. "I love children dearly" (Berebitsky 2000).

Yet, in reality, adoption was growing at an astounding rate. According to the U.S. Children's Bureau, there were approximately 17,000 adoptions in 1937. By 1945 that figure nearly tripled to 50,000, and only twelve years later improved survey methods revised the total upward to 91,000 annually (Melosh 2002). Many different factors converging over several decades produced the steady surge.

Imbued with new ideas about the emotional benefits of parenting described above, couples began rejecting adoption as a charitable gesture and framed it instead as a way to indulge in the rewards of family life. In the words of one adoptive father who published his own story in the 1950s, he and his wife "were dead set against the idea of adoption" because they refused to pick up the pieces of "other people's mistakes." But when their friends began expanding their own households, "we suddenly began to realize that we were missing something in life . . . something that hobbies, entertaining or a three-year-old cocker spaniel could never provide." After adopting their daughter, they often received compliments for being so "nice" to take in a homeless child. "They probably think we are a couple of do-gooders, when actually we are two of the most selfish people in the world," he insisted. "We adopted Barbara because we wanted her, and not because we thought we were doing her a favor" (Bell 1954).

Historians also credit the expansion of adoption to rising rates of illegitimate pregnancy and the compatibility of adoption with American Cold War culture. Barbara Melosh explains that in the postwar era of intense nationalism and pro-democratic fervor, adoption "gained new credibility as a kind of social engineering that appealed to American dreams of upward mobility and self-invention" (Melosh 2002).

DEVELOPING STANDARDS OF PARENTAL "FITNESS," INDEPENDENT BABY BROKERS, AND "BLACK MARKET" BABIES

The transformation of adoption from an act of charity to a legitimate—albeit still inferior—form of family-making went hand in hand with the growing influence of social workers. They became powerful gatekeepers, guiding birthmothers' decisions, meticulously screening prospective parents, and selectively distributing available children. In 1937, Sophie van Senden Theis, a prominent New York adoption advocate, defended the increased prominence of social workers in the field, saying, "Adoption work is not easy, but that is all the more reason for having it in skilled hands" (Theis 1937). By 1941, thirty-four states had amended their adoption statutes to require an official investigation by a social work professional into every adoption (Berebitsky 2000).

As social workers grew more dominant, licensed adoption work became increasingly bureaucratized and the application process for would-be adopters more intrusive. Couples now had to pass psychological muster by submitting to extensive interviews and background checks. Marjorie Winter described the grueling ordeal in a book about adopting her daughter. She recalled how she and her husband behaved as "humble petitioners, prostrate enough, we hoped, to satisfy the power-lust of some of the social workers we had to woo." The marathon application process left them "so thoroughly demoralized by the threat of rejection" that by the end "we had no more character left than a couple of rennet puddings" (Winter 1956). In return for their endurance and cooperation, social workers promised applicants to scientifically evaluate the health, intelligence, and temperament of each baby to ensure that the child selected would match as perfectly as one that might have been born to them (Berebitsky 2000; Melosh 2002). According to Theis and others who trumpeted the merits of "skilled social service," only professionals could provide the "understanding and experience" necessary to "prevent unnecessary and ill-advised adoption placements" (Theis 1937).

Many couples evidently decided, however, that obtaining a baby shortly after its birth and being left alone to pursue their dreams of parenthood were more important than infant IQ tests and guarantees. Independent baby brokers, mostly doctors and lawyers, attracted couples and birthmothers seeking faster transactions with less red tape and greater confidentiality. Their business boomed despite lurid tales of predatory dealers peddling defective babies (Berebitsky 2000; Melosh 2002). In the 1950s, the Kefauver Senate Subcommittee to Investigate Juvenile Delinquency held hearings on the black market that condemned all unlicensed adoption transactions. Nevertheless, illegal trafficking continued to thrive, and professional agencies were forced to compete by relaxing some of their requirements. Their efforts paid off with a steady rise in the number of adoptions transacted through licensed agencies. In 1945 they attracted only about one-fourth of all adoption business. By 1951, however, half of adopters acquired their children through agencies, a ratio that would climb to 80 percent by 1971 (Melosh 2002).

Despite ongoing competition from black market dealers, licensed adoption practitioners enjoyed a huge surplus of applicants from which to select the most desirable parents. Young, infertile couples had the best chance because their family would most closely adhere to the baby-boom mandate of early marriage and pregnancy. Older couples were steered toward hard-to-place children (Berebitsky 2000). Single women, who were once thought to possess useful maternal instincts, found themselves dropped from consideration altogether following the emergence of the "lesbian menace" in the 1920s. Not until the late 1960s, when the increasing frequency of divorce began normalizing the single-parent family, and the women's liberation movement encouraged new expressions of independence and self-sufficiency, were single women again able to adopt (Berebitsky 2000).

TRANSRACIAL AND INTERNATIONAL ADOPTION

Experiments in racial diversity within adoptive families began in earnest after World War II, when some American couples took in Japanese children orphaned by the atomic bomb attacks. Similar efforts followed with Korean children, Afro-German babies (the biracial offspring of black American servicemen stationed overseas), and later with American Indian and Latin American children, as well as Vietnamese refugees (Altstein and Simon 1991; Collmeyer 1995; Melosh 2002). Some advocates of transracial and transnational adoption were politically conscious citizens making a statement in favor of racial integration. Pearl S. Buck, prize-winning author and humanitarian, was one of the first to take a public stand on behalf of homeless children overseas, especially mixed-race "G.I. babies" marginalized and abandoned in their own countries. "We Americans must take up our responsibility because we helped bring these children into the world," she declared. Her adoption agency, Welcome House, founded in 1949, placed children of American-Asian parentage with couples of all racial and religious backgrounds. She and her husband also adopted several themselves. "A child is a child," she insisted, "no matter what his race or religion" ("Pearl Buck" 1958; Rockwell 1972).

Others believed their work was infused with a divine mandate. Harry Holt, an Oregon farmer, embarked on "the work of the Lord," adopting several homeless Korean children and founding his own adoption organization in 1956 that placed some 3,000 mixed-race abandoned Korean youth in American families ("Harry Holt" 1964). Likewise, Helen Doss and her husband, a Methodist minister, adopted a large brood of children from East Asia, Europe, and the Philippines, many of whom were also multiracial. Doss rejected notions of white superiority and racial segregation in adoption on theological grounds. "East may be East and West may be West, but the twain *can* meet and get along with each other" because "God is the father of all mankind; we are all God's children, and all men are brothers" (Doss 1954).

The persistent shortage of healthy white babies on the adoption market also contributed to the willingness of white Americans to transgress racial and national boundaries in search of parenting opportunities. The sexual revolution and the arrival of the birth control pill ushered in a new acceptance of female sexuality outside of marriage, and even of unwed pregnancy. As the stigma of "illegitimacy" faded, mental health experts retreated from their previous assertion that relinquishment was the only viable solution for unwed mothers. One doctor admitted that he had "yet to see any woman willingly relinquish her child" to adoption. "Giving away a baby, even a baby a girl doesn't want," he insisted, "leaves deep emotional scars." Another physician lamented "the heartlessness, the cruelty, and the sadism" foisted on accidentally pregnant women in the interests of adoption. Most of the women he saw "adamantly rejected" suggestions to give birth to a baby "and then hand it over, never to see it again, to someone else to rear" (Solinger 1992). Later, legalized abortion allowed women to avoid altogether the agonizing dilemma of keeping a child they were unready for or relinquishing their newborn to strangers. Maternity homes soon became obsolete. Between 1952 and 1972 over half of all white unwed mothers gave up their babies. By the early 1980s, however, only about 3 percent did so (Berebitsky 2000). For an increasing number of childless couples, overseas adoption provided their best opportunity to achieve the family life they so desired.

Whatever their motives, the number of adopters seeking nonwhite children from other countries grew steadily in the late twentieth century. Their families conspicuously challenged the "as if begotten" model of American adoption, lending credence to the notion that kinship was not so much about biological heredity as selflessly caring for another (Berebitsky 2000; Melosh 2002).

CASE RECORDS, SECRECY, AND DISCLOSURE

Prior to World War II, adoption agencies willingly disclosed case record information. Adoptive parents usually received an extensive medical and social history of their child, and most agencies gladly facilitated meetings between blood relatives separated by adoption.

The first statute protecting records from public view to shield children from the stigma of illegitimacy was the 1917 Children's Code of Minnesota.

By 1938, however, only five other states had adopted similar laws, and not until the 1940s did an amendment to the Social Security Act increase the confidentiality of adoption records in many other states. The practice of issuing a second, falsified birth certificate listing the adoptive parents in place of the child's biological parents was only gradually adopted by individual states beginning in the 1930s (Carp 1998).

Not until the postwar era would adoption proceedings become shrouded beneath a nearly impenetrable veil of silence. Wayne Carp attributes this change in part to the increasingly upscale population of unwed mothers who demanded that the transaction leave no trace in the public record. Social workers became more suspicious of adult adoptees returning for information about biological relatives, and more inclined toward "secrecy and legalism," recasting adoptees' inquiries as a sign of maladjustment (Carp 1998). One psychotherapist proposed that the "antidote" for such inclinations could be found in "a healthy, secure, satisfying relationship between the child and his adoptive parents" (Carp 1998). Withholding identifying information from all parties became the new casework standard.

Social workers did, however, advocate disclosing the fact of the adoption to the child beginning in the preschool years by framing the news within a sanguine "chosen baby" story. Parents were advised to emphasize their earnest quest to find a child, their implicit rejection of other children who did not meet their expectations, and the perfect suitability of the son or daughter they selected for their new adoptive family. Josephine Antoine, opera singer and adoptee, wrote in 1947 of learning the truth when she was still a toddler: "I want to tell you something before anyone else does," her mother began hesitantly. "We adopted you because you were so sweet and dear, and we wanted you so much." She urged her daughter not to feel "different" or "ashamed," but rather "proud" because "We picked you out" (Antoine 1947). By the 1930s the theme had become so widely accepted that when Valentina Wasson's *The Chosen Baby* storybook appeared in 1939 it became an instant success (Wasson 1939).

Critics, on the other hand, felt that lying to children about the adoption process was harmful. Few couples were actually allowed to peruse several babies among the few available and pick their favorite. The first psychiatrist to publicly challenge the "chosen" school of telling, Irene M. Josselyn, warned that children would soon realize "he who has been chosen on account of certain values, while others were rejected, could in turn be rejected if he disappointed his parents" (Carp 1998).

Many parents rejected the idea of telling altogether. They feared disclosing the adoption might result in losing their child's love. A 1959 issue of *McCall's* featured a confessional piece by an adoptive mother entitled "To My Adopted Daughter: I Wish I Hadn't Told You," mourning the many social and psychological troubles her daughter had endured since learning of her true status. Lying is better, she insisted, because "the knowledge that one is adopted creates far more problems than the one it is supposed to solve" (Carp 1998).

Beginning in the 1950s, recalcitrant parents began receiving support from some child development experts who came out against early and frequent disclosure. Psychoanalyst Marshall D. Schechter reported that many disturbed adopted children appeared in his practice suffering from "severe narcissistic injury" because they had been told of their adoption when their "immature ego" could not yet "cope with the knowledge of the rejection by its original parents" (Carp 1998). Thus, according to Carp, parents seeking to adopt in the 1960s and 1970s faced a "cacophony of advice" in both academic and popular literature. Not until the mid-1970s would the voices of the different camps be eclipsed by "a single voice" calling for "openness not only in telling but in all aspects of adoption" (Carp 1998).

ROOTS OF THE ADOPTION RIGHTS MOVEMENT

As adoption surged in the postwar era, the population of adoptees raised with "chosen baby" stories, vague explanations of their backgrounds, and permanently sealed adoption records was large, affluent, and receptive to new interpretations of their experience.

In 1953, Jean M. Paton, a social worker and adoptee, founded the Life History Study Center and shortly afterward the first adoptee search organization, Orphan Voyage (Carp 1998). Her groundbreaking study, *The Adopted Break Silence* (1954), introduced the radical concept that adoptees comprise a community of people oppressed by the legalized gag rules surrounding adoption. "If adopted people wanted to try to build a responsible way of reconciling with natural families, should they not be allowed to try?" she reasoned in her follow-up study, *Three Trips Home.* "Were they inferior people, who must cool their heels outside of the agency office, waiting for a nod?" (Paton 1960). Florence Fisher, who later took up Paton's call and launched ALMA, the Adoptees' Liberty Movement Association, recalled in her autobiography the "strained, tense atmosphere" in her childhood home caused by the fear surrounding the "dark secret" of her adoption that her parents tried to keep from her at all costs. Upon reaching adulthood she tracked down the doctor who had arranged the adoption for her parents. When she pressed him to admit she had another set of parents, he responded indignantly, "Didn't you have a good home? Aren't you grateful?" (Fisher 1973). Paton's groundbreaking notion of facilitating constructive meetings between adoptees and their relatives through centralized reunion registries together with Fisher's righteous militancy would provide an ideological foundation for ARM, the Adoption Rights Movement, which emerged in the early 1970s to shake up the entire adoption community. A few years later, activist birth parents would follow suit by forming their own organization to denounce the "inhumane" system of adoption and demand the right to reunite with their long lost children (Carp 1998).

CONCLUSION

The momentous course of dependent child care from the 1930s through the 1960s laid the groundwork for the profound developments we have witnessed in recent decades, including backlashes against entitlement programs for dependent children; continued conflicts over racial matching in foster care; grassroots rights movements by adoptees, birthmothers, and adoptive parents; custody suits brought by birth parents to reclaim their biological children; open adoption, gay and lesbian adoption, and the proliferation of transracial and transnational adoption opportunities. What began as evangelical child-saving in the mid-1800s was transformed during the course of the twentieth century into a professional, bureaucratized, complex network of efforts to confront illegitimacy and dependency. What has emerged is a new understanding of kinship that at once challenges and upholds the biological nuclear family concept in American culture, and that will continue to shape our responses to dependent children and their caregivers well into the new millennium.

REFERENCES

"Adoption Sought for Older Waifs." 1935. *New York Times*, November 22: 17.

Altstein, Howard, and Rita James Simon. 1991. *Intercountry Adoption: A Multinational Perspective.* New York: Praeger.

Antoine, Josephine. 1947. "I Was an Adopted Child." *Woman's Home Companion* (February): 36–37, 94.

Ashby, LeRoy. 1997. *Endangered Children: Dependence, Neglect, and Abuse in American History.* New York: Twayne.

Bell, Harry. 1954. *We Adopted a Daughter.* Boston: Houghton Mifflin.

Berebitsky, Julie. 2000. *"Like Our Very Own": Adoption and the Changing Culture of Motherhood, 1851–1950.* Lawrence: University Press of Kansas.

Boretz, Mary E. 1938. Untitled Speech. New York: Hebrew Sheltering Guardian Society.

Buchwald, Art. 1993. *Leaving Home: A Memoir.* New York: G. P. Putnam's.

Carp, E. Wayne. 1998. *Family Matters: Secrecy and Disclosure in the History of Adoption.* Cambridge, MA: Harvard University Press.

Cauthen, Nancy K., and Edwin Amenta. 1996. "Not for Widows Only: Institutional Politics and the Formative Years of Aid to Dependent Children." *American Sociological Review* 61, no. 3: 427–48.

Collmeyer, Patricia M. 1995. "From 'Operation Brown Baby' to 'Opportunity': The Placement of Children of Color at the Boys and Girls Aid Society of Oregon." *Child Welfare* 74, no. 1: 242–53.

Doss, Helen G. 1954. *The Family Nobody Wanted*. Boston: Little, Brown.

Fisher, Florence. 1973. *The Search for Anna Fisher*. New York: Arthur Fields Books.

Garner, Suzanne. 1993. "The Indian Child Welfare Act: A Review." *Wicazo Sa Review* 9, no. 1: 47–51.

Gordon, Linda. 1988. *Heroes of Their Own Lives: The Politics and History of Family Violence: Boston, 1880–1960*. New York: Viking.

"Harry Holt, Who Found Parents for 3,000 Korean Orphans, Dies." 1964. *New York Times*, April 29: 41.

Holt, Marilyn Irvin. 1992. *The Orphan Trains: Placing Out in America*. Lincoln: University of Nebraska Press.

Kunzel, Regina G. 1993. *Fallen Women, Problem Girls: Unmarried Mothers and the Professionalization of Benevolence, 1890–1945*. New Haven, CT: Yale University Press.

Leahy, Alice M. 1933. "Some Characteristics of Adoptive Parents." *American Journal of Sociology* 38, no. 4: 548–63.

Melosh, Barbara. 2002. *Strangers and Kin: The American Way of Adoption*. Cambridge, MA: Harvard University Press.

Mink, Gwendolyn. 1995. *The Wages of Motherhood: Inequality in the Welfare State, 1917–1942*. Ithaca, NY: Cornell University Press.

Mintz, Steven, and Susan Kellogg. 1988. *Domestic Revolutions: A Social History of American Family Life*. New York: Free Press.

Morton, Marian J. 2000. "Surviving the Great Depression: Orphanages and Orphans in Cleveland." *Journal of Urban History* 26, no. 4: 438–55.

Paton, Jean M. 1954. *The Adopted Break Silence: Forty Men and Women Describe Their Search for Natural Parents*. Cedaredge, CO: Orphan Voyage.

———. 1960. *Three Trips Home or Oedipus Revisited: Adoption Through the Eyes of the Adopted, a Presentation Organized Around Three Trips to Michigan from Philadelphia, in 1955*. Philadelphia: The Life History Study Center.

"Pearl Buck Meets New Adopted Girl." 1958. *New York Times*, July 19: 16.

Pleck, Elizabeth Hafkin. 1987. *Domestic Tyranny: The Making of Social Policy Against Family Violence from Colonial Times to the Present*. New York: Oxford University Press.

Rockwell, Winthrop A. 1972. "Efforts Grow to Bring Here Babies That G.I.'s Left in Vietnam." *New York Times*, January 3: 22.

Solinger, Rickie. 1992. *Wake Up Little Susie: Single Pregnancy and Race Before* Roe v. Wade. New York: Routledge.

Theis, Sophie van Senden. 1937. *Social Aspects of Child Adoption*. Eastern Regional Conference. New York: Child Welfare League of America.

Wasson, Valentina P. 1939. *The Chosen Baby*. Philadelphia: J. B. Lippincott.

Winter, Marjorie. 1956. *For the Love of Martha*. New York: Julian Messner.

4 Civil Rights, Adoption Rights: Domestic Adoption and Foster Care, 1970 to the Present

Martha Satz and Lori Askeland

"All power to the people!"—the rallying cry of the Black Panther Party—captures the democratic zeal of many activist groups in the 1960s and 1970s. During this period, a variety of grassroots organizations struggled, both in the United States and internationally, to expand the legal, social, and economic standing of ordinary people—especially women, ethnic minorities, young people, and people who do not identify as heterosexual. These movements invigorated several notions related to family-creation, some of which ultimately conflict with one another: that adult women, as well as men, have a right to create a family when and if they so choose; that all people and their families, regardless of color, should be accorded a certain amount of integrity and privacy (especially from public officials); that all children have a right to a stable family; and that we all have a right to "know" our families of origin and our cultures of origin. Moral fervor—distinct from but reminiscent of that which had characterized "child-saving" efforts of the late nineteenth century—returned to the scene in a variety of forms.

Possibly the most tangible effect of the civil rights movements in this arena was on the numbers of infant adoptions taking place each year. The women's movement laid the groundwork for the landmark ruling by the Supreme Court in 1973's *Roe v. Wade* case that legalized women's right to utilize abortion services and, along with the increased availability of contraception, facilitated an unprecedented freedom for women to choose when and whether to have children (see especially Solinger 2001). As a result, the numbers of racially and ethnically "matched" children available for domestic infant adoptions by white middle-class families decreased, and adoptions overall also decreased, having skyrocketed from a low of 50,000 adoptions in 1944 to a century-long high point in 1970 of about 175,000 (Maza 1984/2004; Herman 2004).[1] Since that date adoption numbers have leveled off at about 125,000 each year (Evan B. Donaldson Adoption Institute 2002b; Herman 2004), and, within that figure, the annual number of international adoptions has increased significantly (Herman 2004; U.S. Department of State 2004).

The complexities and the various ethical and legal issues raised by international adoption will be discussed by Elizabeth Bartholet in Chapter 5. This chapter will focus on domestic adoption and foster care. In particular, we will focus on the "Search Movement," sometimes called the "Adoption Rights Movement," and its connection to "open adoption." Prospective adoptive parents, who were largely white, increasingly became interested in adopting nonwhite children, including the growing numbers of foster children served by state welfare systems. Yet, equally a result of the civil rights movements, the adoption of children across ethnic lines—particularly the adoption of African American and American Indian children by white parents—remained controversial. Finally, and most recently, these same progressive movements also helped open the way to adoption and fostering by single adults and gay or lesbian couples—the latter a controversy that remains very much alive at the time of this writing.

THE SEARCH MOVEMENT

In recent history, a strong impulse has developed to dispense with the secrecy that shadowed adoption practice in the last part of the twentieth century. Beginning in the early 1970s, the Search Movement—largely comprised of adults seeking their biological parents and birthmothers seeking the children they had relinquished—culminated in a political movement to open formerly sealed adoption records. Although the controversy remains legally unresolved, the attitudes and pleas which have driven the political movement to open adoption records has resulted in an increasingly popular way of realizing adoption, "open adoption," in which varying degrees of contact exist between birth parents, the child, and adoptive parents. ("Adoption with contact" and "cooperative adoption" are terms for open adoptions with high levels of contact.) More traditional adoptions also have been influenced by this emphasis on openness, as adoptive parents and potential adoptive parents increasingly stress the importance of complete disclosure of the history and medical records of the children they adopt. Yet the practice of open adoption itself remains the subject of considerable disagreement.

Appearing in 1978, a seminal work, *The Adoption Triangle: Sealed or Open Records: How They Affect Adoptees, Birth Parents, and Adoptive Parents* by Arthur Sorosky, Annette Baran, and Reuben Pannor, solidified and publicized a growing unease about adoption. The book diagnosed adoption as a disability that creates vulnerability in all the parties involved, particularly the adoptee, who, the authors claimed, experiences difficulties at all stages of development as a result of adoption. The authors described adoptees as suffering from the handicap of severance from biological kin, a condition they termed "genealogical bewilderment." The authors asserted that an adoptee's "true identity" is stolen in adoption; lifting the veil of secrecy is the only means to a rediscovery of wholeness. Birthmothers, they claimed, suffer a parallel affliction designated "psychological amputation." Even adoptive parents are impaired, they pronounced: "Without the bond of birth, adoptive mothers have an inherently unstable primary identification with their children, even those adopted in infancy" (Sorosky 1978).

The growing Adoption Rights Movement (ARM), whose political aim was to open the records of adult adoptees, served as a background for this book. In the 1970s, adoptees' organizations arose first as "consciousness-raising" groups, like those of the women's rights movement, encouraging the sharing of personal narratives and the search for birth parents. As mentioned in the preceding chapter, an adoptee named Jean Paton interviewed adult adoptees and published the result in *The Adopted Break Silence* (1954). Using highly inflammatory rhetoric, she remarked: "As far as I can determine, as the arrangement stands now, in most places, it [adoption] is rather akin to slavery. The child is given to whoever wants it, with no right to select or reject" (Paton 1954). In her second book, *Orphan Voyage* (1968), which was first published under her birth name Ruthena Hill Kitteson, Paton advocates adoption reform, including the possibility of parents and children having contact after relinquishment, thus sowing the seeds for the practice of open adoption. In 1973, Florence Fisher published one of the first search narratives, *The Search for Anna Fisher*, the chronicle of her attempts to locate her biological mother. At the end of the book, Fisher discusses the organization she founded in 1971, ALMA (Adoptees' Liberty Movement Association), the twofold purpose of which was to advise adoptees and birth parents on how to carry out a search and to advocate the opening of sealed records. Each of these memoirs, and many others, drew upon the language of difference, servitude, severance, and civil rights.

In parallel fashion, birthmothers were producing their own anguished memoirs, the most famous of which are Lorraine Dusky's *Birthmark* (1979) and Carol Schaefer's *The Other Mother* (1991), later a made-for-TV movie. Dusky's torment and longing for the daughter she relinquished at age twenty-three received wide exposure because of a 1992 "My Turn" editorial she published in *Newsweek* expressing her heartbreak, her longing for her daughter, and the need to change laws affecting birth records. In her book, Dusky rails against the role society has consigned to women like her: "They call me 'biological mother.' I hate those words. They make me sound like a baby machine, a conduit, without emotions. They tell me to forget and go out and make a new life. I had a baby and I gave her away. But I am a mother" (Dusky 1979).

Overwhelmingly, the search narratives of both adoptees and birthmothers have similar plots. At some stage, the protagonist comes to understand the gap in her life, her psychological need to find her biological mother or child. Although many different terms are applied, this quest becomes the search for self, the attempt to heal the psyche. Everything and everyone else in her life recedes in importance. Many barriers are thrown in her path— an unjust legal system, unfeeling bureaucrats, the general population and/or family who cannot understand her emotional needs. Birthmothers tell the story of how as young women they were manipulated by their family, their religion, and well-meaning social workers to give up their baby. They are told that they will forget this incident, but in fact they never do so. Adoptees, too, usually have been in conflict with their adoptive families. However, eventually, through perseverance, ingenuity, and luck, the mother finds her child, or the child finds her mother, father, or occasionally some other relative. Although these stories sometimes end with mixed or poignant results, the pilgrimage is always pronounced satisfying—achieving, through openness, a kind of "closure."

Finally, and parallel to these pleas for openness on the part of birth parents and adoptees, adoptive parents have voiced their own distress over agencies concealing their children's medical and psychosocial histories. Ann Kimble Loux published an influential memoir, *The Limits of Hope* (1997), of the extraordinarily difficult time that she had with the daughters she adopted—a predicament she attributed to their neglect and abuse, which was not revealed to her before adoption. Likewise, Michael Dorris, in his memoir *The Broken Cord* (1990), tells of his gradual discovery that his adopted son had Fetal Alcohol Syndrome. And a featured *New York Times* article told of parents who learned that their son's birthmother was a schizophrenic confined to a mental institution only when he himself developed schizophrenia (Belkin 1999).

CONTROVERSIES SURROUNDING THE OPEN RECORDS MOVEMENT

The search narratives and other memoirs served as the raw data for the political movement for open records, which has been carried on by a variety of organizations such as AAC (American Adoption Congress) and CUB (Concerned United Birthparents) and most recently Bastard Nation. Every state now allows nonidentifying information to be released to adoptive parents and adopted children, and Alaska and Kansas have long allowed adult adoptees access to their original birth certificates. But the approval of a ballot initiative in Oregon—which made Oregon the first state to open unconditionally previously sealed records to adult adoptees—was probably the most dramatic victory for this movement (Carp 2004). Likewise, in 2000, Alabama reversed its 1991 sealed records law and granted unrestricted access to original birth and adoption records to adult adoptees (Hollinger 2004).

However, many other states have rejected such dramatic changes (Hollinger 2004), and the political movement for open adoption records has its opponents as well. Once again, evidence for the privacy position makes itself apparent in narratives, most of which also use the language of rights and freedom. In her famous memoir, Fisher unwittingly lays the ground for the opposition. Although she scorns critics who worry about birthmothers' rights to privacy—decrying anyone who thinks that a child might betray her own mother—by the end of the book, she insists that the account of her search be published with all names unchanged in spite of her mother's objections, embarrassment, and fears. For Fisher, it would seem, the truth and cause of open records trump all other considerations. The political stance of Bastard Nation is equally uncompromising (Carp 2004). Moreover, in the follow-up to her editorial, Dusky writes of contacting her biological daughter when the daughter is fifteen. Such an action violates the tacit premise of the open records movement that the right to information and contact be limited to adults. Dusky's account may fuel the fears of adoptive parents that the open records movement might threaten their family life with unanticipated contact with birth parents—contact that they believed the contract of their adoption had excluded.

Sarah Saffian's *Ithaka* (1998), however, breaks the conventions of the adoption-memoir genre. At age twenty-three, Saffian is contacted, out of the blue, by her birth parents. She conveys dismay and disorientation from this experience—her consistent refrain being: "I have a complete life. I don't know where to put you." She turns to her adoptive father for comfort, and depicts reunion with birth parents as disruptive rather than redemptive, thus departing from the usual fantasies of completion that dominate adoption memoirs. In 2004, A. M. Homes, who depicted the searing effect of adoption in her novel *In a Country of Mothers* (1995), wrote an account in *The New Yorker* of her own disturbing, unsought encounter with her birth parents. In 1996, David O. Russell's movie *Flirting with Disaster* spoofed the romantic idealization of the adoptee's search. The main character makes the characteristic complaint of the adoptee—he doesn't know who he is. When he is mistakenly given false leads on the identity of his "real parents," he finds something with which to identify in each case, his identity shifting to conform to what he believes is his "actual" identity. These and other unconventional portrayals of the participants in adoption deflate the notion that all adult adoptees desire to find their birth parents and can be made psychologically whole only when this quest is satisfied. In short, they furnish data for the view opposing the opening of formerly "sealed" adoptions.

The chief political opponent of open records is the National Council for Adoption (NCA). NCA representatives argue that contact between adult adoptees and birth parents should be made only by mutual consent. Other arrangements, they insist, violate the privacy to which parties to the adoption were contractually guaranteed. They maintain that open-records advocates are overrepresented in the media simply because publicity favors those who search. Moves to speak out by those birth parents and adoptees who seek privacy would be self-defeating. NCA reports that 85 to 99 percent of adult adoptees do not search, and further argues that open records would reduce the number of adoptions because some birthmothers consent to adoption only if their privacy can be assured. Further, they claim that ever-increasing openness weakens the strength of adoptive families because the expectation will become that all adoptees eventually reunite with their birth parents. NCA instead advocates a mutual consent registry in which adult adoptees and birth parents could register to indicate their desire to reunite with the other.

OPEN ADOPTION

The Adoption Triangle, so influential in the adoption rights movement, additionally recommended open adoption. The book's conclusion advocated a form of adoption in which "the birth parent meets the adoptive parents, relinquishes all legal, moral, and nurturing rights to the child, but retains the right to continuing contact and knowledge of the child's whereabouts and welfare" (Sorosky 1978)—similar, in fact, to the kind of informal adoption or placing-out that was common in the United States before the mid-twentieth century. During the 1980s the practice of open adoption grew, although its definition and practice varied a great deal. In a widely circulated article in *The New Yorker,* Lincoln Caplan explained the range of options, noting of an attorney who arranges open adoptions: "Almost all the adoptions that Michelsen helps arrange involve a meeting between the birthmother and the adoptive couple; three-fourths involve some continuing contact between the two parties, through exchanges of pictures and letters; and about ten per cent lead to continuing relationships through phone calls and visits" (Caplan 1990).

The open adoption first advocated by adoption rights groups soon became a mainstay of adoption agencies. In this arrangement, it became the task of the potential adoptive couple to "sell themselves" to the birthmother—first through a "Dear Birthmother" letter and then in a meeting. Caplan's *New Yorker* article dwelled upon the combination of artifice and authenticity involved in this process, pausing on the telling details. He described the adoption consultant's advice, which encompassed everything from word choices to the color of the paper used in printing the letters. Of one couple's photos the consultant commented "they are too clingy, exclusive. She wanted a picture that highlighted a beautiful triangle—Lee, Dan, and room for the baby" (Caplan 1990).

Despite its growing popularity, opinions varied on the benefits of open adoption. Adoption rights advocates perceived open adoption as a partial solution to the adoptee's deprivation of identity and the birthmother's psychic wounding. Some feminist theoreticians such as Drucilla Cornell saw the arrangement as a new ideal, in some ways replicating the process of Other Mothering and para-kinship practiced in the African American community (Cornell 1998). Gay adoptive father Dan Savage does not idealize the open adoption relationship in his memoir *The Kid* (1999), but he does assert that seeing the pain of the birthmother on parting with her child was vital to him and his boyfriend as a kind of reality-check, and he believes it will be critical to helping their son deal with the adoption as he grows up.

In contrast, many potential adoptive parents feared the arrangements, raising concerns about interference in their family life and bonding process. Such fears had become especially acute, for virtually all adoptive parents, after widely publicized disputes over "Baby Jessica" in 1993 and "Baby Richard" in 1995, contests that featured images of screaming children wrested from their adoptive parents' arms (Ashby 1997). Additionally, critics in the psychiatric community had hesitations about the practice. Five authors expressed their views in a series of articles in *Child and Adolescent Social Work Journal.* They saw problems with open adoption for each member of the "adoption triad": for birthmothers, openness might inhibit the grieving process; for adoptive parents, anxiety might interfere with attachment to the adopted child; for the adopted child, two sets of parents might engender psychological conflict (Kraft et al., 1985, 1985b, 1985c; Melosh 2002).

Studies of open adoptions have not been definitive (Hollinger 2004c). Counterintuitively, studies show that adoptive parents in open adoptions are actually less likely to fear birth parents reasserting their rights to their child than in closed adoptions (Melosh 2002). However, studies have shown that birthmothers in open adoptions do not adjust better to the relinquishment of their children. In fact, birthmothers seem to suffer more problems; typically, in fact, they desire less contact with their children over time (Melosh 2002). Thus, the jury on open adoptions is still out, especially since the persons who have not yet been studied are the adopted children themselves. Historian Barbara Melosh speculates about the effect of such arrangements on adoptees:

> We know from their own accounts that many adopted persons experience relinquishment as rejection, even if adoptive parents have portrayed birth parents positively and offered empathetic explanations for relinquishment. . . . But in confidential adoption, relinquishment is a decision made once and, usually, on behalf of an infant with whom the mother has had only a brief relationship. In contrast, children in open

adoptions are vulnerable to the withdrawal of a birth mother who could see them but who chooses not to do so. Surely such adopted persons are more, not less, likely to experience separation from the birth mother as a personal rejection, even something for which they are to blame. (Melosh 2002)

It is perhaps not surprising, then, that while open adoption arrangements have become more common over the course of the past twenty-five years, many states still do not legally recognize or enforce these agreements. However, since the mid-1990s, more than twenty states have enacted statutes that allow contact agreements between birth and adoptive parents after adoption, although few are willing to force parental visitation over the objections of adoptive parents (Hollinger 2004c).

ADOPTION AS PROPOSED SOLUTION TO FOSTER CARE CRISIS

During the post-1970 period, poverty rates for women and children remained high, particularly for families headed by a single woman, and the numbers of children requiring foster care also increased dramatically, with around 800,000 children, overall, currently being served each year by an overstretched system (Children's Bureau 2004). Over the last several years, higher numbers of children have entered the system than have left it each year, and around 20,000 children annually "age out" of the foster care system, never having achieved a permanent home (Child Welfare League of America 2004b; Children's Bureau 2004). Meanwhile, about 125,000 children annually wait to be adopted from the foster care system, while only about a third of that number are typically adopted in any given year (Evan B. Donaldson Insitute 2002).

Until the 1980s, parents often sought out the foster care system when they could not cope with severe financial, health, or relationship problems (Hollinger 2004b). However, as a result of renewed public attention to child abuse and a Senate subcommittee hearing on the topic in the early 1970s (Ashby 1997), Congress first passed the Child Abuse Prevention and Treatment Act (CAPTA) in 1974, which sought to increase the identification and treatment of abused children and to collect and disseminate, on a federal level, research and statistics on abuse for distribution nationwide.[2] Today, most children wind up in foster care after a court has found neglect or abuse (Hollinger 2004b).

Not only are foster children thus typically older than the children adopted from abroad; they often face serious emotional and psychological challenges as a result of coming from homes ravaged by drugs, physical or sexual abuse, and other problems (Child Welfare League of America 2004). And often they are children from oppressed groups within American society—African Americans, Hispanic Americans, and Native Americans are all disproportionately represented in the ranks of foster children. Sixty percent of those waiting to be adopted are black and Hispanic children (Evan B. Donaldson Adoption Institute 2002; Hollinger 2004b).

These facts together paint a picture of a system stretched to a breaking point, such that by 1991, a blue ribbon panel warned that the national child protection program was on the verge of collapse. Sensational stories of abuse and neglect of children within the system periodically arose in the popular media, but only a few major, systemic responses from the government or other bodies have worked to address these problems, as all welfare programs were attacked as wasteful and even dangerous to impoverished people throughout the 1980s and 1990s (Ashby 1997). The procedures and regulations governing direct welfare payments, usually in the form of Aid to Families with Dependent Children (AFDC), were dramatically reformed and curtailed in 1996, and state budgets for social welfare have been slashed during financial crises since then.

However, a few major pieces of legislation have recently been enacted that have attempted to address the problems faced by these most vulnerable young citizens. In virtually every case—with a few important exceptions, which we will discuss below—the goal has been to speed the child's transition either to reunification with the birth family or to adoption, if reunion is deemed impossible. Beginning with the first reauthorization of CAPTA in 1978, the federal government encouraged states to enact comprehensive adoption assistance programs and to provide direct grants for the adoption of abused children and those with special needs. By 1980, a new bill, the Adoption Assistance and Child Welfare Act, explicitly focused on "permanency planning" for children, in order to protect them *not* from parental abuse, but from the negative psychological effects of the foster care system itself. Some conservative politicians and scholars, notably Newt Gingrich, even proposed bringing back orphanages as preferable to the foster care system (Ashby 1997). In this case, a conservative desire to cease paying for an "expensive" welfare system combined with the language of freedom from the civil rights era to achieve further emphasis on adoption as the solution for foster children who are caught in a dysfunctional system.

THE TRANSRACIAL ADOPTION CONTROVERSY

Yet, despite the language of rights and freedom, the movement toward adoption as the solution for all displaced children in the United States has also been complicated by the goals and histories of the civil rights movements, especially those of groups within African American and American Indian communities. As Lori Askeland discussed in Chapter 1, these cultures have flexible, strong, complex, and resilient family forms that often, ironically, incorporate formal adoption or quasi-adoptive and fostering relationships. Yet, especially before the 1970s, scholars and policymakers too often viewed these families as simply chaotic or dysfunctional. By contrast, in a parallel trend, whites entrenched in civil rights movements sought a "color-blind" world and idealistically thought race was irrelevant in adoption.

Early in the century, Native American children were often forcibly removed from their "unfit" families' homes and forced into white-managed boarding schools, missions, and orphanages (see, for example, Bonnin 1900). As time went on, adoption and foster care were employed for this "civilizing" function. Scholars estimate that approximately 35 percent of Native American children were placed in white adoptive and foster families between 1969 and 1974; in some states during this period, American Indian communities supplied up to 40 percent of all adoptions, almost all going to white families. Indeed, by 1978, over 90 percent of all Native American adoptees were in non-native families (Ashby 1997).

African American children, too, were often "saved" from families who loved them. Malcolm X's best-selling narrative of his life to Alex Haley in 1964 presented a powerful example of such destruction, as he explained to Haley his belief that "the state Welfare people" seemed to believe "that getting [black] children into foster homes was a legitimate part of their function" (Haley 1964). In fact, after describing his mother's hospitalization and his own demeaning experiences in white foster families, Malcolm X concluded: "We wanted and tried to stay together. Our home didn't have to be destroyed. But the Welfare, the courts, and their doctor, gave us a one-two-three punch" (Haley 1964).

These powerful histories of ethnic and racial oppression within "child-saving" institutions echoed throughout the contemporary period, and created a context in which attempts by white individuals or white-dominated agencies to intervene in the lives and families of nonwhites were often looked upon with deep suspicion; so much so, in fact, that in September 1972, the National Association of Black Social Workers (NABSW) published its now-famous "Position Statement on Trans-Racial Adoption." In this statement, the social workers argued that transracial adoption is best recognizable "as an expedient for white folk," that does not derive from "an altruistic humane concern for black children," but which arose because "[t]he supply of white children for adoption has all but vanished, and adoption agencies, having always catered to middle class whites, developed an answer to their desire for parenthood by motivating them to consider black children" (NABSW 1972/1974). As with the search memoirs, these social workers invoked strong rhetoric, calling transracial adoption a form of "genocide." Some states, as a result, began requiring race-based matching, and many agencies quietly did likewise (Ashby 1997).

A few years later, the Indian Child Welfare Act of 1978 (ICWA) was passed by the U.S. Congress after several investigations into the loss of Indian children from their families. The act stated that "an alarmingly high percentage of Indian families are broken up by the removal, often unwarranted, of their children from them by non-tribal public and private agencies and that an alarmingly high percentage of such children are placed in non-Indian foster and adoptive homes and institutions" (U.S. Code, Title 25). Since children represent a tribe's most precious "resource," the ICWA attempted to set firmer standards for the removal of children from their families, and gave explicit preference first to the extended families of Indian children, then to others within their tribal community, and finally to other Indians for providing foster care or adoptive families for the children—over and against placement in any non-Indian home.

The NABSW's stance and the ICWA itself were responses to the fact that poverty and racism place great stress on nonwhite families, and the foster care and adoption systems were designed by whites who have not been adequately trained in the histories and cultural integrity of nonwhite peoples in the United States, to serve the needs of white adults and children (see Billingsley and Giovannoni 1972). So it is quite possible that some prospective adoptive parents of color are not adequately recruited by the system, as the NABSW continues to assert (Neal 1996). Indeed, the pro-adoption organization, the North American Council of Adoptable Children, recently commissioned a study of this problem, which found several serious, systemic barriers to prospective nonwhite adoptive parents. For instance, due to their deep awareness of the history of slavery, many black adults are very suspicious of adoption fees, which make the process too much like "buying" a baby (Gilles and Kroll 1991). Meanwhile, the educational system continues to fail blacks, Hispanics, and Native Americans, many of whom drop out of the system before completing high school, a fact which continues to hurt their economic status and helps to maintain white domination of the social, legal, and economic institutions, including some child-welfare organizations.

Yet, supporters of transracial adoption counter that studies of children adopted transracially show largely positive results from the practice (Simon and Allstein 2001). And some advocates of transracial adoption such as Elizabeth Bartholet see transracial adoption as projecting a new paradigm of family, "Adoptive parenting may produce parents and children who are unusually open and tolerant of a wider variety of differences" (Bartholet 1993). Moreover, surveys show that the majority of black people in the United States are opposed to racial-matching policies.

We seem to be caught in a system that is designed to perpetuate the "numbers mismatch" identified by Bartholet (1993), whereby large numbers of children of color are trapped in an underfunded and often white-dominated child-welfare system, and where whites also constitute the largest group of adults available and eager for governmentally assisted and enforced adoption. Thus, transracial adoption seems like a logical and simple solution to many scholars, activists, and adoptive parents—one that, they feel, may bring about greater understanding on both sides of the color line. Yet some legal theorists such as Twila Perry acknowledge the deep reality of racism's legacy in this country, which is often invisible to white people, and suggest that it remains true that African American parents can best prepare children to encounter that racism. She also suggests that encouraging transracial adoption inhibits working out the larger problems that produce the necessity of such adoptions (Perry 1993–1994). Others strive for a position that can both recognize the reality of racism and the needs of children in care who might be served by transracial adoption (see Satz 2001).

Thus, while all sides of this debate express deep concern about the plight of the "nearly 500,000" children in foster care, especially the "tens of thousands of foster children . . . waiting for adoption" (U.S. Code, Public Law 103–382, Title V, Section E), they differ on how to respond—with one side urging extensive efforts to recruit fostering and adoptive parents from nonwhite communities and greater support for all impoverished families, and the other arguing for streamlining the process of placement for children, without regard to ethnicity.

THE MULTIETHNIC PLACEMENT ACT OF 1994

Given this impasse, Senator Howard Metzenbaum introduced the Multiethnic Placement Act (MEPA) to congress in 1993, which ultimately attempted to chart a middle way between the two camps described above. When passed in 1994, MEPA denied federal funds to any agency that uses race as a reason to "categorically deny" any child or adult adoption rights, and also that an adoption or foster placement must not be delayed or denied "solely on the basis of race," although race can be considered. It stated both that children in state custody are not exempt from federal antidiscrimination statutes, especially Title VI of the 1964 Civil Rights Act, and that this law did not surpass or alter the special provisions for Native children established by the ICWA (Hollinger 2004e).

Although this bill was supported by many prominent organizations and some black leaders like Jesse Jackson (Ashby 1997), other groups opposed the bill's compromises, and many of those who have to implement the bill remain confused by what it does and does not allow (Hollinger 2004e). As the bill was being considered by Congress, a group of thirty law professors argued that race should not be factored at all in adoption decisions. Harvard professor Randall Kennedy expressed dismay at the continued consideration of race in adoption, seeing it as "affirm[ing] the notion that race should be a cage to which people are assigned at birth and from which people should not be allowed to wander" (Kennedy 1994; Ashby 1997).

ADOPTION AND FOSTERING BY SINGLES, GAY/LESBIAN COUPLES

As mentioned in Chapter 3, before the 1940s, single women had been allowed to adopt children, but during much of the postwar period, only "fit," rigidly heterosexual couples were allowed to adopt. Especially in the 1980s, this began to change. As the traditional, two-parent family became rarer and the crisis in the foster care system deepened, agencies' rules became more flexible on many fronts, especially in the cases of "hard-to-place" children—that is, those with disabilities and older children in the foster care system. Age restrictions on adoptive parents were often relaxed. Single women and, more rarely, single men began to adopt children on their own; every state now allows unmarried persons to adopt. And, for the first time, adoption agencies began accepting applications from gay and lesbian couples. Of course, many gays and lesbians were already parenting children from previous relationships, and a few were becoming parents through surrogacy and insemination (Melosh 2002; Evan B. Donaldson 2003/2005). Yet, many of these couples additionally sought "second-parent adoptions" so that each partner in a relationship would be recognized as a legal parent of the children in the family (Hollinger 2004d).

But none of this happened without generating a controversy that continues to this day, as it is a key component of the struggle over gay marriage. Several major studies, particularly a review of longitudinal studies by the American Psychological Association completed in 1995, suggest that children raised by same-sex couples do well in all areas of development and adjustment. All major child advocacy and child development organizations (the Child Welfare League, the National Association of Social Workers, the American Association of Pediatrics and Family Physicians, etc.) support the view that sexual orientation should not preclude anyone from seeking adoption. But many religious conservatives see the lives of gay and lesbian individuals as inherently sinful and thus bad for the children they raise (see Cameron 2005).

Thus, the legal climate for gays and lesbians as adoptive and fostering parents is very mixed. Most states willingly accept gays and lesbians as adoptive or foster parents for "hard-to-place" children, but states like Florida and Utah categorically deny adoption to gay and lesbian adults—although gay and lesbian people often can and do provide foster care in many such states. Second-parent adoptions are explicitly allowed in some states (California, Connecticut, and Vermont), and individual judges in many states routinely allow them, but other judges have denied them on various grounds (Hollinger 2004d).

CONCLUSION

In each area discussed in this chapter, movements for civil rights by oppressed segments of our society had seismic effects on the shape of the American family and the practices of adoption and foster care. We are, today, still living with those changes, and legal and social welfare agencies are struggling to come to terms with what these changes entail for their charges. While the emphasis on "the best interests of the child" remains the explicit goal for all sides of these various controversies, we have not, as a nation, come to a clear consensus as to what that well-worn phrase means, almost 200 years after it was first used in this country. And, as the next chapter will explore, what constitutes a child's "best interest" is also the subject of considerable debate on an international level, where cultural differences are often more dramatic, and a global variety of legal traditions must also be considered.

NOTES

1. Adoption statistics are notoriously difficult to nail down, as many scholars have noted (see especially Carp 1998; Herman 2004). First, many adoptions are informal and beyond the scope of most statisticians. Second, the federal government ceased collecting comprehensive adoption statistics in 1975, so most adoption statistics since that time have been collected by private agencies. However, since international adoptions require a naturalization process, those statistics are readily available from the U.S. State Department. Moreover, since the passage of the Adoption and Safe Families Act of 1997, the federal government has required states to compile statistics on how many children are adopted from foster care using the annual Adoption and Foster Care Analysis and Reporting System (AFCARS) report of the Children's Bureau. And, for the first time in U.S. history, the category "adopted son/daughter" first appeared on the 2000 Census form (Herman 2004).

2. The various pieces of legislation discussed in this section—including all significant revisions of each act—are summarized by the National Clearinghouse on Child Abuse and Neglect Information (NCCANI), a new agency of the U.S. Department of Health and Human Services, in its document, "Major Federal Legislation Concerned With Child Protection, Child Welfare, and Adoption" (NCCANI 2003).

REFERENCES

Ashby, LeRoy. 1997. *Endangered Children: Dependency, Neglect, and Abuse in American History.* New York: Twayne.

Bartholet, Elizabeth. 1991. "Where Do Black Children Belong: The Politics of Race-Matching in Adoption." *University of Pennsylvania Law Review* 139 (May): 1163–1255.

————. 1993. *Family Bonds: Adoption and the Politics of Parenting.* Boston: Houghton Mifflin.

Belkin, Lisa. 1999. "What the Jumans Didn't Know about Michael." *New York Times Magazine*, March 14: 42–49.

Billingsley, Andrew, and Jeanne M. Giovannoni. 1972. *Children of the Storm: Black Children and American Child Welfare.* New York: Harcourt, Brace, Jovanovich.

Bonnin, Gertrude (Zitkala-Sa). 1900. "The School Days of an Indian Girl." *Atlantic Monthly* 85: 185–94.

Cameron, Paul. 2005. "Gay Adoption Should Not Be Accepted." In *Gay and Lesbian Families*, ed. Kate Burns, 51–54. Detroit: Greenhaven Press.

Caplan, Lincoln. 1990. "A Reporter at Large: An Open Adoption—Parts I & II." *New Yorker*, May 21, 73–95; May 28, 40–68.

Carp, E. Wayne. 1998. *Family Matters: Secrecy and Disclosure in the History of Adoption Matters.* Cambridge, MA: Harvard University Press.

————. 2004. *Adoption Politics: Bastard Nation and Ballot Initiaive 58.* Lawrence: University Press of Kansas.

Child Welfare League of America. 2004. "The Health of Children in Out of Home Care." *Child and Family Development: Health Care: Facts and Figures.* http://www.cwla.org/programs/health/healthcarecwfact.htm.

————. 2004b. "Quick Facts About Foster Care." *Child Welfare: Family Foster Care.* http://www.cwla.org/programs/fostercare/factsheet.htm.

Children's Bureau. 2004. "National Adoption and Foster Care Statistics, 1999–2003." *Adoption and Foster Care Analysis and Reporting System (AFCARS).* August. http://www.acf.hhs.gov/programs/cb/dis/afcars/publications/afcars.htm.

Cornell, Drucilla. 1998. *At the Heart of Freedom: Feminism, Sex, and Equality.* Princeton, NJ: Princeton University Press.

D'Emilio, John. 1983. *Sexual Politics, Sexual Communities.* Chicago: University of Chicago Press.

Dorris, Michael. 1990. *The Broken Cord.* New York: HarperCollins.

Dusky, Lorraine. 1979. *The Birthmark.* New York: M. Evans and Co.

————. 1992. "My Turn: The Daughter I Gave Away." *Newsweek*, March 30: 112.

Evan B. Donaldson Adoption Institute. 2002. "Foster Care Facts." *Facts About Adoption.* http://www.adoptioninstitute.org/FactOverview/foster.html.

————. 2002b. "Overview of Adoption in the United States." *Facts About Adoption.* http://www.adoptioninstitute.org/FactOverview.html.

————. 2003/2005. "Adoption by Lesbians and Gays: A National Survey of Adoption Agency Policies, Practices, and Attitudes." October 29, 2003. http://www.adoptioninstitute.org/whowe/Gay%20and%20Lesbian%20Adoption1.html. Reprinted as "Gay Adoption is Commonly Accepted." In *Gay and Lesbian Families*, ed. Kate Burns, 46–50. Detroit: Greenhaven Press.

Gilles, Tom, and Joe Kroll. 1991. *Barriers to Same Race Placement.* St. Paul, MN: North American Council on Adoptable Children.

Haley, Alex, and Malcolm X. 1964. *The Autobiography of Malcolm X.* New York: Random House.

Herman, Ellen. 2004. "Adoption Statistics." *The Adoption History Project.* Updated: November 15. http://darkwing.uoregon.edu/~adoption/topics/adoption statistics.htm.

Hollinger, Joan Heifetz. 2004. "Adoption and Confidentiality." In *Families by Law: An Adoption Reader,* ed. Naomi R. Cahn and Joan Heifetz Hollinger, 123–24. New York: New York University Press.

———. 2004b. "Foster Care and Informal Adoption." In *Families by Law: An Adoption Reader,* ed. Naomi R. Cahn and Joan Heifetz Hollinger, 91–93. New York: New York University Press.

———. 2004c. "Overview of Legal Status of Post-Adoption Contract Agreements." In *Families by Law: An Adoption Reader,* ed. Naomi R. Cahn and Joan Heifetz Hollinger, 159–63. New York: New York University Press.

———. 2004d. "Second Parent Adoptions Protect Children with Two Mothers or Two Fathers." In *Families by Law: An Adoption Reader,* ed. Naomi R. Cahn and Joan Heifetz Hollinger, 235–38. New York: New York University Press.

———. 2004e. "The What and Why of the Multiethnic Placement Act." In *Families by Law: An Adoption Reader,* ed. Naomi R. Cahn and Joan Heifetz Hollinger, 189–93. New York: New York University Press.

Homes, A. M. 1995. *In a Country of Mothers.* New York: Vintage.

———. 2004. "The Mistress's Daughter: Meeting the Parents." *The New Yorker,* December 20–27: 69–109.

Kennedy, Randall. 1994. "Orphans of Separatism: The Painful Politics of Transracial Adoption." *American Prospect* 17 (Spring): 40–42. Excerpted on *The Adoption History Project,* ed. Ellen Herman. Updated: November 15, 2004. http://darkwing.uoregon.edu/~adoption/archive/KennedyOOS.htm.

Kirk, H. David. 1964. *Shared Fate: A Theory of Adoption and Mental Health.* New York: Free Press.

Kraft, Adrienne D., Joseph Palumbo, Patricia K. Woods, Dorian Mitchell, and Anne W. Schmidt. 1985. "Some Theoretical Considerations on Confidential Adoptions. Part I: The Birth Mother." *Child and Adolescent Social Work* 2, no. 1: 13–21.

———. 1985b. "Some Theoretical Considerations on Confidential Adoptions. Part II: The Adoptive Parent." *Child and Adolescent Social Work* 2, no. 2: 77–81.

———. 1985c. "Some Theoretical Considerations on Confidential Adoptions. Part III: The Adoptive Child." *Child and Adolescent Social Work* 2, no. 3: 139–55.

Loux, Ann Kimble. 1997. *The Limits of Hope: An Adoptive Mother's Story.* Charlottesville: University of Virginia Press.

Maza, Penelope L. 1984. "Adoption Trends: 1944–1975." U.S. Children's Bureau. *Child Welfare Research Notes* 9: 1–4. Reprinted in *The Adoption Project,* ed. Ellen Herman. Updated: November 15, 2004. http://darkwing.uoregon.edu/~adoption/archive/MazaAT.htm.

Melosh, Barbara. 2002. *Strangers and Kin: The American Way of Adoption.* Cambridge, MA: Harvard University Press.

Modell, Judith. 1994. *Kinship with Strangers: Adoption and Interpretations of Kinship in American Culture.* Berkeley: University of California Press.

NABSW (National Association of Black Social Workers). 1972/1974. "Position Statement on Trans-Racial Adoption." In *Children and Youth in America: A Documentary History*. Vol. 3: Parts 1–4, ed. Robert H. Bremner, 777–80. Cambridge, MA: Harvard University Press.

Neal, Leora. 1996. "The Case Against Transracial Adoption." Regional Research Institute for Human Services. http://www.puaf.umd.edu/courses/puaf650/Transracial%20Adoption-Neal.htm.

Novy, Marianne, ed. 2001. *Imagining Adoption: Essays on Literature and Culture*. Ann Arbor: University of Michigan Press.

————. 2005. *Reading Adoption: Family and Difference in Fiction and Drama*. Ann Arbor: University of Michigan Press.

Paton, Jean. 1954. *The Adopted Break Silence: The Experiences and Views of Forty Adults Who Were Adopted as Children*. Philadelphia: Life History Study Center.

———— (Ruthena Hill Kittson). 1968. *Orphan Voyage*. New York: Vantage.

Perry, Twila L. 1993–1994. "The Transracial Adoption Controversy: An Analysis of Discourse and Subordination." *New York University Review of Law and Social Change* 21, no. 1: 33–108.

Russell, David O., director. 1996. *Flirting with Disaster*. Miramax.

Saffian, Sarah. 1998. *Ithaka*. New York: Basic Books.

Sants, H. J. 1965. "Genealogical Bewilderment in Children with Substitute Parents." *Child Adoption* 47: 32–42.

Satz, Martha. 2001. "Should Whites Adopt Black Children: One Family's Phenomenological Response." In *Imagining Adoption: Adoption in Literature and Culture*, ed. Marianne Novy, 267–76. Ann Arbor: University of Michigan Press.

Savage, Dan. 1999. *The Kid: What Happened After My Boyfriend and I Decided to Go Get Pregnant: An Adoption Story*. New York: Dutton.

Schaefer, Carol. 1991. *The Other Mother: A Woman's Love for the Child She Gave Up for Adoption*. New York: Soho Press.

Simon, Rita J., and Howard Allstein. 2001. *Adoption Race and Identity: From Infancy to Young Adulthood*. 2nd ed. New Brunswick, NJ: Transaction Publishers.

Solinger, Rickie. 2001. *Beggars and Choosers: How the Politics of Choice Shapes Abortion, Adoption, and Welfare in the United States*. New York: Hill & Wang.

Sorosky, Arthur D., Annette Baran, and Reuben Pannor. 1978. *The Adoption Triangle: Sealed or Open Records: How They Affect Adoptees, Birth Parents, and Adoptive Parents*. Garden City, NY: Doubleday/Anchor.

U.S. Code, Public Law 103–382, Title V, Section E. 1994. "The Multi-Ethnic Placement Act of 1994." Full-text at http://nccanch.acf.hhs.gov/general/legal/federal/pl103_382.cfm.

U.S. Code, Title 25. 1978. "The Indian Child Welfare Act."

U.S. Department of State. 2004. "Immigrant Visas Issued to Orphans Coming to the United States, 1999–2003." http://travel3.his.com/travel/family/adoption/stats/stats_451.html.

5 International Adoption

Elizabeth Bartholet

International adoption—involving the transfer of children for parenting purposes from one nation to another—presents an extreme form of what is often known as "stranger" adoption, by contrast to relative adoption. Relative adoption refers to situations in which a stepparent adopts the child of his or her spouse, or a member of a child's extended biological family adopts the child whose parents have died or become unable or unwilling to parent. Such adoptions are largely uncontroversial: children stay within the traditional biological family network, and the adoptive parents are generally thought of as acting in a generous, caring manner by taking on the responsibility for these children.

By contrast, in international adoption, adoptive parents and children meet across lines of difference involving not just biology, but also socioeconomic class, race, ethnic and cultural heritage, and nationality. Typically, the adoptive parents are relatively privileged white people from one of the richer countries of the world, and typically they will be adopting a child born to a desperately poor birthmother belonging to one of the less privileged racial and ethnic groups in one of the poorer countries of the world. International adoption is characterized by controversy. Some see it as an extraordinarily positive form of adoption. It serves the fundamental need of some of the world's neediest children for family. The families formed demonstrate our human capacity to love those who are in many senses "other" in a world which is regularly torn apart by the hatred of seemingly alien others. But many see international adoption as one of the ultimate forms of human exploitation, with the rich, powerful and white taking from poor, powerless members of racial and other minority groups their children, thus imposing on those who have little what many of us might think of as the ultimate loss.

International adoption has grown significantly over the last few decades, with many thousands of children now crossing national borders for adoption each year. International law as well as domestic laws within the United States have become generally more sympathetic to international adoption than they have been in the past. But the controversy surrounding such adoption continues, and makes its future uncertain.

HISTORY AND CURRENT TRENDS

International adoption is largely a phenomenon of the last half century, with the numbers of children from other countries coming into the United States rising over the years from negligible to some 20,099 in 2002 and 21,616 in 2003 (U.S. Department of State 2004b).

The numbers and the pattern of international adoption have changed over the years in response not simply to the objective needs of children for homes and of prospective parents for children, but also to the politics of international adoption and to changing cultural attitudes. The poor countries of the world have long had an excess of children for whom they cannot adequately care—children doomed to grow up in grossly inadequate orphanages or on the streets. The rich countries have long had an excess of infertile adults who want to parent and a relatively limited number of homeless children. Yet there was virtually no matching of these children with these adults until after World War I. That war left the predictable deaths and devastation, and made the plight of parentless children in the vanquished countries visible to the world at a time when adoption was beginning to seem like a more viable option to childless adults in more privileged countries who were interested in parenting. Thus began the first wave of international adoptions.

In successive years different countries made their children available for adoption abroad in response to different political crises and cultural changes. The Korean War led to the opening up of South Korea for adoption, and for years it was the source of most of the children coming into the United States for adoption, largely because South Korea designed its international adoption system so as to facilitate the placement of children in need of homes with adults abroad who could provide them. In recent years the fall of the "Iron Curtain" and the dissolution of the former USSR has resulted in the opening up of China, Russia, and various new countries that were formerly part of the USSR. At the same time, China's overpopulation combined with its one-child policy designed to address that problem has resulted in the abandonment of many thousands of baby girls, exacerbating the newly felt need to place children for adoption abroad (Van Leeuwen 1999). While many poor countries in Latin America and Africa have had an extended family caretaking tradition which meant that orphaned children or others who could not be cared for by their parents were taken in by relatives, wars and other crises have created huge numbers of children for whom such family care is unavailable. Economic dislocation has resulted in many parents moving away from their extended families to cities in desperate attempts to find work, and then, if the parents fall victim as they often do to the ravages of ongoing poverty, the children may be abandoned to the streets or to institutional care. The AIDS crisis has now so devastated the adult populations in many African countries that thousands on thousands of "AIDS orphans," some themselves HIV-positive and others not, have been left without any family care. Impoverished Latin American countries have long been sending some of their children abroad for adoption, and while Africa has to date sent very few children, the AIDS crisis there has created new pressures which have begun to increase the flow (Greene 2002).

Countries' felt need to find homes for their children abroad is a factor not just of poverty and crisis, but of cultural attitude. Muslim countries subscribe to a religious faith that makes adoption, in which a child is assigned new legal parents, unacceptable, and so these countries don't permit international adoption. Asian countries tend to value blood-related parenthood even more highly than we do in the United States, and so South Korea was eager to place its children abroad even when it was relatively well off economically, because the government knew that there was little opportunity for the children in its orphanages to find adoptive homes within the country.

In addition, the politics of international adoption creates pressures for countries to close their borders for reasons that have nothing to do with the objective need their homeless children may have for adoptive homes. So, for example, South Korea in recent years has limited the number of children released for adoption abroad not because of any cultural changes making it easier to find domestic adoptive homes, but because political forces opposed to international adoption criticized the government for "selling" its children to foreigners. Romania, after the fall of Ceausescu in December 1989 and the resulting exposure to the world of the horrible orphanage conditions in which thousands of its children were living and dying, opened its doors to international adoption and sent large numbers of children abroad (Hoksbergen 2002).[1] Romania closed those doors again at the end of 2000 and has allowed hardly any children out since (see U.S. Department of State 2004c). This change resulted not from any change in the needs of the country's children. An influx of Western attention and resources has brought some modest improvement in the orphanages, but there are still thousands on thousands of children living in desperately inadequate orphanage conditions. The closing down of international adoption was triggered by a baby-buying scandal in which some Romanian birthmothers received payments in connection with surrendering their babies for adoption. Opponents of international adoption took advantage of this scandal to call for a moratorium on international adoption, pending "reform" of the adoption system. While efforts to enforce rules against baby-buying are appropriate, these so-called reform moves in Romania resulted in denying adoptive homes on an ongoing basis to thousands of children abandoned in institutions for reasons which had nothing to do with any illicit payments to their birth parents (Bartholet 1999). More recently, as discussed below, the country has shut down international adoption entirely as a result of pressure imposed by the European Union in connection with Romania's efforts to join the Union.

At the same time that what are often termed "sending countries" have gone through changes over recent decades that have led generally to an increased willingness to send their children abroad for adoption, the more privileged countries, often termed "receiving countries," have gone through their own cultural changes resulting in an increased willingness on the part of adults interested in parenting to look abroad for children to adopt. In the United States and elsewhere, such adults found fewer infants available domestically to adopt as the use of birth control and abortion expanded, and as the stigma against single parenthood lessened so that more birthmothers felt comfortable keeping their babies to raise themselves. As the stigma against adoption and mixed-race families lessened, adults became more comfortable doing international adoption, which so typically involves children who look physically different thus marking the families as adoptive families, and so typically involves the adoption by whites of black and brown children. Adults interested in parenting were thus conditioned to respond to the signals sent from various other countries that children were in need of homes and would be made available for adoption abroad.

RECENT LEGAL DEVELOPMENTS

Relevant law here in the United States consists both of international law, law purporting to bind all countries or the particular countries that have agreed to it, and domestic law, law passed by a particular country to govern its own affairs. I will deal primarily with recent international law, and with recent domestic law in the United States.

On the international front, law has moved generally in the direction of legitimating international adoption, and of providing general guidelines for its appropriate conduct, but does little to *facilitate* such adoption so as to help ensure that children in need of homes receive them. The first truly significant international documents recognizing international adoption were the 1986 United Nations "Declaration on Social and Legal Principles Relating to the Protection and Welfare of Children, with Special Reference to Foster Placement and Adoption, Nationally and Internationally," and the

1989 United Nations Convention on the Rights of the Child. However, they stopped short of fully legitimating such adoption. The Convention on the Rights of the Child, for example, placed international adoption lower in the hierarchy of approved options for children in need of homes than institutional care in their home countries (Bartholet 1999). Then in 1993, sixty-six countries, including most of the sending and receiving countries in the international adoption world, approved a multilateral treaty called the Hague Convention on Intercountry Adoption. This constitutes the most significant legitimation of international adoption to date, making such adoption a preferred option for children over institutional care in their home countries, although indicating that adoption in-country should be preferred over adoption abroad. The Convention also includes some basic substantive rules designed to ensure that birth parents and their children are protected against wrongful attempts to separate them through, for example, use of financial payments to induce the surrender of parental rights, or coercion as in kidnapping. And it includes some basic procedural rules designed to ensure obedience to the substantive rules, such as requirements that each country create a Central Authority to implement the Convention. The Convention governs only those adoptions that take place between countries that have ratified it. As of mid-October 2004, forty-six countries had become parties to the Convention and six had signed but not yet ratified, with more having indicated that they will become parties in the coming years (see U.S. Department of State 2004). The U.S. Senate has given its advice and consent authorizing the U.S. ratification of the Convention, conditioned on laws and regulations being adopted to enable compliance with the Convention's requirements. Basic enabling legislation called the Intercountry Adoption Act of 2000 has been enacted (U.S. Public Law No. 106-279), and the necessary regulations are in the works, with the final ratification step now anticipated in 2006.

There is reason for optimism that the net impact of the Hague Convention will be favorable to lawful international adoption. First, in legitimating such adoption as a good option for children, it not only reflects widely shared international opinion, but is likely to reinforce such opinion, giving those in a position to influence policy more reason to shape policy in an adoption-friendly way. Second, in reinforcing existing rules against baby-buying and other improper practices, it may help reduce the number of adoption scandals, which are not only problems in their own right but also so often trigger anti-adoption "reforms" closing down or drastically limiting international adoption. Third, the Convention will provide political cover for leaders in sending countries who think international adoption will serve their countries' and their countries' children's interests, but might be afraid of anti-adoption forces' charges that they are "selling" or otherwise exploiting these children, and wasting what are often termed these countries' "most precious resources." The Convention can be used to demonstrate that internationally adopted children will be protected against sale and exploitation, and that the world community approves of such adoption as a good option for children.

There is also reason for concern that the Hague Convention may create additional barriers to international adoption. Some countries may ratify the Convention based on good-faith belief that it is a good idea, but have trouble taking the bureaucratic steps necessary to make it effective, thus locking themselves out of the international adoption business. Anti-adoption forces may see attempts to implement the Convention as an opportunity to mount a battle to limit or close down international adoption, as has occurred recently in Guatemala. Even if the Convention is implemented, the new bureaucratic hurdles it creates will likely increase the expense of international adoption for all prospective parents, as is predicted to be the case in the United States, creating the risk that reduced numbers of prospective parents will step forward, and reduced numbers of children will receive homes. And there is always the risk, as with any law "reform" in the adoption area, that the new legal regimes put in place to accommodate the Convention requirements will result in some children in need of homes being held for even longer periods of time prior to placement, and others being denied placement altogether.

International law has also moved in the direction of increased recognition of children's rights and interests, as has the domestic law of many countries. The U.N. Convention on the Rights of the Child, now ratified by virtually every country in the world except the United States, provides a powerful new international recognition of the primacy of children's rights generally. The new Constitution adopted by the Republic of South Africa provides robust protection for children's rights, significant of things to come elsewhere, given that that Constitution embodies many of the progressive rights movements of recent years (see Woodhouse 1999).[2]

This move, assuming it continues, should encourage facilitation of international adoption as an option for children in need of homes. There is always debate about how to assess children's interests, and many of those who oppose international adoption do so in the name of children's interests. However, adoption advocates make powerful arguments that children's most fundamental interests are in being raised in a loving, nurturing manner, in the context of a permanent family, and that these interests can best be served by giving them the homes that often will only be available in international adoption (see the discussion below).

In the United States, law has moved dramatically in recent years in directions favorable to international adoption specifically, to various other forms of adoption, and to children's rights. On the international adoption front, a federal law called the Child Citizenship Act was passed in 2000, giving internationally adopted children automatic citizenship rights immediately upon adoption (Levy 2001). Previously, their parents had to apply for citizenship for them, a requirement that constituted one more bureaucratic hurdle in a process already characterized by hurdles, and one that if not fulfilled left the children dangerously unprotected. The new Citizenship legislation gives those *adopted* from abroad similar citizenship status with children *born* abroad to U.S. citizens, an important symbolic step toward recognizing the legitimacy of international adoption. Federal income tax law was amended effective 1996 to give tax credits for the first time for expenses for any adoption, including international adoption, for those falling within the income eligibility limits, with the amount of the credit increased from $5,000 to $10,000 per adoption, in 2002 (Hampton 1988–).[3] Again, apart from the practical significance, this was a dramatic move in the direction of reducing disparities in the treatment of biologically related parenthood, always heavily subsidized by tax, employment benefit and health insurance policies, as compared to adoption.

The Hague Convention will result in additional significant changes in U.S. law favorable to international adoption. Most significant is the elimination (for Convention adoptions) of the so-called "orphan" requirement in U.S. Immigration law, which limits those children entitled to immediate entry upon adoption to those who have only one birth parent surrendering them for adoption (Sullivan 2000). Since virtually all countries allow couples who are not in a position to raise their children to surrender them for adoption, this restriction has limited the pool of children available for adoption who could find homes in the United States. It has also caused crises in a number of individual adoption cases in which U.S. citizens unwittingly adopted children who did not fit the orphan definition, only to find that although they were the legal parents of the adopted children, they could not bring them back into the United States.[4] The Intercountry Adoption Act of 2000, the Hague implementing legislation referred to above, amends the Immigration and Nationality Act to eliminate the orphan restriction for those adoptions conducted under and in accord with the Convention. This Act also removes or reduces the need for parents who have adopted in courts abroad to re-adopt in their home state. Parents have to date felt pressure to re-adopt because foreign decrees are not entitled to the "full faith and credit" from courts in the United States that an adoption decree issued by a court here would be. The Act implements the Hague requirement that adoption decrees issued by courts in the sending country in compliance with Hague requirements be recognized and given effect in the receiving country. Such decrees will accordingly be entitled to full faith and credit, and increasing numbers of states should adapt their laws to provide that the foreign decree alone entitles adopting parents to get a birth certificate issued by their local U.S. birth registry, so that their child has the very important practical advantage of an English-language birth certificate issued by a local registry capable of issuing additional "original" copies if the first is lost.

Other legal developments in the United States with no specific impact on international adoption are nonetheless significant in changing the landscape in adoption-friendly directions that may well prove relevant to international adoption's long-term prospects. Congress passed in 1994 and strengthened in 1996 a law called the Multiethnic Placement Act (MEPA), prohibiting foster and adoption agencies receiving federal funds from using race as a factor in child placement. This law was designed to radically change the laws and policies of the fifty states, all of which had traditionally engaged in "race matching," placing children if at all possible with same-race foster and adoptive parents. MEPA constitutes a powerful rejection of the philosophy at the heart of efforts to restrict international adoption—the idea that children are best off if kept within their community of origin, and the related idea that racial and ethnic communities are best off when they keep "their" children within the group. (See also the discussion of this law as it relates to domestic U.S. adoptions in Chapter 4 in this volume.) In 1997, Congress also passed a law called the Adoption and Safe Families Act (ASFA). This law was designed to reduce the emphasis the states had traditionally placed on keeping children with their family of origin, to place a greater emphasis on children's interests in growing up in nurturing, permanent homes, and to ensure that if the family of origin could not provide that kind of home within a reasonable period of time, then children be moved on to adoptive homes rather than held on an ongoing basis in foster or institutional settings. ASFA constitutes a powerful rejection of a regime within the United States that exists in extreme form in most of the sending countries of the international adoption world, where children are held in orphanages for years at a time, technically tied to their birth parents and not free for adoption, even though they may see their parents rarely if ever and may have no hope of returning to live with them. If ASFA's spirit were to spread beyond our borders, it would help animate efforts to free up increased numbers of children for adoption, and to ease the barriers to international adoption so that more of them could be placed.

Finally, there are some very general developments in U.S. law in an adoption-friendly direction that bode well for international adoption also. Traditionally, U.S. parentage law has accorded very significant weight to biology and been heavily biased against the kind of non-biologically linked parenting that is adoption (Bartholet 1999). But the recent trend has been in the direction of reducing the importance of biology as a factor in defining parentage. Increasing emphasis is being placed on established and/or intended *social* as opposed to biological parenting relationships, with these factors sometimes weighing equally with or even outweighing biology (Bartholet 2004b). And there are indications that despite our traditional emphasis on adult rights over children's, we are moving, however slowly, in the same child-friendly direction as the rest of the world (Bartholet 2004).

THE POLITICS OF INTERNATIONAL ADOPTION

Those in favor of international adoption tend to focus, on the one hand, on the best interests of the children in need of homes, and on the other hand, on larger community issues. With respect to children they refer to the social science and the child development expertise that demonstrates how harmful it is to children to grow up in institutional homes or on the streets, and how well children do when placed in international adoptive homes. With respect to the larger community, they argue that international adoptive families, in which parents and children demonstrate the human capacity for love across lines of difference, are a positive force for good in a world torn apart by hatred based on racial, ethnic, and national differences.

Opponents of international adoption also focus on both children's best interests and on larger community issues. With respect to children they argue that children are best served by remaining in their community of origin, where they can enjoy their racial, ethnic, and national heritage, and that they are put at risk when placed with dissimilar adoptive parents in foreign countries. With respect to the larger community they argue that international adoption constitutes a particularly vicious form of exploitation of the impoverished sending countries of the world by the richer countries of the world, and the loss of the poor countries' "most precious resources."

Advocates for international adoption reply that the opponents' claims are based on extreme romanticism, without any grounding in the available evidence and without support in common sense. They question how children doomed to grow up in orphanages or on the streets can expect to enjoy their cultural heritage in any meaningful way, and they question how impoverished communities will in fact be in any way enriched by keeping these children.

Some arguments made by adoption opponents seem harder to answer. They point out that at best international adoption is a band-aid operation providing homes to only a small fraction of the children in need in any sending country, and argue that the funds spent on giving homes to the handful would be much better spent on improving conditions that would benefit the larger group of children in need. A related argument is that the governments of both sending and receiving countries should do more to change the conditions of poverty that result in children being abandoned and surrendered for adoption, rather than making efforts to facilitate the transfer of such a limited number of children to adoptive parents.

These arguments raise hard issues, because it is clearly true not only that limited numbers of children are being placed in international adoption, but that even if laws were changed to facilitate such adoption, the numbers placed would never begin to seriously address the needs for adequate nurturing of all the children at issue. And in any event, the better, more humane solution would obviously be the one that the opponents of international adoption assert as their goal—elimination of the kind of poverty and injustice that causes so many desperately poor people in so many nations to be unable to keep and raise the children that they bear. But it is not clear that eliminating or restricting international adoption does anything to further this goal. It *could* be that international adoption diverts energy and resources that would otherwise be devoted to this goal. But it seems at least as likely that it has no such impact and instead actually operates to improve conditions for children in sending countries wholly apart from the children placed in adoption. Anecdotal evidence indicates that many international adoptive parents emerge from their experience with a much greater sense of commitment to contribute to social services of various kinds in their children's sending countries. They will also be more likely to support efforts by their government to contribute to foreign countries in need or to international organizations devoted to improving the lot of the world's children. Sending-country officials that witness foreign adoptive parents gratefully taking into their homes children of different racial and ethnic backgrounds seem likely to realize new potential for placing these children in their own country. In the meantime, the international adoption fees that parents pay contribute very real funds to the sending countries involved, with such funds often allocated to improving conditions in the orphanages from which children are placed for adoption. For example, it has been reported that more than $10 million were given directly to Chinese orphanages in 1996 as the result of a requirement that adoptive parents make a "donation" of $3,000 to the orphanage from which their child is adopted (Van Leeuwen 1999). Much higher figures have been reported in recent years as the numbers of adoptions out of China have increased.

Given the imponderables involved in deciding whether restricting international adoption would in any way actually improve conditions in sending-countries' orphanages or function more generally to reduce poverty and injustice, the fact that such adoption appears to radically improve life prospects for virtually all those children who are in fact placed provides a powerful argument for moving in the direction of expanding rather than restricting such adoption. (See below for discussion of the benefits for children in being placed in adoptive homes.)

However, the opponents of international adoption have had a major impact on policy. Despite the general increase in such adoption over recent years, and despite the increased sympathy to such adoption reflected in both international and in domestic legal developments, as discussed above, the future of international adoption is uncertain. The opponents' ranks include many of the organizations that see themselves as promoting children's interests. So, for example, international children's human rights organizations succeeded in changing the focus of the Hague Convention negotiations so that the original goal of *facilitating* international adoption, and expediting the placement of children in need, was eliminated. And UNICEF has played a major role in recent attempts to restrict international adoption, including efforts to pass an adoption "reform" law in Guatemala which would significantly restrict international adoption (Dillon 2003). Countries with millions of children growing up or dying in horribly inadequate orphanages or on the streets are regularly passing adoption laws which severely restrict international adoption or eliminate it altogether, in response to opponents' demands. The European Parliament is now dominated by forces which are making countries in Eastern Europe interested in joining the Union agree to outlaw international adoption as a condition for joining (New York Law School Justice Action Center 2004). Romania, where ongoing poverty and dislocation resulting from the disastrous Ceausescu regime mean that vast numbers of children continue to be relegated to orphanages which deny them any decent life prospects, has released few children since the 2000 shutdown triggered by the baby-selling scandal. And, in June 2004—largely as a result of the European Union's pressure—Romania enacted a law eliminating international adoption altogether, except for adoption by a child's grandparents (Evan B. Donaldson Adoption Institute 2004).

CONCLUSION: IMPORTANT ISSUES OF THE DAY

Controversy exists at the heart of international adoption and makes progress hard to define. The world is divided between those who argue that the goal is to open up international adoption to facilitate the placement of children in need of homes, and those who argue that the goal is to close it down to avoid further exploitation of these children, their parents, and their countries. However, focusing on the reality of children's lives and needs may help the warring factions agree on a pathway to reformed policies. Large numbers of children in the poorer countries of the world live in truly desperate circumstances. Too many of those in orphanages spend their infancy having bottles jammed in their mouths and propped, in hopes that some nourishment will happen; and left unattended for hours in between bottle-propping events, so that they learn early that making demands for human attention is meaningless (see Aronson 2004). Largely deprived of the human touch as they grow up, those who survive physically are unlikely to develop emotionally and mentally in ways that will make it possible for them to relate meaningfully and happily to other human beings, or to learn or work in meaningful ways. The longer they spend in such orphanages, the less chance they will have at anything resembling normal development (Bartholet 1988–, 1999; Talbot 1998; Judge 1999; Hoksbergen 2002; Aronson 2004). By contrast, those placed in international adoption flourish. Those placed in infancy will do essentially as well as other children in their new country. Those placed later will do far better than they would in the absence of placement—international adoption has been shown to overcome even very significant deficits caused by early deprivation, with the age of placement overwhelmingly predictive of the chance for normal life (Bartholet 1988–, 1999).

If policymakers were to genuinely commit themselves to improving the lot of the world's children, they might want to listen to the concerns expressed on both sides of the international adoption divide, and consider reforms that would both promote placement in international adoption and promote improvement in conditions in the sending countries. Policymakers committed to these twin goals should consider a variety of legal reforms.

First they need to ensure that children who cannot realistically be cared for by their parents are freed for adoption as promptly as possible. The ASFA legislation recently passed by the U.S. Congress (discussed above) can serve as something of a model for other countries as they look at their domestic laws. Most countries have no adequate system for identifying children in need of adoptive homes and freeing them up from their biological parents so that they can be placed. Orphanages worldwide are filled with children who grow up with no meaningful tie to their parents except the technical tie that means they cannot be placed with adoptive parents. The same is true for street children. Law reform efforts need to focus on creating systems for identifying and freeing up children who have been effectively permanently abandoned, and they need to create realistic methods of expediting the process, so that children are placed in adoptive homes as early in life as possible. Ironically, and tragically, much of what now goes under the name of "adoption reform" pushes in the exact opposite direction. Countries regularly react to international adoption critics by passing laws eliminating private adoption, in which children are transferred more or less directly from birth parents to adoptive parents, insisting that children instead be placed in orphanages, and then often increasing the bureaucratic barriers between orphanage children and adoptive placement. The net effect is that infant adoptions are almost unknown today in the international adoption world, although they used to occur frequently, and that children released from orphanages today are generally many months and years older than they used to be. Insisting that children spend additional months and years in the conditions of the typical orphanage, or on the streets, is inhumane in the short term, and destructive in the long term of children's opportunities to live happy and fulfilling lives, assuming that they even survive, as many will not.

Second, policymakers in both sending and receiving countries need to facilitate the adoption process so that it better serves the needs of prospective adopters. This will not only promote their legitimate interest in parenting, but will maximize the numbers of parents for the children in need.

But policymakers also need to link these kinds of adoption reform efforts with initiatives designed to address the baby-buying and kidnapping problems that exist in the international adoption world. International adoption's opponents have grossly exaggerated the scope of these problems, using them deliberately to promote restrictive adoption rules to suit their larger anti-adoption agenda. But taking children from loving birth parents by applying improper financial or other pressures victimizes not only the particular parents and children involved, but the larger group of children and parents whose opportunities for legitimate international adoption are thwarted by the negative regulation that is so often triggered by adoption abuses.

Finally, policymakers need to work to improve conditions for the children who will not be adopted and for their birth parents. International adoption's opponents are correct in arguing that it can never provide homes for all the children in need, and that we must address the problems of poverty and injustice that result in children being abandoned in large numbers in the poor countries of the world. International adoption provides a natural trigger for such broad efforts at social reform. Adoptive parents and their governments become more aware of the problems of the countries from which international adoptees come by virtue of the adoption process. With this knowledge, and with the privilege of caring for these children, comes new responsibility for the children left behind.

NOTES

1. An estimated 120,000–150,000 abandoned children were living in 600–800 Romanian orphanages as of 1989, with approximately 10,000 institutionalized children placed in international adoption between 1990 and 2000 (Hoksbergen 2002).

2. See also, for example, the 1991 Children Act in the United Kingdom, which gave children the right to sue on their own behalf in family law matters (Millar 1993).

3. The credit is reduced if the adoptive parents' modified adjusted gross income (AGI) is more than $150,000, and eliminated entirely if their modified AGI is more than $190,000. IRS publication 968, Cat. No. 23402W (Hampton 1988–).

4. The U.S. government has now taken steps, first initiated in 2003, to enable prospective adopters to ensure that foreign children available for adoption fit the orphan definition before the adopters go abroad to take custody (Friess 2003).

REFERENCES

Aronson, Jane. 2004. "Medical Considerations in EU Adoptions." Presentation at "Intercountry Adoption Conference: Intercountry Adoption, the European Union, and Transnational Law." Justice Action Center, New York Law School, May 21. http://www.nyls.edu/pages/2305.asp.

Bartholet, Elizabeth. 1988–. "International Adoption: Overview." In *Adoption Law and Practice*, ed. Joan H. Hollinger et al., 1–43. New York: Matthew Bender.

————. 1993. "International Adoption: Current Status and Future Prospects." *The Future of Children* 1 (Spring): 89–103.

————. 1995. "Beyond Biology: The Politics of Adoption and Reproduction." *Duke Journal of Gender Law and Policy* 2 (Spring): 5–14.

————. 1996. "International Adoption: Propriety, Prospects and Pragmatics." *Journal of the American Academy of Matrimonial Lawyers* 13 (Winter): 181–210.

————. 1996b. "What's Wrong with Adoption Law?" *The International Journal of Children's Rights* 4, no. 3: 263–72.

————. 1999. *Family Bonds:Adoption, Infertility, and the New World of Child Production.* Boston: Beacon Press.

————. 2004. "The Challenge of Children's Rights Advocacy: Problems and Progress in the Area of Child Abuse and Neglect." *Whittier Journal of Child and Family Advocacy* 3 (Spring): 215–30.

————. 2004b. "Guiding Principles for Picking Parents." *Harvard Women's Law Journal* 27 (Spring): 323–44.

Dillon, Sarah. 2003. "Making Legal Regimes for Intercountry Adoption Reflect Human Rights Principles: Transforming the United Nations Convention on the Rights of the Child with the Hague Convention on Intercountry Adoption." *Boston University International Law Journal* 21 (Fall): 179–257.

Evan B. Donaldson Adoption Institute. 2004. "Romania Enacts Law Ending Nearly All Intercountry Adoptions." June E-Newsletter. http://www.adoption institute.org/newsletter/2004_06.html.

Friess, Steve. 2003. "Government Program Aims to Curtail Fraud in Foreign Adoptions; Goal Is to Reduce Parental Heartache." *USA Today*, May 27: D6.

Greene, Melissa Fay. 2002. "What Will Become of Africa's AIDS Orphans?" *New York Times Magazine*, December 22: 50–55.

Hampton, Lawrence P. 1988–. "Economic Consequences: Adoption Tax Credits 12.05[1][c]." In *Adoption Law and Practice*, ed. Joan H. Hollinger et al., 77–79. New York: Matthew Bender.

Hoksbergen, Rene. 2002. "Experiences of Dutch Families Who Parent an Adopted Romanian Child." *Journal of Development and Behavioral Pediatrics* 6 (December): 403–9.

Judge, Sharon Lesar. 1999. "Eastern European Adoptions: Current Status and Implications for Intervention." *Topics in Early Childhood Special Education* 19 (Winter): 244–52.

Levy, Daniel. 2001. "The Child Citizenship Act of 2000." *Bender's Immigation Bulletin* 6, no. 6: 293–304.

Maravel, Alexandra. 1996. "The U.S. Convention and Co-operation on the Rights of the Child and the Hague Conference on Private International Law: The Dynamics of Children's Rights Through the Legal Strata." *Journal of Transnational Law and Contemporary Problems* 6 (Fall): 309–28.

Millar, Fiona. 1993. "Children: A Law that Cares at Last." *The Guardian*, January 4: E10.

New York Law School Justice Action Center. 2004. "Intercountry Adoption Conference: Intercountry Adoption, the European Union, and Transnational Law." May 21. http://www.nyls.edu/pages/2305.asp.

Seftel, Joshua. 1992. *Lost and Found: The Story of Romania's Forgotten Children.* Somerville, MA: Seftel Productions.

Sullivan, Kathleen. 2000. "Intercountry Adoption Act Becomes Law." *Bender's Immigration Bulletin* 5, no. 23: 977.

Talbot, Margaret. 1998. "The Disconnected; Attachment Theory: The Ultimate Experiment." *New York Times,* May 24 (Sec. 6): 24.

U.S. Department of State. 2004. "Hague Convention on Intercountry Adoption." http://www.travel.state.gov/family/adoption_hague.html.

———. 2004b. "Immigrant Visas Issued to Orphans Coming to the United States, 1999–2003." http://travel3.his.com/travel/family/adoption/stats/stats_451.html.

———. 2004c. "Update on Romanian Moratorium on International Adoption." http://www.travel.state.gov/family/adoption_romania.html.

U.S. Public Law No. 106-279, 114 Stat. 825. "Intercountry Adoption Act of 2000." http://frwebgate.access.gpo.gov/cgi-bin/getdoc.cgi?dbname=106_cong_public_laws&docid=f:publ279.106.pdf.

Van Leeuwen, Michelle. 1999. "The Politics of Adoptions Across Borders: Whose Interests are Served? A Look at the Emerging Markets of Infants from China." *Pacific Rim Law and Policy Journal* 8 (January): 189–218.

Woodhouse, Barbara B. 1999. "The Constitutionalization of Children's Rights: Incorporating Emerging Human Rights into Constitutional Doctrine." *University of Pennsylvania Journal of Constitutional Law* 2 (December): 1–52.

6 The Orphan in American Children's Literature

Claudia Nelson

Across many centuries and within many cultures, parentless children have served as symbols of human individuality, independence, and strength. We have only to invoke folk tale and myth to recognize the prevalence of the pattern: a virtuous protagonist is temporarily or permanently orphaned, thus becoming exposed to the cruelties and dangers of the world, but finally triumphs over circumstance by finding a safe haven and secure position. It is no accident that in his classic study of the structure of Russian fairy tales, Vladimir Propp begins his list of characteristic plot elements with "One of the members of a family absents himself from home" and notes that "An intensified form of absentation is represented by the death of parents" (Propp 1968/1994). Whether our protagonist is Moses or Snow White, King Arthur or Luke Skywalker, Sara Crewe or Harry Potter, the loss of home and family is often depicted as the gateway to full engagement with life.

The degree to which the orphan is characterized as vulnerable, however, differs from text to text. Sometimes these differences have to do with gender. As feminist critics have been pointing out for decades, Rapunzel and her fairy-tale sisters are often represented as victims; bereft of their natural protectors, they wait more or less passively for new protectors to appear. In contrast, orphan boys in fiction frequently become their own saviors, striking out to seek their fortunes à la Dick Whittington, Horatio Alger's boy heroes, or such non-Western examples as Kibun Daizin, title character of Meiji writer Gensai Murai's fact-based novel about an upwardly mobile Japanese kite seller. A pair of orphan novels by French author Hector Henri Malot, *Sans Famille* (1878, translated into English as *Nobody's Boy*) and *En Famille* (1893, *Nobody's Girl*), offer a characteristic contrast: in the words of the foreword to the American edition of *Nobody's Girl, Nobody's Boy* is "a wide-ranging adventure tale," while the heroine of *Nobody's Girl*, although intelligent and resourceful, repeatedly voices her fears about being alone, and gratefully accepts the bounty of her grandfather (whose emotional life she reawakens in payment) at the end of the tale. Such protagonists model for children the gender roles their culture expects them to take up, although in adult literature, as critic Claudia Mills has observed, orphan boys such as Oliver Twist may have no more agency—or may even have less—than orphan girls such as Jane Eyre (Mills 1987).

Our culture perennially returns to the question of what should be done with displaced children. Yet, like the symbolic uses to which it puts accounts of displaced children's experiences, its answers to this question vary, as do the characterizations of the children themselves. American texts for children about orphans and quasi-orphans, like their counterparts in other countries, embrace both the vulnerable and the competent child, Cinderella retreads and picaresque survivors. This diversity mirrors the conflicting attitudes present within the surrounding culture. From the mid-nineteenth century onward, as the number of displaced children grew alongside urbanization and immigration, the question of what society should do with such children not only became more urgent, but also met with new responses. Colonial America's solution to the problem of abandoned or orphaned children had typically been to place them with employers, who would provide room and board in exchange for labor. This system, known as "binding-out" or "placing-out," remained operational throughout the nineteenth century, but it was increasingly challenged by two other ways of handling the children, namely, adoption (formal or informal) and institutionalization. A look at the fiction of the time suggests that all three offered opportunities for a culture confronted with rapid industrialization and population growth to meditate upon the relationship both between needy child and established adult, and between individual and society.

BINDING-OUT: THE WORKING ORPHAN

Today, the binding-out system, as described in the first two chapters of this volume, may strike privileged observers as impossibly outmoded, if not downright barbaric. Late-twentieth-century children's books on binding-out are necessarily historical in tone; they often focus on the phenomenon of the orphan trains, instituted by George Merrill in 1850 (and quickly imitated by Merrill's more famous contemporary Charles Loring Brace) to send urban slum children, many of them immigrants, to rural homes in locations ranging from New England to the Southwest, where they might be resocialized to absorb the values of the American heartland. Works such as Eve Bunting's picture book *Train to Somewhere* (1996) and Joan Lowery

Nixon's novel *A Family Apart* (1987) foreground the pain felt by children and biological parents separated by poverty—a pain that Brace, for one, played down in his published writings. Conversely, Bunting and Nixon end these tales by allowing their protagonists to find new homes in which they will be cherished. As the following passage from *A Family Apart* suggests, the emphasis is not on work but on emotion:

> Frances held Margaret [her new mother] tightly, the love she felt melting away all the mixed-up feelings that had been tormenting her. She would always love Ma, whether she could be with her or not, but she had a new home with people who loved her, too, who generously shared their life with Petey [her biological brother] and her. (Nixon 1987)

Here the displaced child of the past is used to reassure today's readers (whose own family stability may be threatened by divorce) that even when children's lives are changed in fundamental and dramatic ways, love will be present.

In contrast, orphan fiction published during and immediately after the Civil War tended to illustrate the qualities demanded of penniless young people in a society largely without child labor laws or welfare benefits. Children's stories aimed at a middle-class readership during this era often highlight neither the child's emotional needs, which may seem secondary to practical considerations, nor the disastrous consequences attendant upon failing to earn one's own way. Rather, what is emphasized is frequently how independence and diligence permit one to succeed. Hence, some young protagonists make do entirely without adult assistance. In Laura Elmer's "The Devoted Brother and Sister," for example, published in *Merry's Museum* in 1860, twelve-year-old Frank and ten-year-old Lucy rear their infant sister and care for a feeble grandfather, Frank supporting the four by running errands and Lucy conserving his meager earnings by thrifty housekeeping. That charity in this instance is neither necessary nor welcome associates orphanhood with the work ethic, to the greater glory of both and the edification of the reader. Since Frank and Lucy model an industry and frugality far more extreme than that demanded of the middle-class children who typically read *Merry's*, the story not only instructs young consumers in principles of household economy (a frequent preoccupation of the day; see, e.g., Pascoe 1994), but also assures them that the poor children who labored so publicly in the nineteenth century as bootblacks, newspaper vendors, crossing sweepers, and the like could live comfortably if their characters were good.

But if sturdy children apparently don't need adults, other deserving fictional waifs find adoptive homes, such as "Patches" in Rosa Graham's 1876 *St. Nicholas* story by the same name, whose honesty in the face of starvation attracts the interest of a kindly housewife. Yet here too, orphans are workers who expect to repay the benevolence offered to them: in later life, "in-dustrious" Patches does "her best to lighten the labors of the good woman to whom she owed so much" (Gannon 1997). In such tales, the relation-ship between respectable adults and the displaced children of the poor is neither that of patron and pensioner nor that of loving parent and treas-ured child; rather, it recapitulates and idealizes that of employer and em-ployee, representing the one as enlightened and the other as devoted. And as Susan Gannon argues, "the fiction of benevolent intervention . . . allowed adult and child readers to reflect on the issues of power and dependency so central to their relations" (Gannon 1997). In class terms, such fiction both educates child readers into understanding their responsibilities as members of the privileged order and assures them that their privileges are seemly.

Thus, when the fiction of this era represents the orphan as exploited, the exploitation typically occurs at the hands of the poor, not the comfort-ably off. Take Caroline Howard's "A Modern Cinderella" (*Our Young Folks*, 1867), which introduces a German cinder-picker with an unusually sweet singing voice who lives with a hard-drinking woman she calls "Granny." A shrewd middle-class observer concludes, "She could not belong to that old woman—of course not. Never was such beauty born of such ugliness. . . . She might be a stolen child," and indeed, it turns out that six-year-old Kohlasche is no blood kin to Granny, but merely the daughter of a defunct lodger. The observer tries to sever the relationship by paying Granny off and sending Kohlasche to a homelike school for poor children, but Granny subsequently kidnaps the little girl, "perhaps, for her clothes—perhaps to hire out for her voice" (Howard 1867). In either case, what motivates Granny cannot be love. While fiction of this period approves of middle-class adults who give orphans suitable employment, it strongly disapproves of working-class adults, from Granny to Mark Twain's Pap Finn, who seek to profit from the children in their power. It is evidently a middle-class pre-rogative to control children's labor, and the poor who usurp this privilege may be labeled child abusers.

Nonfiction social commentary in the nineteenth century often viewed displaced children as a threat to the country, carriers of criminality and lack of enterprise. Binding-out fiction, in contrast, ascribes these traits to working-class adults but suggests that even when marginalized young peo-ple have developed unsavory habits, they may nonetheless be socialized into decency by contact with the right kind of middle-class employer. In *Jack Hazard and His Fortunes*, a serial published in *Our Young Folks* in 1871 by the magazine's coeditor, J. T. Trowbridge, the eponymous hero begins as a foul-mouthed petty thief—yet the narrative assures readers that these traits are attributable not to Jack's innate defects but to his upbringing by his brutish stepfather and only surviving family member, Cap'n Berrick. After Jack flees Berrick's canal-boat and finds sanctuary with a farm family in an arrangement that mingles informal adoption with employment, he learns that Berrick is about to be tried for murder, the alleged victim being Jack himself. Metaphorically, the accusation functions as a condemnation of Berrick's handling of his stepson, a suggestion that to treat children in a way that encourages profanity, dishonesty, illiteracy, and other social problems is tantamount to killing them.

Yet this "murder" is merely temporary, since Jack effectively resurrects himself by climbing into the middle class. Once he is scrubbed and outfitted into decency, Jack not only "look[s] as well as anybody's boy," but also manages to "put off all [his] bad habits with [his] old clothes, and put on new behavior with this clean suit." As soon as he finds respectable people who believe in him, reformation becomes child's play. Even Berrick turns over a new leaf, signaled by his statement that Jack "was always too good for the canal. For my part, I'm glad as anybody that he has done better for himself; and I cheerfully give up my claim to him here and now." No shady lower-class relations will hamper Jack's inevitable rise, and this is as it should be, since, as Jack's new foster father moralizes, "birth and education sometimes have [little] to do with a young man's turning out well or ill . . . a man's destiny lies in his own character—and in Providence, which helps those who help themselves" (Trowbridge 1871). This moral places responsibility firmly on the individual. In nineteenth-century America, it does not "take a village" to bring up a child. Rather, the figure of the self-sufficient orphan who earns by honest toil all the benefits he receives from his new parents embodies the sturdy independence and upward mobility that Victorian America persistently valorized.

MASS-PRODUCED CHILDREN: THE ORPHANAGE IN FICTION

If fiction about working orphans permitted authors to highlight individual resilience and the American dream, fiction about orphanages permitted them to turn this attitude inside out. As noted in Chapter 3 of this volume, the population of institutions designed for the mass care of dependent children peaked shortly after the turn of the twentieth century (Ashby 1984; Hacsi 1997). Along with this boom came considerable anxiety about the long-term effects of institutionalization on the child's psyche. In particular, commentators bemoaned the regimentation demanded by orphanage routine, which, they charged, sapped inmates' enterprise and individuality. But that such lamentations were couched in language studded with comparisons to factories and mechanization may encourage us to view them as something more than responses to the specific social problem of children in congregate care. They also functioned as thinly veiled expressions of anxiety about the ever-increasing standardization of American life in the machine age (see Nelson 2003b).

There are comparatively few novels set primarily in orphanages; the best known today is Jean Webster's *Dear Enemy* (1915), which I have discussed at length elsewhere (see Nelson 2003). Many turn-of-the-century orphan fictions, however, use the orphanage as a departure point for their protagonists, who invariably have only negative things to say about their stint in the institution. Judy Abbott, for instance, the protagonist of Webster's earlier orphan novel *Daddy-Long-Legs* (1912), leaves the John Grier Home for college after the first chapter, but dots her letters to the anonymous benefactor who is paying for her education with acerbic remarks about "that Dreadful Home looming over my childhood." She comments that "The aim of the John Grier Home . . . is to turn the ninety-seven orphans into ninety-seven twins"; that "I'd rather die than go back"; that "My childhood was just a long, sullen stretch of revolt" (Webster 1912). If the Home is hostile to individuality, the individual is at least equally hostile to the Home.

Although Judy christens her benefactor "Daddy-Long-Legs," frequently shortens this title to "Daddy," and receives from him the college tuition money that her classmates receive from their fathers, their arrangement is not an adoption. As her undergraduate career advances, Judy becomes increasingly likely to reject her "Daddy's" decisions about where she shall spend her time and whether the money he advances her is to be considered a gift or (as she prefers) a loan; eventually he can retain title to his high-spirited protégée only by marrying her. On the one hand, this marriage recapitulates a plot device common in nineteenth-century orphan romances such as Susan Warner's best-seller *The Wide, Wide World* (1850). On the other, it seems a necessary recompense to Judy for the degree of control asserted over every aspect of her childhood by the John Grier Home: once she has escaped the congregate environment (if only for another group setting, that of college), she deserves complete autonomy.

And lest the reader doubt that a marriage between a penniless twenty-one-year-old and an autocratic millionaire fourteen years her senior will be an equal partnership, the happy ending stipulates not only that Judy has begun to sell her stories and thus has the potential for financial independence, but also that her future husband has recently been gravely ill and must have her love if his health is to be restored. Judy thus represents not neediness but dynamism; although many contemporaneous commentators feared that orphanages would eradicate their inmates' energy, the John Grier Home has plainly been unable to diminish Judy's. The novel nonetheless established that such fears were by no means baseless. While Judy is characterized as a talented writer with a lively sense of humor and a strong personality, Webster indicates that these traits exist despite the orphanage, not because of it, and that the institution would indeed like to extirpate the very signs of individuality that we are asked to value in her.

This contrast between the delightful, unusual child and the unappreciative, soulless institution was a stock beginning-point in sentimental orphan fiction at the turn of the twentieth century. Canadian author L. M. Montgomery provided a famous example in *Anne of Green Gables* (1908), whose eponymous heroine, "no commonplace soul," considers her four months in the orphan asylum "worse than anything you could imagine . . . there is so little scope for the imagination in an asylum." Like Judy Abbott, Anne Shirley overflows with personality, which has been cramped and thwarted by institutional life. The "very short, very tight, very ugly dress of yellowish gray wincey" (Montgomery 1908) that she wears on her departure from the orphanage functions as a metaphor for the shortcomings and emotional inadequacies of the communal existence. Somewhat similarly, the hero of Kate Douglas Wiggin's *Timothy's Quest* (1890) has escaped from a baby farm in an effort to find a younger, more obviously adoptable child a home. Timothy's rebellion against the lovelessness and hopelessness of his early childhood is an important mechanism in establishing his own worthiness and in transforming into a real home the austere household to which he comes.

It is characteristic, however, that these narratives use baby farms and orphanages to epitomize emotional deprivation. At the time in which Wiggin and Montgomery were writing, such symbols would have been readily interpretable—and, given the boom in the population of orphanages during this period, would have chastised society for its inability to appreciate and nurture the deserving individual. Indeed, we may sometimes find this trope in much later novels such as Zilpha Keatley Snyder's *Gib Rides Home* (1998), inspired by the "terrible childhood" of the author's father, which was spent partly in an orphanage and partly as a bound-out boy: "Required to do a man's work when he was eight years old, beaten [and] mistreated . . . he survived to become a kind-hearted patient man with an unquenchable sense of humor and an uncanny ability to communicate with horses" (Snyder 1998). If the rebuke to society here comes long after the fact, clearly it is still deeply felt.

THE PRICELESS INDIVIDUAL: ADOPTION STORIES

Although the otherwise brutal institution featured in Snyder's novel contains one devoted staff member, a point that nearly every orphan story written before the mid-twentieth century makes about any orphanage it may mention is that such institutions are devoid of love. Conversely, as early as the middle of the nineteenth century, decades before the approach to displaced children in real life became predominantly emotional rather than utilitarian, adoption in fiction became a common way of conveying the power of love, and especially the ability of the loving individual to redress social problems. If fictional representations of orphanages criticize society, fictional representations of adoption often hold out the possibility of society's redemption—and they do so, as Julie Berebitsky has observed, not by "reflect[ing] the normative family" but by "defin[ing] the ideal" (Berebit-sky 2000).

Thus, antebellum adoption novels such as Maria Cummins's popular melodrama *The Lamplighter* (1854) established a pattern that flourished until at least the 1920s. Gerty, the novel's protagonist, is an orphan whose life since her mother's death has been one of neglect and abuse. When the harridan with whom she lives drops her kitten into boiling water to punish the child for a minor infraction, this parody of the parent–child relationship comes to an end, and Gerty, then aged eight, finds an infinitely superior home with the kindly lamplighter Trueman Flint. Flint's profession is symbolic; the love and care that he provides for Gerty begin her transformation from an outcast convinced of her own ugliness into a spiritually advanced being, just as Flint's blind patroness Emily Graham "impart[s] light to the child's dark soul." The novel thus urges upon its readers an active compassion for America's discarded children, in part because such compassion gives significance to one's own life: even after death, Uncle True's "lamp still burns brightly in heaven . . . and its light is not yet gone out on earth!" (Cummins 1854/1968).

Yet Gerty is by no means only a victim, a poor child to be patronized by a stronger society. As Nina Baym observes, everyone in the novel is vulnerable to some extent, and "The characters league together for mutual aid in a world characterized by illness, poverty, accident, death, and separation of loved ones." Moreover, Baym continues, "Cummins' purpose is . . . to persuade woman that she is responsible for saving herself and equal to the demand" (Baym 1978). Gerty eventually gains the upper hand in the novel, acting as benefactor to her erstwhile patrons and proving her ability to earn her own way before entering into a desirable marriage. The erring and tempestuous waif of the novel's beginning has developed by its end into a self-sacrificing and brave woman. As so often in American orphan fiction, Gerty's lack of protectors serves to highlight the power of the self; as her future husband sums her up, she may be "without family, wealth or beauty; but [possesses] a spirit so elevated as to make her great, a heart so noble as to make her rich, a soul so pure as to make her beautiful" (Cummins 1854/1968).

It is this emphasis on Gerty's spirit, heart, and purity of soul that makes *The Lamplighter* so characteristic of its era. This work is part of the nineteenth-century form known as the sentimental novel, a genre that primarily addressed female readers, saw human nature as essentially good rather than (as in Calvinist theology) depraved, and stressed the value of emotion in determining one's course of action. Orphan fiction, which often seeks to elicit the reader's sympathy for a child whose situation is presented as deeply pathetic, was a significant component of sentimental literature. Yet the sentimental adoption novel changes over time. For instance, in the early twentieth century, authors downplay the adoptive parent's role in socializing the child. Whereas the loving and nurturing adult was to return in the "new realism" characteristic of children's literature in the 1960s and 1970s, the orphan novel of the turn of the twentieth century presents the child, not the adult, as the source of emotional bounty. To quote the slogan of the "child-rescue" campaign mounted by one women's magazine, the *Delineator*, in 1907, the issue was not simply "The Child That Needs a Home" but also "The Home That Needs a Child."

Thus, the Progressive Era adoption tale revises the utilitarian attitude often taken toward displaced children in real life. No longer was the exchange presented as one in which the child received food, shelter, and basic socialization in return for manual labor. In sentimental fiction, the orphan's labor is emotional much more than it is physical. As children's-literature scholar Perry Nodelman describes "the warmhearted world of the traditional [orphan] novel for girls," the narrative centers on the interaction of orphan and caregivers. The latter

> will be old, or they will act as if they are old. They will be stiff and unfriendly, very strict about themselves and others. They will have suffered greatly in the past, probably because of thwarted love, and they will be unmarried or widowed. They will probably have a strong sense of duty. And the child . . . will transform their lives and make them happy. (Nodelman 1982)

In the nineteenth century, prestige literature and the sentimental mode could coexist, enabling the orphan-savior to figure in novels by revered authors such as George Eliot, whose 1861 adult novel *Silas Marner* considers just such a redemption as Nodelman sketches above. The twentieth century, however, redefined the emotional range appropriate to realistic fiction, a shift that led to a boom in a more low-key style of orphan. In works such as Elizabeth Enright's *Then There Were Five* (1944), the adopted child is significant not because he "transforms [the] lives" of his new family but rather because his inclusion in that family helps to illustrate the bounty and warmth that it already displayed. Abused and neglected by his original guardian (a distant cousin), Enright's Mark Herron accedes to his adoption by the Melendy family with a gratitude that shows that both he and the Melendys know what a true family means; the novel ends with Mark's words "Home again," spoken "as solemnly and joyfully as if he had said the word 'Amen' " (Enright 1944/1987). In Enright's rendition, this religion of home, characterized by loyalty, love, mutual help, and humor, not only nurtures individuality but also enables the entire group to weather traumas ranging from straitened financial circumstances to the extended absence of the Melendy children's one surviving parent, who has been called away to do war work in Washington, D.C. Mark and the Melendys' resilience and optimism thus models for the child reader of the 1940s the spirit that is expected of Americans in general during times of national crisis.

The same point could be made of other well-known literary orphans of the period. Many appeared in historical fiction, a device that enabled authors to highlight the stalwart independence of the Americans of the past; from the 1930s to the 1950s, the orphan was frequently an archetype for instilling patriotism in young readers. Examples of this type include Rachel Field's *Calico Bush* (1931), about the Americanization of a bound-out French girl; Esther Forbes's *Johnny Tremain* (1943), whose title character rises above a crippling accident to further the cause of Revolutionary America; and Jean Lee Latham's *Carry On, Mr. Bowditch* (1955), one of a series of fictionalized biographies by this author featuring "men who had it 'rough' and yet still managed to achieve something worthwhile, despite overwhelming setbacks" (Latham, quoted in Hoyle 1978). Like Enright's Mark Herron, and unlike many of their nineteenth-century predecessors, Field's, Forbes's, and Latham's protagonists are shown to need family more than family needs them. At the same time, that their emotional deprivation goes hand in hand with talent and strength of character suggests to the reader that cultural or individual investment in the orphan will be repaid many times over, a theme common in orphan fiction from the Civil War onward.

MULTIETHNIC ADOPTION IN THE LATE TWENTIETH CENTURY

The adaptability of the displaced child as a literary figure continues: responding to the importance of international adoption over the past decades, authors have produced any number of chapter books and picture books affirming the strength of the multiracial and/or multinational adoptive home, and frequently also the home headed by a single adoptive parent, usually female. An early example is Helen Doss's 1954 memoir *The Family Nobody Wanted*, which recounts her and her husband's joyful adoption of twelve children, most of them of East Asian, Filipino, and/or American Indian ancestry. More recent entrants are typified by Elisabet McHugh's trilogy of novels from the 1980s about a single woman veterinarian who adopts two Korean daughters; Rose Lewis's autobiographical picture book *I Love You Like Crazy Cakes* (2000), which describes her adoption of a Chinese infant; and, more metaphorical in strategy, Keiko Kasza's *A Mother for Choco* (1992, but published earlier in a different form in Japan), the tale of a single bear who adopts her children from a wide range of species, including alligators and birds. Invariably, the message of this type of modern text is that love transcends racial and national boundaries, a theme that speaks to the preoccupations of post–World War II America as well as to the personal experience of many of today's adoptive parents.

It is worth noting that this theme is far more common in works produced after 1950 than it is in works of an earlier day, which in turn contain messages that do not invariably appear in more recent adoption stories. Examples provided elsewhere in this chapter illustrate as well that orphan novels perennially respond to the influence of new genres that have gradually entered children's literature, from historical fiction to the late-twentieth-century "problem novel." For instance, the current emphasis on multiculturalism is not only visible in stories about contemporary multiethnic adoptive families. We might also see it at work in, say, a novel such as Sally Watson's *To Build a Land* (1957), which describes the experience of a group of young emigrants to Palestine in 1947, or in the many other historical accounts of children displaced from their original families by World War II. Such tales have a clear social purpose—they may be designed to educate readers about the past, to encourage respect for different groups, or to widen readers' horizons in other ways. The purposes may alter from generation to generation, but the existence of social content remains a constant. As this chapter has sought to illustrate, displaced children have historically served a variety of functions within American children's literature, functions that reflect the changing requirements and concerns of American culture. Both the continuities and the variations apparent over time in the American literary orphan, and indeed in the literary orphan of other cultures, have much to tell us about ourselves.

REFERENCES

Ashby, LeRoy. 1984. *Saving the Waifs: Reformers and Dependent Children, 1890–1917.* Philadelphia: Temple University Press.

Baym, Nina. 1978. *Woman's Fiction: A Guide to Novels by and about Women in America, 1820–1870.* Ithaca, NY: Cornell University Press.

Berebitsky, Julie. 2000. *Like Our Very Own: Adoption and the Changing Culture of Motherhood, 1851–1950.* Lawrence: University Press of Kansas.

Bunting, Eve. 1996. *Train to Somewhere.* New York: Clarion.

Cummins, Maria Susanna. 1854/1968. *The Lamplighter.* Omnibus edition with *Tempest and Sunshine*, by Mary Jane Holmes. Edited by Donald A. Koch, 211–552. New York: Odyssey Books.

"The Delineator Child-Rescue Campaign: For the Child That Needs a Home and the Home That Needs a Child." 1907. *Delineator* 70, no. 5: 715–19.

Doss, Helen. 1954/2001. *The Family Nobody Wanted.* Boston: Northeastern University Press.

Eliot, George. 1861/1999. *Silas Marner.* Edited by Elizabeth Seely. Hauppage, NY: Barron's.

Elmer, Laura. 1860. "The Devoted Brother and Sister." *Merry's Museum* 60, no. 2: 103–5.

Enright, Elizabeth. 1944/1987. *Then There Were Five.* New York: Dell Publishers.

Field, Rachel. 1931. *Calico Bush.* New York: Macmillan.

Forbes, Esther. 1943/2004. *Johnny Tremain.* Waterville, ME: Thorndike Press.

Gannon, Susan R. 1997. " 'The Best Magazine for Children of All Ages': Cross-Editing *St. Nicholas Magazine* (1873–1905)." *Children's Literature* 25: 153–80.

Graham, Rosa. 1876. "Patches." *St. Nicholas* 3, no. 12 (October): 774–76.

Hacsi, Timothy. 1997. *Second Home: Orphan Asylums and Poor Families in America.* Cambridge, MA: Harvard University Press.

Howard, Caroline A. 1867. "A Modern Cinderella." *Our Young Folks* 3, no. 5: 280–84.

Hoyle, Karen Nelson. 1978. "Latham, Jean Lee." In *Twentieth-Century Children's Writers*, ed. D. L. Kirkpatrick, 730–34. New York: St. Martin's Press.

Kasza, Keiko. 1992. *A Mother for Choco.* New York: Putnam.

Latham, Jean Lee. 1955. *Carry On, Mr. Bowditch.* Boston: Houghton, Mifflin.

Lewis, Rose. 2000. *I Love You Like Crazy Cakes.* Boston: Little, Brown.

Malot, Hector Henri. 1878/1916. *Nobody's Boy (Sans Famille).* Translated by Florence Crewe Jones. New York: Cupples & Leon Company.

———. 1893/1962. *Nobody's Girl (En Famille).* Translated by Florence Crewe Jones. New York: Platt and Munk.

Mills, Claudia. 1987. "Children in Search of a Family: Orphan Novels Through the Century." *Children's Literature in Education* 18: 227–39.

Montgomery, L. M. 1908/1976. *Anne of Green Gables.* New York: Bantam Books.

Nelson, Claudia. 2003. " 'In These Days of Scientific Charity': Orphanages and Social Engineering in *Dear Enemy.*" In *Children's Literature and the Fin de Siècle*, ed. Roderick McGillis, 91–100. Westport, CT: Praeger.

———. 2003b. *Little Strangers: Portrayals of Adoption and Foster Care in America, 1850–1929.* Bloomington: Indiana University Press.

Nixon, Joan Lowery. 1987. *A Family Apart.* The Orphan Train Quartet, Book 1. New York: Bantam Books.

Nodelman, Perry. 1992. "Progressive Utopia: Or, How to Grow Up without Growing Up." In *Such a Simple Little Tale: Critical Responses to L. M. Montgomery's* Anne of Green Gables, ed. Mavis Reimer, 29–38. Metuchen, NJ: Scarecrow Press.

Pascoe, Judith. 1994. "Tales for Young Housekeepers: T. S. Arthur and the American Girl." In *The Girl's Own: Cultural Histories of the Anglo-American Girl, 1830–1915*, ed. Claudia Nelson and Lynne Vallone, 34–51. Athens: University of Georgia Press.

Propp, V. 1968/1994. *Morphology of the Folktale.* 2nd ed. Translated by Laurence Scott. Edited by Louis A. Wagner. Austin: University of Texas Press.

Snyder, Zilpha Keatley. 1998. *Gib Rides Home.* New York: Bantam Books.

Trowbridge, J. T. 1871. *Jack Hazard and His Fortunes.* Serialized in *Our Young Folks* 7 (January–December).

Warner, Susan. 1850/1987. *The Wide, Wide World.* Edited by Jane Tompkins. New York: Feminist Press.

Watson, Sally. 1957. *To Build a Land.* New York: Holt.

Webster, Jean (Alice Jane Chandler). 1912/1987. *Daddy-Long-Legs.* New York: Dell Publishers.

Webster, Jean. 1915/2004. *Dear Enemy.* In *Daddy Long Legs and Dear Enemy.* Edited by Elaine Showalter. New York: Penguin.

Wiggins, Kate Douglas. 1890. *Timothy's Quest: A Story for Anybody, Young or Old, Who Cares to Read It.* Boston: Houghton, Mifflin.

II Documents

7 Multicultural Forms of Adoption and Foster Care before 1850

The following sources include stories, laws, letters, contracts, and narratives that demonstrate the variety of approaches to adoption and foster care before adoption laws began to be modernized in the 1850s and before legalized slavery was ended in 1863. They are derived from Native American, European American, and African American sources.

1. Seneca Tale, "The Origin of Stories"

A native Senecan, Arthur C. Parker was also an eminent archeologist and ethnologist. He collected Senecan stories and worked for their preservation. This story tells the story of how all Seneca stories came to be. To this day, the Seneca people still call their most important stories of the past "Gă' kāā," from the name of the orphaned boy who brought the stories to the people.

There was once a boy who had no home. His parents were dead and his uncles would not care for him. In order to live this boy, whose name was Gaqka, or, Crow, made a bower of branches for an abiding place and hunted birds and squirrels for food.

He had almost no clothing but was very ragged and dirty. When the people from the village saw him they called him Filth-Covered-One, and laughed as they passed by, holding their noses. No one thought he would ever amount to anything, which made him feel heavy-hearted. He resolved to go away from his tormentors and become a great hunter.

One night Gaqka found a canoe. He had never seen this canoe before, so he took it. Stepping in he grasped the paddle, when the canoe immediately shot into the air, and he paddled above the clouds and under the moon. For a long time he went always southward. Finally the canoe dropped into a river and then Gaqka paddled for shore.

On the other side of the river was a great cliff that had a face that looked like a man. It was at the forks of the river where this cliff stood. The boy resolved to make his home on the top of the cliff and so climbed it and built a bark cabin.

The first night he sat on the edge of the cliff he heard a voice saying, "Give me some tobacco." Looking around the boy, seeing no one, replied, "Why should I give tobacco?"

There was no answer and the boy began to fix his arrows for the next day's hunt. After a while the voice spoke again, "Give me some tobacco."

Gaqka now took out some tobacco and threw it over the cliff. The voice spoke again: "Now I will tell you a story."

Feeling greatly awed the boy listened to a story that seemed to come directly out of the rock upon which he was sitting. Finally the voice paused, for the story had ended. Then it spoke again saying, "It shall be the custom hereafter to present me with a small gift for my stories." So the boy gave the rock a few bone beads. Then the rock said, "Hereafter when I speak, announcing that I shall tell a story you must say, 'Nio,' and as I speak you must say 'Hĕⁿ'" that I may know that you are listening. You must never fall asleep but continue to listen until I say 'Dā'neho nigagā'is.' (So thus finished is the length of my story). Then you shall give me presents and I shall be satisfied."

The next day, the boy hunted and killed a great many birds. These he made into soup and roasts. He skinned the birds and saved the skins, keeping them in a bag.

That evening the boy sat on the rock again and looked westward at the sinking sun. He wondered if his friend would speak again. While waiting he chipped some new arrow-points, and made them very small so that he could use them in a blow gun. Suddenly, as he worked, he heard the voice again. "Give me some tobacco to smoke," it said. Gaqka threw a pinch of tobacco over the cliff and the voice said, "Hau'nio"," and commenced a story. Long into the night one wonderful tale after another flowed from the rock, until it called out, "So thus finished is the length of my story." Gaqka was sorry to have the stories ended but he gave the rock an awl made from a bird's leg and a pinch of tobacco.

The next day the boy hunted far to the east and there found a village. Nobody knew who he was but he soon found many friends. There were some hunters who offered to teach him how to kill big game, and these went with him to his own camp on the high rock. At night he allowed them to listen to the stories that came forth from the rock, but it would speak only when Gaqka was present. He therefore had many friends with whom to hunt.

Now after a time Gaqka made a new suit of clothing from deer skin and desired to obtain a decorated pouch. He, therefore, went to the village and found one house where there were two daughters living with an old mother. He asked that a pouch be made and the youngest daughter spoke up and said, "It is now finished. I have been waiting for you to come for it." So she gave him a handsome pouch.

Then, the old mother spoke, saying, "I now perceive that my future son-in-law has passed through the door and is here." Soon thereafter, the younger woman brought Gaqka a basket of bread and said, "My mother greatly desires that you should marry me." Gaqka looked at the girl and was satisfied, and ate the bread. The older daughter was greatly displeased and frowned in an evil manner.

That night the bride said to her husband, "We must now go away. My older sister will kill you for she is jealous." So Gaqka arose and took his bride to his own lodge. Soon the rock spoke and began to relate wonder stories of things that happened in the old days. The bride was not surprised, but said, "This standing rock, indeed, is my grandfather. I will now present you with a pouch into which you must put a trophy for every tale related."

All winter long the young couple stayed in the lodge on the great rock and heard all the wonder tales of the old days. Gaqka's bag was full of stories and he knew all the lore of former times.

As springtime came the bride said, "We must now go north to your own people and you shall become a great man." But Gaqka was sad and said, "Alas, in my own country I am an outcast and called by an unpleasant name."

The bride only laughed, saying, "Nevertheless we shall go north."

Taking their pelts and birdskins, the young couple descended the cliff and seated themselves in the canoe. "This is my canoe," said the bride. "I sent it through the air to you."

The bride seated herself in the bow of the canoe and Gaqka in the stern. Grasping a paddle he swept it through the water, but soon the canoe arose and went through the air. Meanwhile the bride was singing all kinds of songs, which Gaqka learned as he paddled.

When they reached the north, the bride said, "Now I shall remove your clothing and take all the scars from your face and body." She then caused him to pass through a hollow log, and when Gaqka emerged from the other end he was dressed in the finest clothing and was a handsome man.

Together the two walked to the village where the people came out to see them. After a while Gaqka said, "I am the boy whom you once were accustomed to call 'Cia"dōdă'.' I have now returned." That night the people of the village gathered around and listened to the tales he told, and he instructed them to give him small presents and tobacco. He would plunge his hand in his pouch and take out a trophy, saying, "Ho ho'! So here is another one!" and then looking at his trophy would relate an ancient tale.

Everybody now thought Gaqka a great man and listened to his stories. He was the first man to find out all about the adventures of the old-time people. That is why there are so many legends now.

Source: Arthur C. Parker, "Origin of Folk Stories," *Seneca Myths and Folk Tales* (Buffalo, NY: Buffalo Historical Society, 1923).

2. English Children Involuntarily Transported to Virginia, 1620

The following act authorized the City of London's Common Council to "bind out" poor, unattended children to the new American colony of Virginia. While most of the English settlers in the New England colonies were families, in the southern colonies, most emigrants were single persons, many of whom were under eighteen years old. These "transported" children were required to complete much hard labor and faced a short life expectancy in their new-world situations.

January 31, 1620.

Whereas we are informed that the City of London hath, by an act of the Common Council, appointed one hundred children, out of the multitudes that swarm in that place, to be sent to Virginia, there to be bound apprentices for certain years with very beneficial conditions for them afterwards, and have moreover yielded to a levy of five hundred pounds for the appareling of those children and towards the charge of their transportation; wherein, as the City deserveth thanks and commendations for redeeming so many poor souls from misery and ruin and putting them in a condition of use and service to the State; so forasmuch as information is likewise made that among that number there are divers unwilling to be carried thither and that it is conceived that both the City wanteth authority to deliver and the Virginia Company to receive and carry out these persons against their wills, we have thought meet, for the better furtherance of so good a work, hereby to authorize and require as well such of the City as take charge of that service as the Virginia Company, or any of them, to deliver, receive, and transport into Virginia all and every the foresaid children as shall be most expedient. And if any of them shall be found obstinate to resist or otherwise to disobey such directions as shall be given in this behalf, we do likewise hereby authorize such as shall have the charge of this service to imprison, punish, and dispose any of those children, upon any disorder by them or any of them committed, as cause shall require, and so to ship them out for Virginia with as much expedition as may stand with conveniency. For which this shall be unto all persons whom the same may any way concern a sufficient warrant.

Source: Great Britain, Privy Council, *Acts of the Privy Council of England, 1619–1621* (London: Spottiswood and Eyre, 1890), vol. 5.

3. Standard Apprenticeship Indentures, Virginia, 1659

Apprenticeships, while not legal adoptions, were common for children of all economic classes, although the profession typically varied depending on the child's family's economic class.

This indenture made the 6th day of June in the year of our Lord Christ 1659, witnesseth, that Bartholomew Clarke the son of John Clarke of the City of Canterbury, sadler, of his own liking and with the consent of Francis Plumer of the City of Canterbury, brewer, hath put himself apprentice unto Edward Rowzie of Virginia, planter, as an apprentice with him to dwell from the day of the date above mentioned unto the full term of four years from thence next ensuing fully to be complete and ended, all which said term the said Bartholomew Clarke well and faithfully the said Edward Rowzie as his master shall serve, his secrets keep, his commands most just and lawful he shall observe, and fornication he shall not commit, nor contract matrimony with any woman during the said term; he shall not do hurt unto his master, nor consent to the doing of any, but to his power shall hinder and prevent the doing of any; at cards, dice or any unlawful games he shall not play; he shall not waste the goods of his said master nor lend them to anybody without his master's consent; he shall not absent himself from his master's service day or night, but as a true faithful servant, shall demean himself. And the said Edward Rowzie in the mystery, art, and occupation of a planter . . . the said Bartholomew shall teach or cause to be taught, and also during said term shall find and allow his apprentice, competent meat, drink, apparel, washing, lodging with all other things fitting for his degree, and in the end thereof, fifty acres of land to be laid out for him, and all other things which according to the custom of the country is or ought to be done.

Source: Philip A. Bruce, *Economic History of Virginia* (New York: Macmillan, 1896), vol. 2.

4. Richard Frethorne, Letter to His Parents, Virginia, 1623

This is a letter from an indentured servant in Virginia to his parents in England, begging them to redeem him from his service and bring him back home.

. . . All these died out of my master's house, since I came; and we came in but at Christmas, and this is the 20th day of March. And the sailors say that there is two-thirds of the 150 dead already. And thus I end, praying to God to send me good success that I may be redeemed out of Egypt. So vale in Christo.

Loving father, I pray you to use this man very exceeding kindly, for he hath done much for me, both on my journey and since. I entreat you not to forget me, but by any means redeem me; for this day we hear that there is 26 of Englishmen slain by the Indians. And they have taken a pinnace of Mr. Pountis, and have gotten pieces, armor, swords, all things fit for war; so that they may now steal upon us and we cannot know them from English till it is too late—that they be upon us—and then there is no mercy. Therefore if you love or respect me as your child, release me from the bondage and save my life. Now you may save me, or let met be slain with infidels. Ask this man—he knoweth that all is true and just that I sat here. If you do redeem me, the Company must send for me to my Mr. Harrod; for so is this Master's name. April, the second day,

Your loving son,
Richard Frethorne

Moreover, on the third day of April we heard that after these rogues had gotten the pinnace and had taken all furnitures [such] as pieces, swords, armor, coats of mail, powder, shot and all the things that they had to trade withal, they killed the Captain and cut off his head. And rowing with the tail of the boat foremost, they set up a pole and put the Captain's head upon it, and so rowed home. Then the Devil set them on again, so that they furnished about 200 canoes with above 1000 Indians, and came, and thought to have taken the ship; but she was too quick for them-which thing was very much talked of, for they always feared a ship. But now the rogues grow very bold and can use pieces, some of them, as well of better than an Englishman; for an Indian did shoot with Mr. Charles, my master's kinsman, at a mark of white paper, and he hit it at the first, but Mr. Charles could not hit it. But see the envy of these slaves, for when they could not take the ship, then our men saw them threaten Accomack, that is the next plantation. And now there is no way but starving; . . . For they had no crop last year by reason of these rogues, so that we have no corn but as ships do relieve us, nor we shall hardly have any crop this year; and we are as like to perish first as any plantation. For we have but two hogsheads of meal left to serve us this two months, . . . that is but a halfpennyloaf a day for a man. Is it not strange to me, think you? But what will it be when we shall go a month or two and never see a bit of bread, as my master doth say we must do? And he said he is not able to keep us all. Then we shall be turned up to the land and eat barks of trees or molds of the ground; therefore with weeping tears I beg of you to help me. Oh, that you did see my daily and hourly sighs, groans, and tears, and thumps that I afford mine own breast, and rue and curse the time of my birth, with holy Job. I thought no head had been able to hold so much water as hath and doth daily flow from mine eyes.

But this is certain: I never felt the want of father and mother till now;

but now, dear friends, full well I know and rue it, although it were too late before I knew it . . .

Your loving son,
Richard Frethorne, Virginia, 3rd April, 1623

Source: Excerpted from *The Records of the Virginia Company of London* (Washington, DC: Government Printing Office, 1935), vol. 4.

5. Frederick Douglass, "The Author's Childhood"

In this passage, Douglass explains what his experience of family was like under slavery, and the kinship care he experienced from his grandmother. This slave narrative, along with many others, is available online at the "Documenting the American South" project of the University Library at the University of North Carolina–Chapel Hill, at http://docsouth.unc.edu/neh/douglass55/menu.html.

Genealogical trees do not flourish among slaves. A person of some consequence here in the north, sometimes designated *father*, is literally abolished in slave law and slave practice. It is only once in a while that an exception is found to this statement. I never met with a slave who could tell me how old he was. Few slave-mothers know anything of the months of the year, nor of the days of the month. They keep no family records, with marriages, births, and deaths. They measure the ages of their children by spring time, winter time, harvest time, planting time, and the like; but these soon become undistinguishable and forgotten. Like other slaves, I cannot tell how old I am. This destitution was among my earliest troubles. I learned when I grew up, that my master—and this is the case with masters generally—allowed no questions to be put to him, by which a slave might learn his age. Such questions are deemed evidence of impatience, and even of impudent curiosity. From certain events, however, the dates of which I have since learned, I suppose myself to have been born about the year 1817.

The first experience of life with me that I now remember—and I remember it but hazily—began in the family of my grandmother and grandfather, Betsey and Isaac Bailey. They were quite advanced in life, and had long lived on the spot where they then resided. They were considered old settlers in the neighborhood, and, from certain circumstances, I infer that my grandmother, especially, was held in high esteem, far higher than is the lot of most colored persons in the slave states. She was a good nurse, and a capital hand at making nets for catching shad and herring; and these nets were in great demand, not only in Tuckahoe, but at Denton and Hillsboro, neighboring villages. . . . In the time of planting sweet potatoes,

"Grandmother Betty," as she was familiarly called, was sent for in all directions, simply to place the seedling potatoes in the hills; for superstition had it, that if "Grandmamma Betty but touches them at planting, they will be sure to grow and flourish." This high reputation was full of advantage to her, and to the children around her. Though Tuckahoe had but few of the goof things of life, yet of such as it did possess grandmother got a full share, in the way of presents. If good potato crops came after her planting, she was not forgotten by those for whom she planted; and as she was remembered by others, so she remembered the hungry little ones around her.

The dwelling of my grandmother and grandfather had few pretensions. It was a log hut, or cabin, built of clay, wood, and straw. At a distance it resembled—though it was much smaller, less commodious and less substantial—the cabins erected in the western states by the first settlers. To my child's eye, however, it was a noble structure, admirably adapted to promote the comforts and conveniences of its inmates. A few rough, Virginia fence-rails, flung loosely over the rafters above, answered the triple purpose of floors, ceilings, and bedsteads. To be sure, this upper apartment was reached only by a ladder—but what in the world for climbing could be better than a ladder? To me, this ladder was really a high invention, and possessed a sort of charm as I played with delight upon the rounds of it. In this little hut there was a large family of children: I dare not say how many. My grandmother—whether because too old for field service, or because she had so faithfully discharged the duties of her station in early life, I know not—enjoyed the high privilege of living in a cabin, separate from the quarter, with no other burden than her own support, and the necessary care of the little children, imposed. She evidently esteemed it a great fortune to live so. The children were not her own, but her grandchildren—the children of her daughters. She took delight in having them around her, and in attending to their few wants. The practice of separating children from their mothers and hiring the latter out at distances too great to admit of their meeting, except at long intervals, is a marked feature of the cruelty and barbarity of the slave system. But it is in harmony with the grand aim of slavery, which, always and everywhere, is to reduce man to a level with the brute. It is a successful method of obliterating from the mind and heart of the slave, all just ideas of the sacredness of *the family*, as an institution.

Most of the children, however, in this instance, being the children of my grandmother's daughters, the notions of family, and the reciprocal duties and benefits of the relation, had a better chance of being understood than where children are placed—as they often are—in the hands of strangers, who have no care for them, apart from the wishes of their masters. The daughters of my grandmother were five in number. Their names were JENNY, ESTHER, MILLY, PRISCILLA, and HARRIET. The daughter last named was my mother, of whom the reader shall learn more by and by.

Living here, with my dear old grandmother and grandfather, it was a long time before I knew myself to be *a slave*. I knew many other things before I knew that. Grandmother and grandfather were the greatest people in the world to me; and being with them so snugly in their own little cabin—I supposed it be their own—knowing no higher authority over me or the other children than the authority of grandmamma, for a time there was nothing to disturb me; but, as I grew larger and older, I learned by degrees the sad fact, that the "little hut," and the lot on which it stood, belonged not to my dear old grandparents, but to some person who lived a great distance off, and who was called, by grandmother, "OLD MASTER." I further learned the sadder fact, that not only the house and lot, but that grandmother herself, (grandfather was free), and all the little children around her, belonged to this mysterious personage, called by grandmother, with every mark of reverence, "Old Master." Thus early did clouds and shadows begin to fall upon my path. Once on the track—troubles never come singly—I was not long in finding out another fact, still more grievous to my childish heart. I was told that this "old master," whose name seemed ever to be mentioned with fear and shuddering, only allowed the children to live with grandmother for a limited time, and that in fact as soon as they were big enough, they were promptly taken away, to live with the said "old master." These were distressing revelations indeed; and though I was quite too young to comprehend the full import of the intelligence, and mostly spent my childhood days in gleesome sports with the other children, a shade of disquiet rested upon me.

The absolute power of this distant "old master" had touched my young spirit with but the point of its cold, cruel iron, and left me something to brood over after the play and in moments of repose. Grandmammy was, indeed, at that time, all the world to me; and the thought of being separated from her, in any considerable time, was more than an unwelcome intruder. It was intolerable.

Children have their sorrows as well as men and women; and it would be well to remember this in our dealings with them. SLAVE-children *are* children, and prove no exceptions to the general rule. The liability to be separated from my grandmother, seldom or never to see her again, haunted me. I dreaded the thought of going to live with that mysterious "old master" whose name I never heard mentioned with affection, but always with fear. I look back to this as among the heaviest of my childhood sorrows. My grandmother! my grandmother! and the little hut, and the joyous circle under her care, but especially *she*, who made us sorry when she left us but for an hour, and glad on her return,—how could I leave her and the good old home?

Source: Excerpted from *My Bondage and My Freedom* (New York: Miller, Orton, and Mulligan, 1855), 34–40.

8 "Orphan Trains," Child-Saving, and the Modernization of Adoption Law, 1851–1929

The documents in this chapter relate to the beginnings of modern adoption, with a ground-breaking 1851 Massachusetts law and the almost simultaneous beginning of the "orphan train" phenomenon, which finds an important root in the 1853 founding of the Children's Aid Society of New York (CAS), whereby thousands of mostly poor, white children were transported on trains to homes in the West and Midwest. The darker side of the moral fervor that characterized this period is illustrated by the story of Zitkala-Sa (Gertrude Bonnin), a Souix teacher and activist who, as a child, was also transported by train, to the East and away from her family in order to be educated and "civilized" by European Americans.

1. "An Act to provide for the adoption of children," 1851

The English Common Law tradition discouraged adoption, so it was not until the mid-nineteenth century that adoption laws began to be passed in the United States. This Massachusetts act emphasized both the child's consent, where appropriate, and fitness of the parents, and was thus the first truly modern adoption law.

Any inhabitant of this Commonwealth may petition the judge of probate, in the county wherein he or she may reside, for leave to adopt a child not his or her own by birth.

If both or either of the parents of such child shall be living, they or the survivor of them, as the case may be, shall consent in writing to such adoption; if neither parent be living, such consent may be given by the legal guardian of such child; if there be no legal guardian, no father nor mother, the next of kin of such child within the State may give such consent; and if there be no such next of kin, the judge of probate may appoint some discreet and suitable person to act in the proceedings as the next friend of such child, and give or withhold such consent.

If the child be of the age of fourteen years or upwards, the adoption shall not be made without his or her consent. . . .

If, upon such petition, so presented and consented to as aforesaid, the judge of probate shall be satisfied of the identity and relations of the persons, and that the petitioner, or, in case of husband and wife, the petitioners, are of sufficient ability to bring up the child, and furnish suitable nurture and education, having reference to the degree and condition of its parents, and that it is fit and proper that such adoption should take effect, he shall make a decree setting forth the said facts, and ordering that, from and after the date of the decree, such child should be deemed and taken, to all legal intents and purposes, the child of the petitioner or petitioners.

A child so adopted, as aforesaid, shall be deemed, for the purposes of inheritance and succession by such child, custody of the person and right of obedience by such parent or parents by adoption, and all other legal consequences and incidents of the natural relation of parents and children, the same to all intents and purposes as if such child had been born in lawful wedlock of such parents or parent by adoption, saving only that such child shall not be deemed capable of taking property expressly limited to the heirs of the body or bodies of such petitioner or petitioners.

The natural parent or parents of such child shall be deprived, by such decree of adoption, of all legal rights whatsoever as respects such child; and such child shall be freed from all legal obligations of maintenance and obedience, as respects such natural parent or parents. . . .

Source: *Massachusetts Acts and Resolves* (Boston, 1851), 815–16.

2. Charles Loring Brace, "The Children's Aid Society," 1853

In this, the initial circular announcing the founding of the Children's Aid Society (CAS)—and seeking charitable contributions to the association from the public—the focus is on the moral imperative of charity, especially for orphaned and "vagrant" children. CAS has provided city-based services to poor children in New York since its inception and continues to do so today.

This society has taken its origin in the deeply settled feelings of our citizens, that something must be done to meet the increasing crime and poverty among the destitute children of New York. Its objects are to help this class by opening Sunday Meetings and Industrial Schools, and, gradually as means shall be furnished, by forming Lodging-houses and Reading-rooms for children, and by employing paid agents whose sole business shall be to care for them.

As Christian men, we cannot look upon this great multitude of unhappy, deserted, and degraded boys and girls without feeling our responsibility to GOD for them. We remember that they have the same capacities, the same need of kind and good influences, and the same Immortality as the little ones in our own homes. We bear in mind that One died for them, even as for the children of the rich and happy. Thus far, alms-houses and prisons have done little to affect the evil. But a small part of the vagrant population can be shut up in our asylums, and judges and magistrates are reluctant to convict children so young and ignorant that they hardly seem able to distinguish good and evil. The class increases. Immigration is pouring in its multitude of poor foreigners, who leave these young outcasts everywhere abandoned in our midst. For the most part, the boys grow up utterly by themselves. No one cares for them, and they care for no one. Some live by begging, by petty pilfering by bold robbery; some earn an honest support by peddling matches, or apples, or newspapers; others gather bones and rags in the street to sell. They sleep on steps, in cellars, in old barns, and in markets, or they hire a bed in filthy and low lodging-houses. They cannot read; they do not go to school or attend a church. Many of them have never seen the Bible. Every cunning faculty is intensely stimulated. They are shrewd and old in vice, when other children are in leading-strings. Few influences which are kind and good ever reach the vagrant boy. And, yet, among themselves they show generous and honest traits. Kindness can always touch them.

The girls, too often, grow up even more pitiable and deserted. Till of late no one has ever cared for them. They are the crosswalk sweepers, the little apple-peddlers, and candy-sellers of our city; or, by more questionable means, they earn their scanty bread. They traverse the low, vile streets alone, and live without mother or friends, or any share in what we should call a *home*. They also know little of God or Christ, except by name. They grow up passionate, ungoverned, with no love or kindness ever to soften the heart. We all know their short wild life—and the sad end.

These boys and girls, it should be remembered, will soon form the great lower class of our city. They will influence elections; they may shape the policy of the city; they will, assuredly, if unreclaimed, poison society all around them. They will help to form the great multitude of robbers, thieves, vagrants, and prostitutes who are now such a burden upon the law-respecting community.

In one ward alone of the city, the Eleventh, there were, in 1852, out of 12,000 children between the ages of five and sixteen, only 7,000 who attended school, and only 2,500 who went to Sabbath School; leaving 5,000 without the common privileges of education, and about 9,000 destitute of public religious influence.

WANTED
HOMES for CHILDREN

A company of homeless children from the East will arrive at

TROY, MO., ON FRIDAY, FEB. 25th, 1910

These children are of various ages and of both sexes, having been thrown friendless upon the world. They come under the auspices of the Childern's Aid Society of New York. They are well disciplined, having come from the various orphanages. The citizens of this community are asked to assist the agent in finding good homes for them. Persons taking these children must be recommended by the local committee. They must treat the children in every way as a member of the family, sending them to school, church, Sabbath school and properly clothe them until they are 17 years old. The following well-known citizens have agreed to act as local committee to aid the agents in securing homes:

O. H. AVERY E. B. WOOLFOLK H. F. CHILDERS
WM. YOUNG   G. W. COLBERT

Applications must be made to, and endorsed by, the local committee.

An address will be made by the agent. Come and see the children and hear the address. Distribution will take place at the

Opera House, Friday,
Feb. 25, at 1:30 p. m.

B. W. TICE and MISS A. L. HILL, Agents, 105 E. 22nd St., New York City. Rev. J. W. SWAN, University Place, Nebraska, Western Agent.

This advertisement, announcing the arrival of a CAS "orphan train," was placed in a Troy, Missouri, newspaper in 1910.

In view of these evils we have formed an Association which shall devote itself entirely to this class of vagrant children. We do not propose in any way to conflict with existing asylums and institutions, but to render them a hearty co-operation, and, at the same time, to fill a gap, which, of necessity, they all have left. A large multitude of children live in the city who cannot be placed in asylums, and yet who are uncared-for and ignorant and vagrant. We propose to give to these work, and to bring them under religious influence. As means shall come in, it is designed to district the city, so that hereafter every Ward may have its agent, who shall be a friend to the vagrant child. "Boys' Sunday Meetings" have already been formed, which we hope to see extended until every quarter has its place of preaching to boys. With these we intend to connect "Industrial Schools," where the great temptations to this class arising from want of work may be removed, and where they can learn an honest trade. Arrangements have been made with manufacturers, by which, if we have the requisite funds to begin, five hundred boys in different localities can be supplied with paying work. We hope, too, especially to be the means of draining the city of these children, by communicating with farmers, manufacturers, or families in the country, who may have need of such for employment. When homeless boys are found by our agents, we mean to get them homes in the families of respectable, needy persons in the city, and put them in the way of an honest living. We design, in a word, to bring humane and kindly influences to bear on this forsaken class—to preach in various modes the gospel of Christ to the vagrant children of New York.

Numbers of our citizens have long felt the evils we would remedy, but few have the leisure or the means to devote themselves personally to this work with the thoroughness which it requires. This society, as we propose, shall be a medium through which all can, in their measure, practically help the poor children of the city.

We call upon all who recognize that these are the little ones of Christ; all who believe that crime is best averted by sowing good influences in childhood; all who are the friends of the helpless, to aid us in our enterprise. We confidently hope this wide and practical movement will have its full share of Christian liberality. And we earnestly ask the contributions of those able to give, to help us in carrying forward the work.

Source: *The Dangerous Classes of New York and Twenty Years' Work Among Them* (New York: Wynkoop, 1872).

3. "Orphan Children Find Homes"

The following article indicates the entirely voluntary, public, and, by modern standards, somewhat haphazard nature of the "orphan train" placements conducted by

CAS during much of the 75-year existence of its "emigration scheme" for placing impoverished children in "Christian homes" in the West.

The Children's Aid Society of New York brought fifteen children to Fredonia Friday under the care of Miss Anna Hill, and a number of the youngsters have already been given homes by people in the county. Each family which took a child can not adopt the little person for at least a year, and at no time is adoption required, the children being removed upon notification of the family given to the society. Occasionally a representative of the society will visit the section to see that the youngsters are being treated properly.

[The original article included, here, a list of all the children, their ages, and the names and addresses of the adults with whom they were placed.]

Persons interested may see Miss Hill who is in charge of the party, at the Loether.

Little Helen Irene Leschander, aged four years, one of the orphans brought to Fredonia by the Children's Aid Society, of New York, last week died at the Loether hotel yesterday morning, after a few days illness, acute laryngitis being the contributing cause of the child's death. The funeral was held yesterday afternoon, Rev. John Carretson of the Presbyterian Church officiating.

The little girl, was an unusually bright and beautiful child and had she lived she would have been adopted by Mr. & Mrs. J. J. Piepmeyer, who have been greatly interested in the little girl since the party arrived in Fredonia.

Source: *The Wilson County* (Kansas) *Citizen*, June 2, 1916.

4. Various Letters to the Children's Aid Society (CAS)

What follows are several pages from the Appendix to an early report of CAS, which typically included entries from the CAS record books, reports from CAS agents describing their journeys, letters from children and foster parents. Although the goal of publishing these letters was, in large part, to emphasize the success of the program and encourage financial contributions to CAS, a few of the letters are surprisingly ambivalent about the process.

a) John D—'s Story

John D—, is an Irish boy of 12 years old, and was brought to the office by Rev. Mr. GERRY. He has friends at No. 40 O— street. Mother is living. Sent Feb. 13th, 1855, to S. S. D—, I—, Pa.

In June, 1856, the following good news was received from Mr. D—, and from John himself.

J—, June 19, 1856.

Dear Sir: We are well pleased with John D—. He is a good boy, and uses good language. He attends Sunday School and Meeting every Sunday. He goes to school in the winter steady; in the summer not so much. If he stays with me, I will do well by him.

Yours truly,
S.S.D—.

Dear Sir: I am happy to say that I have abstained from all bad language, and it was by the means of God's holy word, that made me do so. I have read the Bible through, and by so doing got presented with a nice gilt Bible of my own. I live about two miles from another boy that came from the city. Dear sir, I should like to know where my brother and sister are; and if you find them, I should like to have you tell them to write me a letter, and let me know how they are getting along. I am well pleased with the country. I am now where I get plenty to eat. I can *eat any time in the day, and that is a great privilege.* I think since I have lived here, I have got quite a lot of money. I have now got in my possession $10. 10, all on my own, I am very thankful to my friends of the Children's Aid Society, and I advise all boys running round the 4th and 7th Wards of New York City, I advise them by all means to come into the country, where they see good examples set at every turn, and if every boy, that you gentlemen are so good to find homes for, have as good a home as I have got, I think they would not ask any more, but I presume that half of them do not have half as good a chance as I do. I have got everything comfortable. I give my respects to all my enquiring friends, likewise to my friends of the Children's Aid Society. No more to say at present, but I remain,

Yours truly,
John J. D—.

b) A Fourth Ward Child

Nov. 4th 1856.

DEAR MR. MACY: I thank you for your kind letter. I have a good home, and many kind friends to care for me. I think the country is a beautiful place. I wish little children would go in the country; there are many things they can get here without stealing or begging, for we have got a nice orchard full of nice fruit. I go out some days nutting. Mrs. F— says, she is going to dress me warm this winter, and take me a sleigh-riding. Mrs. F— took me in the carriage about two weeks ago, to hear Mr. F—, a Missionary, address the Sabbath School at W—; he told us some pretty stories; I hope I shall profit by it.

MR. MACY, I want to tell you what Mrs. F— has taught me to do. I can make coffee, and milk the cow, and make buckwheat cakes. I think it is better for little children to be in the country, and learn all these pretty things, than to be in that wicked city. I love the country; and think I am a good girl Mrs. F— tells me I am sometimes. The young ladies teach me, and bear me my lessons; and teach me to sew. Please give my love to MR. GERRY, and the ladies, and my teachers, and the children, with much respect.

A.F.

P.S. (In Mrs. F—'s handwriting.) This is an original document, MR. MACY and Annie's first letter, remember.

c) "The Other Side"

PEORIA, Aug. 27, 1856.

Dear Sir: I hardly know how to reply to your letter, asking for information about Elizabeth W; but shall endeavor to tell you both *pro* and *con*, and then leave you to weigh one against the other.

1st. She is a very bad girl. I cannot say that she is *immoral.* I have had fears and suspicions, but she assures me that she is not guilty of indecency in speech or conduct. She is bad in the sense of impudent, stubborn, disobedient, hot tempered, and ungrateful; and on this account, she has made us all lead an unhappy life. Indeed it would be impossible to tell you what a trial she has been to us.

2nd. She is a very good girl. By this, I mean that at times she has given us perfect satisfaction, thus showing what she *can* be, and do, when she *will.* I must say too, that she has greatly improved, and occasionally at least, tries to resist her besetting sins.

3d. She is very smart, though very ignorant, *she is one of the smartest girls I ever saw.* At her work she is quick and thorough; and particularly her mind is of far more than ordinary caliber. She is a musical genius in her studies, and she is very ready, discerning, and inquiring.

4th. Physically, she is very weak. Her health is by no means robust, and hard work and exposure would soon bring her to the grave.

And now, dear sir, when I tell you that I have young children, of whom it is necessary that Elizabeth should take much charge, and that I am burdened with anxiety with regard to the influence such a girl must exert on them, you will understand why I am not desirous to keep her. I say nothing about the peace of my family or the trouble the girl causes me; but the question is—*Is it my duty to risk the ruin of my children?* Every conscientious parent can appreciate my anxiety, but on the other hand, because she is bad, I wish to make her good; because she has unusual talent, I wish to cultivate it; because she is not strong, I wish to save her from hard work; because she is friendless, I wish to give her a home; and most of all, because she has a soul, I wish to save it. We have concluded then to try her still further, but, if you can place her in a *pious* family who will certainly care for her in the manner above indicated, I shall be satisfied to give her up. But it will never do to cut her adrift again; she would seek low company, and soon perish forever. With regard to her instruction, she attends regularly my Sabbath School and Church; and during the week, is taught in History, Arithmetic, &c., by my wife and myself.

With regard to her position in my family, I have not adopted her as my child but we wish to make her, and have her consider herself, as one of the family; not, as a servant. And just in this particular, we have great difficulty with her; she persists in the closest intimacy with our kitchen servant, which for her own sake, and for the sake of order in our household, we cannot allow.

With regard to my treatment of her, it is as though she were my own child. Hence, I have on two occasions, inflicted a slight punishment. This was absolutely necessary, for she boasted that we could not punish her. The result has been good. I would not treat a *servant* so; but my children often need and receive chastisement. If I have done wrong in this matter, please inform me; for I have acted conscientiously, and not in a spirit of cruelty.

With regard to her future, I have proposed to her to get her to become a teacher, and then she can either follow this pursuit, or have a home with us, as long as she lives.

Thus, my dear sir, I have written to you freely, fully, and I hope satisfactorily. If in anything I have transgressed the requirements of your society, please to let me know. We shall be glad to have a reply to this communication.

Elizabeth shall write soon; with prayers for the blessing of *that* "Friend" that sticketh closer than a brother,

I am very Respectfully,

R.P.F.

Source: *The Fourth Annual Report of the Children's Aid Society* (New York: Wynkoop, 1857), 48–52.

5. Minnesota Adoption Law, 1917

Minnesota's 1917 adoption law was among the earliest to require that a state agency verify that a child was a "proper subject for adoption" and that the proposed adoptive home was "suitable." It was also an early proponent of explicitly sealed records.

Adoption; petition and consent.—Any resident of the State may petition the district court of the county in which he resides for leave to adopt any child not his own. If the petitioner be married the spouse shall join in the petition. All petitions for the adoption of a child who is a ward or pupil of the State public school shall be made jointly by the person desiring to adopt such child and the superintendent of the State public school. . . .

Investigation by board of control.—Upon the filing of a petition for the adoption of a minor child the court shall notify the State board of control. It shall then be the duty of the board to verify the allegations of the petition, to investigate the condition and antecedents of the child for the purpose of ascertaining whether he is a proper subject for adoption, and to make appropriate inquiry to determine whether the proposed foster home is a suitable home for the child. The board shall as soon as practicable submit to the court a full report in writing, with a recommendation as to the granting of the petition and any other information regarding the child or the proposed home which the court shall require. No petition shall be granted until the child shall have lived for six months in the proposed home: *Provided, however,* That such investigation and period of residence may be waived by the court upon good cause shown, when satisfied that the proposed home and the child are suited to each other.

Consent, when necessary.—Except as herein provided, no adoption of a minor shall be permitted without the consent of his parents, but the consent of a parent who has abandoned the child, or who can not be found, or who is insane or otherwise incapacitated from giving such consent, or who has lost custody of the child through divorce proceedings or the order of a juvenile court, may be dispensed with, and consent may be given by the guardian, if there be one, or, if there be no guardian, by the State board of control. In case of illegitimacy, the consent of the mother alone shall suffice. In all cases where the child is over fourteen years old his own consent must be had also. . . .

Decree; change of name.—If upon the hearing the court shall be satisfied as to the identity and relationship of the persons concerned, and that the petitioners are able to properly rear and educate the child, and that the petition should be granted, a decree shall be made and recorded in the office of the clerk, setting forth the facts and ordering that from the date thereof the child shall be the child of the petitioners. If desired, the court, in and by said decree, may change the name of the child. . . .

Annulment.—If within five years after his adoption a child develops feeble-mindedness, epilepsy, insanity, or venereal infection as a result of conditions existing prior to the adoption, and of which the adopting parents had no knowledge or notice, a petition setting forth such facts may be filed with the court which entered the decree of adoption, and if such facts are proved the court may annul the adoption and commit the child to the guardianship of the State board of control. In every such proceeding it shall be the duty of the county attorney to represent the interests of the child.

Records of adoption.—The files and records of the court in adoption proceedings shall not be open to inspection or copy by other persons than the parties in interest and their attorneys and representatives of the State board of control, except upon an order of the court expressly permitting the same.

Source: *Session Laws of Minnesota for 1917*, Chapter 222; Section 1-7151-1761.

6. Zitkala-Sa (Gertrude Bonnin), "The Land of Red Apples"

In this selection, Zitkala-Sa (whose name means "Red Bird") describes her experience as an eight-year-old girl being seduced into following missionaries East to Wabash, Indiana, away from her mother and the traditional Sioux life she has known on the Pine Ridge Reservation in South Dakota. Such attempts at "civilizing" Native children will be viewed as a form of cultural genocide by activists in the latter part of the century (see Chapter 4).

There were eight in our party of bronzed children who were going East with the missionaries. Among us were three young braves, two tall girls, and we three little ones, Judéwin, Thowin, and I.

We had been very impatient to start on our journey to the Red Apple Country, which, we were told, lay a little beyond the great circular horizon of the Western prairie. Under a sky of rosy apples we dreamt of roaming as freely and happily as we had chased the cloud shadows on the Dakota plains. We had anticipated much pleasure from a ride on the iron horse, but the throngs of staring palefaces disturbed and troubled us.

On the train, fair women, with tottering babies on each arm, stopped their haste and scrutinized the children of absent mothers. Large men, with heavy bundles in their hands, halted near by, and riveted their glassy blue eyes upon us.

I sank deep into the corner of my seat, for I resented being watched. Directly in front of me, children who were no larger than I hung themselves upon the backs of their seats, with their bold white faces toward me. Sometimes they took their forefingers out of their mouths and pointed at my moccasined feet. Their mothers, instead of reproving such rude curiosity, looked closely at me, and attracted their children's further notice to my blanket. This embarrassed me, and kept me constantly on the verge of tears.

I sat perfectly still, with my eyes downcast, daring only now and then to shoot long glances around me. Chancing to turn to the window at my side, I was quite breathless upon seeing one familiar object. It was the telegraph pole which strode by at short paces. Very near my mother's dwelling, along the edge of a road thickly bordered with wild sunflowers, some poles like these had been planted by white men. Often I had stopped, on my way down the road, to hold my ear against the pole, and, hearing its low moaning, I used to wonder what the paleface had done to hurt it. Now I sat watching for each pole that glided by to be the last one. . . .

It was night when we reached the school grounds. The lights from the windows of the large buildings fell upon some of the icicled trees that stood beneath them. . . . Entering the house, I stood close against the wall. The strong glaring light in the large whitewashed room dazzled my eyes. The noisy hurrying of hard shoes upon a bare wooden floor increased the whirring in my ears. My only safety seemed to be in keeping next to the wall. As I was wondering in which direction to escape from all this confusion, two warm hands grasped me firmly, and in the same moment I was tossed high in midair. A rosy-cheeked paleface woman caught me in her arms. I was both frightened and insulted by such trifling. I stared into her eyes, wishing her to let me stand on my own feet, but she jumped me up and down with increasing enthusiasm. My mother had never made a plaything of her wee daughter. Remembering this I began to cry aloud.

They misunderstood the cause of my tears, and placed me at a white table loaded with food. There our party were united again. As I did not hush my crying, one of the older ones whispered to me, "Wait until you are alone in the night."

It was very little I could swallow besides my sobs, that evening.

"Oh, I want my mother and my brother Dawée! I want to go to my aunt!" I pleaded; but the ears of the palefaces could not hear me.

From the table we were taken along an upward incline of wooden boxes, which I learned afterward to call a stairway. At the top was a quiet hall, dimly lighted. Many narrow beds were in one straight line down the entire length of the wall. In them lay sleeping brown faces, which peeped just out of the coverings. I was tucked into bed with one of the tall girls, because she talked to me in my mother tongue and seemed to soothe me.

I had arrived in the wonderful land of rosy skies, but I was not happy, as I had thought I should be. My long travel and the bewildering sights had exhausted me. I fell asleep, heaving deep, tired sobs. My tears were left to dry themselves in streaks, because neither my aunt nor my mother was near to wipe them away.

Source: "School-Days of an Indian Girl," *Atlantic* 85 (1900): 185–94. Reprinted in *American Indian Stories* (Washington, DC: Hayworth, 1921).

9 Science and Secrecy: Adoption, Orphanages, and Foster Care, 1930–1969

The documents in this chapter relate to the beginnings of federal subsidies for dependent children during the Depression and New Deal era, increasing standardization of the adoption process, and a new imposition of secrecy onto infant adoption procedures after World War II. A few adult adoptees began to publicly assert that this intense secrecy was damaging to them as children, as suggested in the excerpt from Jean Paton's groundbreaking work, *The Adopted Break Silence* (1954). Meanwhile, Art Buchwald's moving story of his placement into foster care as a child—out of his original placement in the Hebrew Orphan Asylum—reminds us that the orphanage continued to be a viable, if ever-diminishing form of child care in America throughout the twentieth century, as foster care, in particular, became more widespread, formalized, and bureaucratized.

1. "Title IV-Grants to States for Aid to Dependent Children," Social Security Act of 1935

This part of the "New Deal" established aid for children deprived of parental support, but still living with relatives, as a federal entitlement.

SECTION 401. For the purpose of enabling each State to furnish financial assistance, as far as practicable under the conditions in such State, to needy dependent children, there is hereby authorized to be appropriated for the fiscal year ending June 30, 1936, the sum of $24,750,000, and there is hereby authorized to be appropriated for each fiscal year thereafter a sum sufficient to carry out the purposes of this title. The sums made available under this section shall be used for making payments to States which have submitted, and had approved by the Board, State plans for aid to dependent children.

STATE PLANS FOR AID TO DEPENDENT CHILDREN

SEC. 402.

(a) A State plan for aid to dependent children must

(1) provide that it shall be in effect in all political subdivisions of the State, and, if administered by them, be mandatory upon them;

(2) provide for financial participation by the State;

(3) either provide for the establishment or designation of a single State agency to administer the plan, or provide for the establishment or designation of a single State agency to supervise the administration of the plan;

(4) provide for granting to any individual, whose claim with respect to aid to a dependent child is denied, an opportunity for a fair hearing before such State agency;

(5) provide such methods of administration (other than those relating to selection, tenure of office, and compensation of personnel) as are found by the Board to be necessary for the efficient operation of the plan; and

(6) provide that the State agency will make such reports, in such form and containing such information, as the Board may from time to time require, and comply with such provisions as the Board may from time to time find necessary to assure the correctness and verification of such reports.

(b) The Board shall approve any plan which fulfills the conditions specified in subsection (a) except that it shall not approve any plan which imposes as a condition of eligibility for aid to dependent children, a residence requirement which denies aid with respect to any child residing in the State

(1) who has resided in the State for one year immediately preceding the application for such aid or

(2) who was born within the State within one year immediately preceding the application, if its mother has resided in the State for one year immediately preceding the birth.

SEC. 403.

(a) From the sums appropriated therefor, the Secretary of the Treasury shall pay to each State which has an approved plan for aid to dependent children, for each quarter, beginning with the quarter commencing July 1, 1935, an amount, which shall be used exclusively for carrying out the State plan, equal to one-third of the total of the sums expended during such quarter under such plan, not counting so much of such expenditure with respect to any dependent child for any month as exceeds $18, or if there is more than one dependent child in the same home, as exceeds $18 for any month with respect to one such dependent child and $12 for such month with respect to each of the other dependent children. . . .

DEFINITIONS
SEC. 406. When used in this title—
(a) The term dependent child means a child under the age of sixteen who has been deprived of parental support or care by reason of the death, continued absence from the home, or physical or mental incapacity of a parent, and who is living with his father, mother, grandfather, grandmother, brother, sister, stepfather, stepmother, stepbrother, stepsister, uncle, or aunt, in a place of residence maintained by one or more of such relatives as his or their own home;
(b) The term aid to dependent children means money payments with respect to a dependent child or dependent children.

Source: Available online as part of "The History of Social Security" on the Social Security Administration's website, at http://www.ssa.gov/history/35activ.html.

2. Child Welfare League of America, "Minimum Safeguards in Adoption," 1938

These standards were among the first to emphasize a need for secrecy in adoption procedures. Note also the emphasis on adoption's purpose being the "completion" of a family group, not labor or any other tangible benefit.

I. The safeguards that the child should be given are:
   1. That he be not unnecessarily deprived of his kinship ties.
   2. That the family asking for him have a good home and good family life to offer and that the prospective parents be well adjusted to each other.
   3. That he is wanted for the purpose of completing an otherwise incomplete family group, in which he will be given support, education, loving care, and the feeling of security to which any child is entitled.
II. The safeguards that the adopting family should expect are:
   1. That the identity of the adopting parents should be kept from the natural parents.
   2. That the child have the intelligence and the physical and mental background to meet the reasonable expectations of the adopting parents.
   3. That the adoption proceedings be completed without unnecessary publicity.
III. The safeguards that the state should require for its own and the child's protection are:
   1. That the adopting parents should realize that in taking the child for

adoption they assume as serious and permanent an obligation as do parents rearing their own children, including the right to inherit.

2. That there be a trial period of residence of reasonable length for the best interests of the family and the child whether there be a legal requirement for it or not.

3. That the adoption procedure be sufficiently flexible to avoid encouragement of illegitimacy on the one hand and trafficking in babies on the other.

4. That the birth records of an adopted child be so revised as to shield him from unnecessary embarrassment in case of illegitimacy.

These safeguards are best provided to the natural parents and also to those asking adoption if they turn to a well established children's organization which has a reputation in this field for good advice and good results.

Source: Washington, DC: CWLA Press, 1938.

3. Jean Paton, "Being Told and Finding Out"

Paton's book, which was based on a survey of forty adopted children, provided the foundation for the Adoption Rights Movement, described in Chapters 3 and 4. Paton's work was deeply attentive to the individual stories of adopted persons, and quoted from them at length. Its sensitive portrayal of the pain that was often associated with the intense secrecy that characterized adoption during this period remains powerful to readers today.

> . . . I myself think that if I ever decide to adopt a child, I'll tell him, as best I can, that he is adopted. But, what will I do when the child starts thinking of the real mother and father, of why they abandoned him, of what they looked like, of how and why?
>
> . . . I've not been hurt at all by the process. I am glad that I was told and I am glad that I was told when I was. I'm sure that I would have found it out by accident later on anyway.

One study is unlikely—that of the adopted who do not know they are adopted. Of us who know, now, those who learned in highly conscious years can conceive only dimly of the continuous form of life that is possible to the unadopted. Other adopted have learned more gradually, or earlier, and their own form of continuity is perhaps almost identical with that of the unadopted; and they may, therefore, sense the discontinuity that other adopted know, only on such occasions of unusual disturbance as life presents to them. Then, not having used the symbols of adoption in earlier distress, they will not do so in the later times of trouble. Thus might run one thesis.

Whatever that may be, all forty reporting herein know their adoptive status, or they would not be with us. But there the resemblance among them ends. In this consideration of how they became aware of their adoption, there is much variety. Only a few, those who seem to have absorbed the knowledge gradually and young, resemble one another. The others, from a variety of sources, by all manner of means, and at a range in age from 5 to 43 years, report abrupt and, usually difficult revelation of status as adopted individuals.

Yet for all their variation, they agree in one particular. Tell children, and tell them from the beginning that they are adopted. And tell them something of whence, they came and why. Beyond that, they ask only what all children ask-to be loved, to be wanted. No claim is made by them or for them that this is all that is necessary. But it is all that the adopted here reporting ask of adopted parents. The rest, each in their own way, as individuals, they will conjure with.

Yet more is asked—but not of the parents. More is asked of the community. The best efforts of the parents are reduced in their good effects by the approach of the curious and aggressive friend, neighbor, stranger. These are often the agents of discovery. The parents who plan to "tell" the child tomorrow, may find they are not in full control of the situation.

This is what we asked:

> When did you first learn that you were adopted? _____ Who told you? _____ (relationship to you). Do you know why they told you? What brought it about? Was it a crisis in the home, or did it break out without apparent cause? Or were you told from the beginning, and never received a shock in the telling?
>
> If you were told suddenly, do you remember your reaction, and can you describe it accurately?

At this point, we wish to digress. We wish to explain why we asked such a difficult question (among other difficult questions); and to ask; as we do so, that the reader consider what has taken place in this study. It is so natural to pick up a study of some human problem, where the book is full of tables and charts and numbers; and to forget somehow, in reading the pages, that people have been disturbed in their routines by the question-man. This can be, in fact, such a painful experience, provided that the areas that are touched are vulnerable, that it is often a process which takes place only under carefully controlled conditions. Some of this control is supposed to exist for the benefit of the truth. Often, we suspect, it fulfills no function except to make people feel less pain, and to be more ready to answer the questionnaire. Whether true answers can be reached by such cautious and limited methods is to be questioned.

"Is adoption freely discussed?" is one question we asked. Consider replies such as these:

> . . . No. There is a decided shyness, almost shame, on my parents' part. Even with me they are very hesitant to discuss it. For a long time I felt it was a terrible thing to *have* to be adopted.
>
> . . . Never in my presence, even in adult life (foster father) never discussed it in my presence except in lawyer's office in 19__ when adult adoption agreement was made to establish date of birth for my use.

Assuming that the crux of satisfactory adoption is the ability to sustain the knowledge of it with relative ease, we shall proceed to review the rather complex nature of this education. The age at which adoption occurs is an important factor; the quality of the transition to the new home is also (but we seldom have anything more than a clue to that, and for such detail must wait for the contributions of adoptive parents in equally sober questionnaires); the choice of the occasion for presenting not only the word "adopted," but all the context making it significant; the unknown, unpredictable re-working in the mind of the adopted child, upon receipt of information; the holding of it secret, despite questions, or the sharing of it, unpredictably, with friends and associates—so the list of factors continues. *Realization* of adoption comes subsequent to *knowledge,* and ripens with life experience. The child sees adoption as:

> "I am what they decided."

Presumably if parents appear to a child as persons of bearable, fortunate-outcome choices, this particular one may also appear to have favorable overtones. Otherwise, it may not.

There are a certain number, of course, who were not informed by their adoptive parents, but by natural parent or agent prior to or at the time of adoption. There is a different quality in these.

There is a second group where no distinct time of telling is recalled. These clearly belong together.

There is a third group, the largest, where the onset of information is clear, is subsequent to adoption, and full of variety. There are several subgroups within this category. . . .

Those Who Overheard

Still another mode of discovery is through the medium of the human voice, as in the above examples, but now voices not intended for the ears of the children con-

DON'T FORGET

This picture was originally included in the chapter, "Being Told and Finding Out," of Jean Paton's book, The Adopted Break Silence. *It was drawn by a six-year-old girl, a foster child, on the day she went from agency care in a temporary boarding home to an adoptive home in 1940. The girl gave it to Paton, her social worker, on that day. It says: "Don't Forget."*

cerned. There are two instances where the information was overheard and understood by the adopted child. Who knows how many others overheard it without understanding?

(Age 9–10)

. . . Foster mother and foster grandmother were wrangling. Grandmother said "You are no fit mother. You shouldn't have adopted that boy."

(Age 8)

> . . . I heard someone say that my parents were nice to have taken into their home a fatherless child whose mother was common. I was, of course, shocked when I heard that. I never told anyone, but I tried to commit suicide. Till this date, no one knows.

And therein is the confirmation (whether true or not an 8-year-old will not discriminate) of one's deepest fear that one's mother was of low degree. Few get such a dose at once, so young. . . .

Those Who Found Adoption Papers at Home

The remaining three people describe their experience in detail, as remembered and as felt. The youngest is now a man of 28, next a woman of 31, and last a woman of 61. They were 10 to 12 when discovery took place. It strikes us that this is a hard way to find out. There is no one around to break the sense of isolation which follows. It is similar, perhaps, to the reaction of the child whose parents explain his status to him, believing he is satisfied, whereas he feels they have rejected him and therefore he is alone; and is similar, too, to the reaction of the child who has overheard—for seeing papers is a little like overhearing. Adoption papers were stumbled upon by these last three:

(Age 12)

> . . . One day I was searching for my father's discharge papers in the family strong box and I accidentally came upon the adoption papers. I remember I was alone in the house and that I cried. I felt very hurt, as though I had been cheated, but since my mother had shown resentment of my father's affection for me, it did help to clear up that puzzle in my young mind. I thought I knew why. It was because I wasn't her own child.
>
> Because I never felt true security in this home, I think it helped me to learn I was adopted. I remember thinking that I must be a very evil little girl because my mother hadn't married before bearing me.

(Age 10)

> . . . I ran into a legal document "Petition for Adoption and Change of Name", etc., lying on the kitchen table with other papers and keepsakes from a metal box, one Sunday afternoon when I came home from Junior Endeavour, entering the back door as my parents were entertaining visitors in the parlor. I seemed to know instantly the meaning of the document without reading more than the description on the cover, but I gave no sign I had noticed the papers when I duly admired the gar-

net brooches etc., and helped return them to the box. It was not until months later when "momma", in one of her rages, dramatically informed me that I was not her own child and was plainly dumfounded that I took the news so calmly, merely saying "I've known that for a long time."

The immediate effect of learning I was adopted was rather absurd. I became obsessed with the idea that I must cost my parents as little as possible, eating as little as possible, and agonizing over having to ask for a nickel for a tablet for school. I remember I kept borrowing a sheet of paper from this one and that in the school room when papa as usual took me with him to pay the grocery bill Saturday night, I said I did not want the little sack of candy the grocer always gave me, but would much rather have a tablet for school.

Earning my way became almost a complex so that it was a long, long time before I learned how to accept gifts and favors gracefully.

It is possible that this detailed story of a child's reaction and subsequent adjustment is not unusual. It is the only such account that we have been presented with. Her verdict is one with which we may agree:

Of one thing I am very sure; it would have been much, much better for all concerned—in my case, at least—had I known I was an adopted child from the first.

Our final example:
  (Age 12)

... Up until the night I accidentally discovered my birth certificate, I had firmly believed that I was their natural child. Gum was a favorite of mine and when I would ask mother for some she went to her dresser drawer and gave it to me. One night (as was so often done) I was alone, wanting gum I was enterprising enough to seek it myself in its obvious location. While rummaging through the drawers in search of some, I came across some old snapshots (not concerned with the story). They were interesting enough to take out and look at. Underneath these photos were some old letters. Being of a very curious nature, I started to look through them and discovered the birth certificate. It read _____ and of course it did not make sense that they should have another boy's certificate there (who was he?) I examined it further and found the birth date which turned out to be my own. I, of course, knew now the whole story, as I was always *too* bright for my age. When I had come to the full realization of facts I ran into my bedroom, crying, and through myself across the bed and cried myself to sleep. Later my mother came home and found me asleep with my clothes on. She asked me what was wrong and I challenged her about the adoption. She then told me briefly what had happened. It is very difficult to give in a few words the whole meaning and importance of these events as they had a profound effect on my whole life and character . . . I had a sinking feeling, and all of the security that they had built up over the years was destroyed. Also, I became rebellious, intolerant, insolent, and almost wholly unmanageable. It is the pivotal point in my life.

Comment:

We have presented the evidence that we have on the point that there are numerous ways by which an adopted person can come to know his status. We have tried to show what we believe to be true and to be borne out by this account, namely, that there is no one right way, but that many people have found the methods used with them rather uneventful, others terribly urgent and oppressive. There are clues as to the personalities involved and as to influence of other factors and persons in each situation. Further studies, with longer summations of individual factors, may be enlightening as to other important causes. Here we are classifying and assembling, suggesting by limited comparison what things matter to adopted people. In subsequent sections, where other factors are analyzed, we will attempt some cross-reference to the experiences above. We believe that valuable people derive out of any of these types of experience, as out of any type of family, but that out of some situations, more strength is required for that personal achievement.

From the point of view of these adoptive parents, have they not in the main been influenced by their cultures in what they decided or neglected to do? Those who were adequate as parents may be more adequate either in telling, or in helping their children who learned on the outside. But this is by no means the prime test of parental adequacy. In reviewing these records, we are impressed that there is little accusation of the parents for not telling, but rather a statement that telling is a better way of handling the situation. It is lack of love, and personal inadequacy that are the main complaints of these adopted people. Somehow, they do not expect adoptive parents to realize as deeply as themselves the importance of telling, and telling young. Though they wish they would.

Yet we would raise a question against this view that early telling does the job. We would like to suggest that it is the *reason* for not telling so many of these cases that does the damage, rather than the mere omitting of the deed. If the parents are not overcome by the stigma of adoption cause, or by whatever it is that keeps them silent, they have a better chance of conveying the facts to their adopted child, whenever and however they so do.

Nonetheless, there still is, and we shall see, a question which even this does not answer. The question is: If there is no stigma, why is there adoption? We have no found the answer. We think the stigma may still be there, unacknowledged to a large extent; and that children whose adoptive parents love and possess them by deeds subsequent to adoption are told easily enough, and they leave the stigma on one side, as have the parents. For most such adopted people, perhaps, this arrangement can work. Perhaps it can be modified as they mature and work throughout their lifetimes. This will be touched upon again in: Search.

Source: *The Adopted Break Silence: The Experiences and Views of Forty Adults Who Were Once Adopted Children* (Philadelphia: The Philadelphia Life History Study Center, 1954), 54–73.

4. Art Buchwald, from *Leaving Home: A Memoir*

Buchwald's memoir of his childhood in Depression-era New York City, after his mother became ill, includes stories of institutional care in the Hebrew Orphan Asylum (HOA) and his placement in foster care, along with his sisters. Their father maintained contact with the children, visiting them in the Asylum and in foster care, and he never relinquished custody. This excerpt describes Buchwald's initial placement with the Morais family, and his shame at being pitied for his situation.

I had been in the HOA for two months and one day when I was called into a receiving room with my three sisters. They scrubbed us up so we would look better, in case someone wanted to take us home. I sat on the wooden bench, just happy to be with my sisters.

"Did they dress us nice?" I asked the girls during our talk at the Regency.

"No, why would they dress us nice?" Alice said. "We weren't up for adoption."

A middle-aged woman with glasses and wearing a large brimmed hat and a double breasted suit came in with a young man in his twenties. She was very businesslike and examined us as she would a Friday night chicken. She was smiling, though I had no idea what she had to do with me. Finally, she said, "How would you like to live with me?"

I replied, "I don't eat meat and I don't eat fish."

She said, "Well, we'll soon change that." Instead of protesting, I just looked down at my shoes.

As far as I was concerned, this woman was one more stranger asking me dumb questions. But she was also possibly my only ticket out of the HOA. I thought that it wouldn't hurt to be nice to her, just in case she had something to do with my freedom.

Her name was Stella Morais, and then she talked to my sisters, who were thinking the same thing I was. If this lady wanted to take us out of the HOA, she was welcome to do it.

She said to me, "You're going to be my foster child."

I just smiled and nodded my head.

Her son Harold said, "I'll teach you how to play baseball and stickball." He was a dapper, good-looking man.

"I'd like that," I assured him. "But I don't have a glove."

"I'll buy you one," he told me.

I was ready to leave with him immediately.

Apparently all the paperwork had been done because we were told to get our things. Except for the HOA clothes, we had no more luggage than when we arrived. . . .

We took the subway to Penn Station and got on the Long Island Rail Road-an hour's journey to Hollis, in Queens.

The lady told us to call her Aunt Stella and the man said we could call him Harold.

On the train, she said, "I expect you children in bed by four o'clock." This was such a weird statement that I recently checked with my sister Edith and asked if she remembered Aunt Stella telling us that.

"Yes," she told me. "I also remember me saying to her, 'Morning or afternoon?' and she said, 'I'll tell you later.' "

It wasn't until years later that I discovered that people took foster children into their homes to supplement their incomes. We were worth twenty-five dollars a month per child, and for many foster parents that paid the rent and the mortgage.

Once they realized that, foster children became very suspicious about why they had been placed in a particular home. We felt that if we were there for the support of their families, there was no sense becoming too friendly. But the Depression made people desperate. I never experienced any cruelty from the people I lived with, except when I was unhappy and invented it. So even if people were in it for the money, they were never unkind. When we arrived in Hollis we were escorted into the living room, where Aunt Stella and Uncle Cyril's children were waiting for us. There was Harold, who had come with us; Ray, who had the best job in the family, selling fabrics to Broadway shows; Ira, who was a press agent; and Caroline, a secretary. They were all dressed nicely and greeted us warmly. No problem here, I thought to myself.

Aunt Stella said we would eat alone in the breakfast nook. That arrangement suited us fine because it meant that we wouldn't have to worry about table manners. The four of us agreed that things could be a lot worse. . . .

The one critical incident in my childhood that I have never forgotten took place on Red Brick Hill in Hollis on a bright, clear winter night. The ground was covered with snow and all the kids were laughing and shouting as they rode their sleds down the hill. I must have been seven or eight. I still remember how wonderful it all felt. The snow made everything glisten. I was feeling happy. I did not own a sled of my own, so I said to two boys standing next to me, "Can I borrow your sled?" One of them answered, "No." The other boy told him, "Let him have it. He doesn't have a mother."

Tears rolled down my cheeks as I rode down the hill on that borrowed sled. Those words have never left me. I wanted to yell that I did have a mother, but only a few people knew where she was and I was in no position to tell them. Sniffling quietly, I dragged the sled up the hill and gave it back.

I'm certain it was on that night on that hill that I vowed I would never ask anybody for anything again.

Source: New York: G. P. Putnam's Sons, 1993, 52–59.

10 Contemporary Issues in Domestic Adoption, 1970 to the Present

T he contemporary period has been marked by a variety of social justice movements, in which groups traditionally disempowered within the broader culture have worked for increased civil and social rights: including many rights related to adoption, foster care, and family formation in general. African Americans, Native Americans, same-sex couples, and all the members of the adoption triad have sought legal and political means by which to claim and protect their rights—and also to claim a basic sense of integrity. These movements have contributed to the rising numbers of open adoption agreements, and other legal developments on a federal and state level that are addressed in the following documents.

1. National Association of Black Social Workers, Statement on Trans-racial Adoption, 1972

This statement, released in the waning days of the mass movements for civil rights and increased autonomy for black people in the United States during the late 1950s, 1960s, and early 1970s, urges our society to recognize the strengths, survival skills, and values of African American families. Using fervent language, it calls for the preservation of black families, whenever possible, and for a recognition of the continuing pervasiveness of racism in the broader American culture.

The National Association of Black Social Workers has taken a vehement stand against the placement of black children in white homes for any reason. We affirm the inviolable position of black children in black families where they belong physically, psychologically and culturally in order that they receive the total sense of themselves and develop a sound projection of their future.

Ethnicity is a way of life in these United States, and the world at large; a viable, sensitive, meaningful and legitimate societal construct. This is no less true nor legitimate for black people than for other ethnic groups. Ethnic identification is an old concept and entrenched practice in the total society, but on some levels appears to be new as it moves from a negative into a positive light. Overt ethnic identification, especially for blacks, was long suppressed by the social and political pressures speaking to total assimilation of all peoples in that great melting pot. We were made, by devious devices, to view ethnic identification as a self defeating stance, prohibiting our acceptance into the mainstream. Black people are now developing an honest perception of this society; the myths of assimilation and of our inferiority stand bare under glaring light. We now proclaim our truth, substance, beauty and value as ourselves without apology or compromise. The affirmation of our ethnicity promotes our opposition to the trans-racial placements of black children.

The family is the basic unit of society; one's first, most pervasive and only consistent culturing life experience. Humans develop their sense of values, identity, self concept, attitudes and basic perspective within the family group. Black children in white homes are cut off from the healthy development of themselves as black people, which development is the normal expectation and only true humanistic goal.

Identity grows on the three levels of all human development; the physical, psychological and cultural and the nurturing of self identity is a prime function of the family. The incongruence of a white family performing this function for a black child is easily recognized. The physical factor stands to maintain that child's difference from his family. There is no chance of his resembling any relative. One's physical identity with his own is of great significance. Until quite recently adoption agencies went to great lengths to match children with adopting parents in an effort to reach as perfect a picture of resemblance as possible. The rationale for that policy was positive; soundly rooted in the importance of family resemblance. Although we applaud the relaxation of the extreme nature of that procedure, we regard trans-racial adoption of black children as another extreme movement, dangerous in it's exact opposite direction with the exact opposite quality—negative.

The historically established and cultivated psychological perceptions and social orientation of white America have developed from their social, political, educational and religious institutional systems. Consequently these are the environmental effects they have to transmit and their teachings are not consistent with the realities of the social system for the black child. He assumes, then, their posture and frame of reference, different from and often antithetical to that of his ethnics which can only result in conflict and confusion when he does become aware of the social system in which he lives. Further internal conflict is inevitable by his minority status within his own family. Such status is normal in school, employment and some communities but in one's most intimate personal group such oddity status is neither normal nor anticipated.

The socialization process for every child begins at birth and includes his cultural heritage as an important segment of the process. In our society, the developmental needs of Black children are significantly different from those of white children. Black children are taught, from an early age, highly sophisticated coping techniques to deal with racist practices perpetrated by individuals and institutions. These coping techniques become successfully integrated into ego functions and can be incorporated only through the process of developing positive identification with significant black others. Only a black family can transmit the emotional and sensitive subtleties of perception and reaction essential for a black child's survival in a racist society. Our society is distinctly black or white and characterized by white racism at every level. We repudiate the fallacious and fantasied reasoning of some that whites adopting black children will alter that basic character.

We fully recognize the phenomenon of trans-racial adoption as an expedient for white folk, not as an altruistic humane concern for black children. The supply of white children for adoption has all but vanished and adoption agencies, having always catered to middle class whites developed an answer to their desire for parenthood by motivating them to consider black children. This has brought about a re-definition of some black children. Those born of black–white alliances are no longer black as decreed by immutable law and social custom for centuries. They are now black-white, inter-racial, bi-racial, emphasizing the whiteness as the adoptable quality; a further subtle, but vicious design to further diminish black and accentuate white. We resent this high-handed arrogance and are insulted by this further assignment of chattel status to black people.

Citation of a few of the problem areas that have surfaced in our discussions with proponents of trans-racial adoption provides it's own basis for the moral imperative for cessation of the practice. Trans-racial adoption of black children has frequently been accomplished at the expense of the parents having to sever all connections with their own families. Such estrangement leaves scars on those directly involved and unquestionably reaches beyond them, as a negative factor, to their children. This is most conflictual and disturbing when there are biological children who are suddenly deprived of their loving relatives; a destructive situation for them and their black sibling who happens to be the "cause of it all." . . .

We denounce the assertions that blacks will not adopt; we affirm the fact that black people, in large number, cannot maneuver the obstacle course of the traditional adoption process. This process has long been a screening out device. The emphasis on high income, educational achievement, residential status and other accoutrements of a white middle class life style eliminates black applicants by the score.

The National Association of Black Social Workers asserts the conviction that children should not remain in foster homes or institutions when adoption can be a reality. We stand firmly, though, on conviction that a white home is not a suitable placement for black children and contend it is totally unnecessary.

Source: Abridged and reprinted with permission of NABSW.

2. "Indian Child Welfare Act of 1978"

Inspired by the American Indian movement, and horrified by the reality of massive numbers of Native children being pulled out of Indian families to be raised by white families, Native Americans successfully lobbied Congress to federally institute some limitations on such practices.

§1901. Congressional findings

Recognizing the special relationship between the United States and the Indian tribes and their members and the Federal responsibility to Indian people, the Congress finds—

(1) that clause 3, section 8, article I of the United States Constitution provides that "The Congress shall have Power * * * To regulate Commerce * * * with Indian tribes [1]" and, through this and other constitutional authority, Congress has plenary power over Indian affairs;

(2) that Congress, through statutes, treaties, and the general course of dealing with Indian tribes, has assumed the responsibility for the protection and preservation of Indian tribes and their resources;

(3) that there is no resource that is more vital to the continued existence and integrity of Indian tribes than their children and that the United States has a direct interest, as trustee, in protecting Indian children who are members of or are eligible for membership in an Indian tribe;

(4) that an alarmingly high percentage of Indian families are broken up by the removal, often unwarranted, of their children from them by nontribal public and private agencies and that an alarmingly high percentage of such children are placed in non-Indian foster and adoptive homes and institutions; and

(5) that the States, exercising their recognized jurisdiction over Indian child custody proceedings through administrative and judicial bodies, have often failed to recognize the essential tribal relations of Indian people and

the cultural and social standards prevailing in Indian communities and families.

§1902. Congressional declaration of policy

The Congress hereby declares that it is the policy of this Nation to protect the best interests of Indian children and to promote the stability and security of Indian tribes and families by the establishment of minimum Federal standards for the removal of Indian children from their families and the placement of such children in foster or adoptive homes which will reflect the unique values of Indian culture, and by providing for assistance to Indian tribes in the operation of child and family service programs.

Source: U.S. Code Title 25, Chapter 21, Sections 1901–1902 (Washington, DC: Government Printing Office). Available online at: http://www.access.gpo.gov/uscode/title25/title25.html.

3. Janine Baer et al., Bastard Nation: The Adoptee Rights Organization, "Mission Statement," and excerpts from "The Basic Bastard" (2005)

Bastard Nation (BN) is, as its name implies, an organization that lobbies for the rights of adoptees, especially the right to access as adults any information related to their births—particularly their original birth certificates. In 1998, BN successfully campaigned for the first citizen-enacted adoption initiative in the nation, Oregon's Ballot Measure 58. All adult Oregonians now have the right to access their birth certificates. Such laws remain controversial, as the next entry, by the National Council for Adoption, suggests.

Bastard Nation is dedicated to the recognition of the full human and civil rights of adult adoptees. Toward that end, we advocate the opening to adoptees, upon request at age of majority, of those government documents which pertain to the adoptee's historical, genetic, and legal identity, including the unaltered original birth certificate and adoption decree.

Bastard Nation asserts that it is the right of people everywhere to have their official original birth records unaltered and free from falsification, and that the adoptive status of any person should not prohibit him or her from choosing to exercise that right. We have reclaimed the badge of bastardy placed on us by those who would attempt to shame us; we see nothing shameful in having been born out of wedlock or in being adopted. Bastard Nation does not support mandated mutual consent registries or intermediary systems in place of unconditional open records, nor any other system that is less than access on demand to the adult adoptee, without condition, and without qualification.

THE BASIC BASTARD

I. Open Records: Why It's an Issue

Adult adoptees in all but four states and two commonwealths in the United States (Kansas, Alaska, Oregon, Alabama, Puerto Rico and the U.S. Virgin Islands) and in all Canadian provinces are forbidden unconditional access to their original birth certificates. Outmoded Depression-era laws create "amended" birth certificates that replace the names of the adoptee's biological parents with those of the adoptive parents as well as frequently falsify other birth information. The adoptee's original birth certificate and records of adoption are permanently sealed in closed records states by laws passed largely after World War II. These laws are a relic of the culture of shame that stigmatized infertility, out-of-wedlock birth and adoption. Even those adoptees now being raised in open adoptions, in which there is some contact between birth and adoptive families, are not allowed access to their original birth records when they reach adulthood.

In Scotland adoptee records have been open since 1930 and in England since 1975. Sweden, The Netherlands, Germany, South Korea, Mexico, Argentina and Venezuela are only a few of the many nations that do not prevent adult adoptees from accessing their own birth records. The United States and Canada lag far behind the rest of what we used to call the "Free World" in opening closed birth and adoption records to those to whom they pertain. This is largely because well-funded and well-connected lobbies representing certain adoption agencies and lawyers have a vested interest in keeping adoptee records closed. These special interest groups want to continue to deprive adult adoptees of their rights, presumably to prevent the disclosure of controversial past practices such as baby-selling, coercion and fraud which are now hidden by state-sanctioned secrecy.

While many adoptees search for their biological relatives to discover the answers to questions regarding medical history and family heritage, all adoptees should be able to exercise their right to obtain the original government documents of their own birth and adoption whether they choose to search or not. At stake are the civil and human rights of millions of American and Canadian citizens. To continue to abrogate these rights is to perpetuate the stigmatization of illegitimacy and adoption, and the relegation of an entire class of citizens to second-class status.

What's with the name?

The half-century old practice of impounding and sealing an adopted person's original birth records in perpetuity has had the disastrous effect of breeding deep and long lasting attitudes of shame in all areas of the adoption process. Secrets and lies abound. So we decided to reclaim the term "Bastard"—to take it back and make it ours. In so doing, we hope to explode the myths of shame surrounding adoption and focus attention on the absolute necessity of changing the laws.

We at Bastard Nation believe that there is NOTHING shameful about having been born out of wedlock or about being adopted. We selected our name because we will no longer be made to feel shamed by the odious state laws that permanently seal our original birth records. We do not fling the word "bastard" at anyone. Rather, we wear it proudly as we work to achieve our goal of equal and unconditional access to original birth records for all adult adoptees.

Why are you so angry?

We are angry that we continue to be treated as second-class citizens, as dirty little secrets, long after most of the world has recognized the rights of adult adoptees to knowledge of their origins and equal access to government-held documents which pertain to them. We are angry at those self-interested sections of the adoption industry which continue to lobby for sealed records, hiding their own past misdeeds under a cloak of "birth parent privacy," and implying that adoptees are potential stalkers who would harm their birth parents if they had access to their own records. We are angry that the media still portrays us far too often as "adopted children," refusing to let us grow up and take our places as full citizens of this country.

Source: Reprinted, with permission, from the BN website, http://www.bastards.org/.

4. National Council for Adoption (NCFA), "Mission and Agenda," "Why Privacy?", and "Correct Adoption Terminology" (2005)

In contrast to BN, NCFA takes a much more conservative approach to open records, particularly to the opening of previously closed records, in the interests of protecting birth parents' rights to privacy.

Mission: Founded in 1980, the National Council For Adoption (NCFA) is a research, education, and advocacy organization whose mission is to promote the well-being of children, birthparents, and adoptive families by advocating for the positive option of adoption. NCFA is an adoption advocate and expert in the halls of power and the courts of public opinion, on behalf of all parties to adoption and its member adoption agencies around the country.

Agenda: Following is a summary of NCFA's adoption agenda to put children first

- Train pregnancy counselors and health care workers in infant adoption awareness, so women and teens with unplanned pregnancies can freely consider the loving option of adoption.
- Advance policies and recruit and prepare parents to promote adoptions out of foster care, so children in need can have loving, permanent families.
- Protect birthmothers and make adoptions secure through putative father registries, so uninvolved birthfathers cannot block birthmothers' adoption plans for their children.
- Strengthen the adoption tax credit and advance other pro-adoption fiscal policies, so more families can afford to adopt.
- Support Safe Havens, so desperate birthmothers can place their children safely and legally with authorized caregivers, rather than abandoning them, or worse.
- Reduce obstacles to transracial adoption, so children are not denied loving families on account of race.
- Work with the US and foreign governments to establish sound policies for intercountry adoption, so foreign orphans can be placed with loving, permanent families.
- Protect the principles of mutual consent and the option of privacy in adoption, so parties to adoption do not have their privacy breached without their consent.
- Serve as an authoritative information clearinghouse on adoption statistics, policies, and practices, so policy makers, adoption professionals, the media, and the public are well informed regarding trends in adoption.
- Provide to our adoption agency members training and education in the latest in adoption practices and regulations, so they can provide excellent adoption services.
- Promote adoption in the media with facts and insight, so Americans will recognize adoption as the loving option it is.

Why Privacy?

The right to maintain or waive one's privacy in adoption is essential to the human rights and personal dignity of adopted persons, birthparents, and adoptive parents. Adoption policy and practice should not empower one party to adoption to receive identifying information or unilaterally impose contacts without the consent of another party.

Search and reunion advocacy is commonplace in the media, but the range of views regarding privacy in adoption is actually as varied and personal as there are parties to adoption. In the context of the media's fascination with openness in adoption, it is important to remember that the many who prefer privacy cannot discuss their views publicly without sacrificing the very privacy they desire to protect. Birthparents and adult adopted persons who desire to have contact should be able to do so, when both agree. Otherwise, both should be able to control the release of their identifying information and whether and when contacts are to occur.

NCFA supports the use of mutual consent registries as a fair way to facilitate contact between adult adopted persons and birthparents. These registries allow adult adopted persons and birthparents to register their interest in making contact with the other. When both parties have indicated their desire to meet, the state facilitates the process by providing contact information.

Correct Adoption Terminology

Words not only convey facts they also evoke feelings. For example, when a TV or movie talks about a 'custody battle' between 'real parents' and 'other parents' this reinforces the inaccurate notion that only birth parents are real parents and that adoptive parents aren't real parents. Members of society may also wrongly conclude that all adoptions are 'battles.'

Accurate adoption language can stop the spread of misconceptions such as these. By using accurate language, we educate others about adoption. We choose emotionally 'correct' words over emotionally-laden words. We speak and write in appropriate adoption language with the hopes of influencing others so that this language will someday be the norm.

Accurate Language	Inaccurate Language
Birthparent	Real parent, natural parent
My child	Adopted child; Own child
Choosing an adoption plan	Giving away, Giving up your child
Finding a family to parent your child	Putting your child up for adoption
Deciding to parent the child	Keeping your baby
Person/Individual who was adopted	Adoptee
To parent	To keep
Child in need of a family	Adoptable child; Available child
Parent	Adoptive parent
International or intercountry adoption	Foreign adoption
Child who has special needs	Handicapped child, hard to place
Child from another country	Foreign child
Was adopted	Is adopted
Birthrelative	Blood relative

Source: Reprinted with permission from NCFA's website, http://www.ncfa-usa .org/.

5. Adoptions from the Heart, Sample Open Adoption Contract (2005)

Given the controversy over sealed records, and certain high-profile media stories of conflict between adoptive parents and birth parents, many adoptive parents and birth parents began to seek arrangements that would allow for some degree of openness in the adoptive relationship. This sample document is used as a starting point by one New York agency that facilitates such agreements; it is then modified to suit the particular situations of all the persons involved.

State of New York: Future Contact Agreement

Adoptions from the Heart acknowledges that adoption is a life-long process and because of this encourages the adult parties of the adoption triangle to mutually determine what type of ongoing contact will best meet their needs.

On the ___ day of _____, 20 by and between _____ and _____ the prospective adoptive parents, and _____ and _____ the birth parents and *Adoptions from the Heart*, who is acting as an Intermediary in the adoption process.

It is hereby understood that the following are the responsibilities of the parties:

1. *Adoptions from the Heart* shall receive and be responsible for the exchange of all correspondence, except in cases where the other parties desire to do this directly.

2. The adoptive parents shall:

   a. Provide to the birth parents, through the Agency, a written letter and pictures of the baby/child to the birth parents regarding the emotional, social and physical well being of the child placed with them, at the following intervals for the next 18 years:

      1. Once a month for the first 6 months

      2. Once a year, a week before the baby's birthday for the next 18 years

      3. ___ visits per year for a mutually acceptable date, time and location

   b. The adoptive parents agree to keep the agency informed of their current address. They also agree to inform the birth parent(s) of the child's death or any serious illness or injury.

3. The birth parent(s) shall:

   a. Provide to *Adoptions from the Heart*, each year by the child's birthday, an update of their current address and telephone number (if it has changed). Any correspondence should include the birth parents' name at the time of placement. Failure by the birth parent(s) to keep the Agency informed of their whereabouts and wishes may cause the Agency to close the files.

b. Respond to the yearly updates with any important medical or social information that would assist the adoptive family in raising and caring for this child.

The adoptive parent(s) hereby acknowledge that by the laws of the state of New York the birthparent's Surrender will contain the terms of this agreement and will be legally binding. Failure to abide by these terms could have legal implications.

The birth parent(s) hereby acknowledge that despite the terms of this agreement, *all* of their *legal rights* relating to the child have been or will be terminated and that the understanding of this writing *does not* affect the legal status of termination but imposes solely a moral obligation. They also acknowledge that this agreement is not a condition of agreeing to terminate their parental rights.

This agreement will become invalid if the birth parents assume an adversarial relationship with the adoptive parents. The adoptive parents will then *not* have to comply with the communication and/or visitation clauses.

All parties to this Agreement are setting their signatures as evidence of their moral commitments to one another and they all realize the grave and binding promises that they are making.

Source: Reprinted with the permission of "Adoptions from the Heart."

6. "The Multi-Ethnic Placement Act of 1994"

The following act by Congress remains controversial to this day. It sought to attend to a perceived crisis of foster care "drift"—whereby children in need of permanent homes were too often passed from one foster home to another. High rates of poverty and persistant racism together work to keep children of color overrepresented in the fostering system. This bill sought to move children more quickly into permanent homes, regardless of the new family's ethnic background, and, simultaneously to acknowledge some need to protect African American families from continued active discrimination against them.

This subpart may be cited as the "Howard M. Metzenbaum Multiethnic Placement Act of 1994."

SEC. 552. FINDINGS AND PURPOSE.

(a) FINDINGS—The Congress finds that—

(1) nearly 500,000 children are in foster care in the United States;

(2) tens of thousands of children in foster care are waiting for adoption;

(3) 2 years and 8 months is the median length of time that children wait to be adopted;

(4) child welfare agencies should work to eliminate racial, ethnic, and national origin discrimination and bias in adoption and foster care recruitment, selection, and placement procedures; and

(5) active, creative, and diligent efforts are needed to recruit foster and adoptive parents of every race, ethnicity, and culture in order to facilitate the placement of children in foster and adoptive homes which will best meet each child's needs.

(b) PURPOSE—It is the purpose of this subpart to promote the best interests of children by—

(1) decreasing the length of time that children wait to be adopted;

(2) preventing discrimination in the placement of children on the basis of race, color, or national origin; and

(3) facilitating the identification and recruitment of foster and adoptive families that can meet children's needs.

SEC. 553. MULTIETHNIC PLACEMENTS.

(a) ACTIVITIES—

(1) PROHIBITION—An agency, or entity, that receives Federal assistance and is involved in adoption or foster care placements may not—

(A) categorically deny to any person the opportunity to become an adoptive or a foster parent, solely on the basis of the race, color, or national origin of the adoptive or foster parent, or the child, involved; or

(B) delay or deny the placement of a child for adoption or into foster care, or otherwise discriminate in making a placement decision, solely on the basis of the race, color, or national origin of the adoptive or foster parent, or the child, involved.

(2) PERMISSIBLE CONSIDERATION—An agency or entity to which paragraph (1) applies may consider the cultural, ethnic, or racial background of the child and the capacity of the prospective foster or adoptive parents to meet the needs of a child of this background as one of a number of factors used to determine the best interests of a child.

(3) DEFINITION—As used in this subsection, the term 'placement decision' means the decision to place, or to delay or deny the placement of, a child in a foster care or an adoptive home, and includes the decision of the agency or entity involved to seek the termination of birth parent rights or otherwise make a child legally available for adoptive placement. . . .

(e) NONCOMPLIANCE DEEMED A CIVIL RIGHTS VIOLATION—Non-compliance with this subpart is deemed a violation of title VI of the Civil Rights Act of 1964.

(f) NO EFFECT ON INDIAN CHILD WELFARE ACT OF 1978—Nothing in this section shall be construed to affect the application of the Indian Child Welfare Act of 1978 (25 U.S.C. 1901 et seq.).

Source: The "Improving America's Schools Act," U.S. Public Law 103-382. Available online from the National Clearinghouse on Child Abuse and Neglect Information: http://nccanch.acf.hhs.gov/general/legal/federal/pl103_382.cfm.

11 International Adoption Law

As adoptive parents in the United States and Europe have become increasingly open to intercountry adoption, laws governing the practice have become formalized and standardized on both an international and federal level.

1. The Hague Convention on Intercountry Adoption, 1993

This agreement, which the United States has signed, represents a milestone for international adoption, as it seeks to protect the rights of all children, and balance the interests of the citizens of poorer "sending" nations, whose children are adopted in large numbers, and those of the "receiving," usually wealthier, nations, who typically adopt these children. It standardizes procedures by which adoption agencies are to be certified and institutes several steps to ensure that children are not taken from parents illegally.

The States signatory to the present Convention,

Recognizing that the child, for the full and harmonious development of his or her personality, should grow up in a family environment, in an atmosphere of happiness, love and understanding,

Recalling that each State should take, as a matter of priority, appropriate measures to enable the child to remain in the care of his or her family of origin,

Recognizing that intercountry adoption may offer the advantage of a permanent family to a child for whom a suitable family cannot be found in his or her State of origin,

Convinced of the necessity to take measures to ensure that intercountry adoptions are made in the best interests of the child and with respect for his or her fundamental rights, and to prevent the abduction, the sale of, or traffic in children,

Desiring to establish common provisions to this effect, taking into account the principles set forth in international instruments, in particular the United Nations Convention on the Rights of the Child, of 20 November 1989, and the United Nations Declaration on Social and Legal Principles relating to the Protection and Welfare of Children, with Special Reference to Foster Placement and Adoption Nationally and Internationally (General Assembly Resolution 41/85, of 3 December 1986),

Have agreed upon the following provisions—

CHAPTER I—SCOPE OF THE CONVENTION

Article 1: The objects of the present Convention are—

a) to establish safeguards to ensure that intercountry adoptions take place in the best interests of the child and with respect for his or her fundamental rights as recognized in international law;

b) to establish a system of co-operation amongst Contracting States to ensure that those safeguards are respected and thereby prevent the abduction, the sale of, or traffic in children;

c) to secure the recognition in Contracting States of adoptions made in accordance with the Convention.

Article 2:

(1) The Convention shall apply where a child habitually resident in one Contracting State ("the State of origin") has been, is being, or is to be moved to another Contracting State ("the receiving State") either after his or her adoption in the State of origin by spouses or a person habitually resident in the receiving State, or for the purposes of such an adoption in the receiving State or in the State of origin.

(2) The Convention covers only adoptions which create a permanent parent-child relationship. . . .

CHAPTER II—REQUIREMENTS FOR INTERCOUNTRY ADOPTIONS

Article 4: An adoption within the scope of the Convention shall take place only if the competent authorities of the State of origin—

a) have established that the child is adoptable;

b) have determined, after possibilities for placement of the child within the State of origin have been given due consideration, that an intercountry adoption is in the child's best interests;

c) have ensured that

(1) the persons, institutions and authorities whose consent is necessary for adoption, have been counselled as may be necessary and duly informed of the effects of their consent, in particular whether or not an adoption will result in the termination of the legal relationship between the child and his or her family of origin,

(2) such persons, institutions and authorities have given their consent freely, in the required legal form, and expressed or evidenced in writing,

(3) the consents have not been induced by payment or compensation of any kind and have not been withdrawn, and

(4) the consent of the mother, where required, has been given only after the birth of the child; and

d) have ensured, having regard to the age and degree of maturity of the child, that

(1) he or she has been counselled and duly informed of the effects of the adoption and of his or her consent to the adoption, where such consent is required,

(2) consideration has been given to the child's wishes and opinions,

(3) the child's consent to the adoption, where such consent is required, has been given freely, in the required legal form, and expressed or evidenced in writing, and

(4) such consent has not been induced by payment or compensation of any kind.

Article 5: An adoption within the scope of the Convention shall take place only if the competent authorities of the receiving State—

a) have determined that the prospective adoptive parents are eligible and suited to adopt;

b) have ensured that the prospective adoptive parents have been counselled as may be necessary; and

c) have determined that the child is or will be authorized to enter and reside permanently in that State. . . .

Article 9: Central Authorities shall take, directly or through public authorities or other bodies duly accredited in their State, all appropriate measures, in particular to—

a) collect, preserve and exchange information about the situation of the child and the prospective adoptive parents, so far as is necessary to complete the adoption;

b) facilitate, follow and expedite proceedings with a view to obtaining the adoption;

c) promote the development of adoption counselling and post-adoption services in their States;

d) provide each other with general evaluation reports about experience with intercountry adoption;

e) reply, in so far as is permitted by the law of their State, to justified requests from other Central Authorities or public authorities for information about a particular adoption situation.

Article 10: Accreditation shall only be granted to and maintained by bodies demonstrating their competence to carry out properly the tasks with which they may be entrusted.

Article 11: An accredited body shall—

a) pursue only non-profit objectives according to such conditions and within such limits as may be established by the competent authorities of the State of accreditation

b) be directed and staffed by persons qualified by their ethical standards and by training or experience to work in the field of intercountry adoption; and

c) be subject to supervision by competent authorities of that State as to its composition, operation and financial situation.

CHAPTER IV—PROCEDURAL REQUIREMENTS IN INTERCOUNTRY ADOPTION

Article 14: Persons habitually resident in a Contracting State, who wish to adopt a child habitually resident in another Contracting State, shall apply to the Central Authority in the State of their habitual residence.

Article 15:

(1) If the Central Authority of the receiving State is satisfied that the applicants are eligible and suited to adopt, it shall prepare a report including information about their identity, eligibility and suitability to adopt, background, family and medical history, social environment, reasons for adoption, ability to undertake an intercountry adoption, as well as the characteristics of the children for whom they would be qualified to care.

(2) It shall transmit the report to the Central Authority of the State of origin.

Article 16:

(1) If the Central Authority of the State of origin is satisfied that the child is adoptable, it shall—

a) prepare a report including information about his or her identity, adoptability, background, social environment, family history, medical history including that of the child's family, and any special needs of the child;

b) give due consideration to the child's upbringing and to his or her ethnic, religious and cultural background;

c) ensure that consents have been obtained in accordance with Article 4; and

d) determine, on the basis in particular of the reports relating to the child and the prospective adoptive parents, whether the envisaged placement is in the best interests of the child.

(2) It shall transmit to the Central Authority of the receiving State its report on the child, proof that the necessary consents have been obtained and the reasons for its determination on the placement, taking care not to reveal the identity of the mother and the father if, in the State of origin, these identities may not be disclosed.

Article 17: Any decision in the State of origin that a child should be entrusted to prospective adoptive parents may only be made if—

a) the Central Authority of that State has ensured that the prospective adoptive parents agree;

b) the Central Authority of the receiving State has approved such decision, where such approval is required by the law of that State or by the Central Authority of the State of origin;

c) the Central Authorities of both States have agreed that the adoption may proceed; and

d) it has been determined, in accordance with Article 5, that the prospective adoptive parents are eligible and suited to adopt and that the child is or will be authorized to enter and reside permanently in the receiving State.

Article 18: The Central Authorities of both States shall take all necessary steps to obtain permission for the child to leave the State of origin and to enter and reside permanently in the receiving State.

Article 19:

(1) The transfer of the child to the receiving State may only be carried out if the requirements of Article 17 have been satisfied.

(2) The Central Authorities of both States shall ensure that this transfer takes place in secure and appropriate circumstances and, if possible, in the company of the adoptive or prospective adoptive parents.

(3) If the transfer of the child does not take place, the reports referred to in Articles 15 and 16 are to be sent back to the authorities who forwarded them.

Article 20: The Central Authorities shall keep each other informed about the adoption process and the measures taken to complete it, as well as about the progress of the placement if a probationary period is required.

Article 21:

(1) Where the adoption is to take place after the transfer of the child to the receiving State and it appears to the Central Authority of that State that the continued placement of the child with the prospective adoptive parents

is not in the child's best interests, such Central Authority shall take the measures necessary to protect the child, in particular—

a) to cause the child to be withdrawn from the prospective adoptive parents and to arrange temporary care;

b) in consultation with the Central Authority of the State of origin, to arrange without delay a new placement of the child with a view to adoption or, if this is not appropriate, to arrange alternative long-term care; an adoption shall not take place until the Central Authority of the State of origin has been duly informed concerning the new prospective adoptive parents;

c) as a last resort, to arrange the return of the child, if his or her interests so require.

(2) Having regard in particular to the age and degree of maturity of the child, he or she shall be consulted and, where appropriate, his or her consent obtained in relation to measures to be taken under this Article.

CHAPTER V—RECOGNITION AND EFFECTS OF THE ADOPTION

Article 23: An adoption certified by the competent authority of the State of the adoption as having been made in accordance with the Convention shall be recognized by operation of law in the other Contracting States. The certificate shall specify when and by whom the agreements under Article 17, sub-paragraph c), were given.

Article 24: The recognition of an adoption may be refused in a Contracting State only if the adoption is manifestly contrary to its public policy, taking into account the best interests of the child.

Article 25: Any Contracting State may declare to the depositary of the Convention that it will not be bound under this Convention to recognize adoptions made in accordance with an agreement concluded by application of Article 39, paragraph 2.

Article 26:

(1) The recognition of an adoption includes recognition of

a) the legal parent-child relationship between the child and his or her adoptive parents;

b) parental responsibility of the adoptive parents for the child;

c) the termination of a pre-existing legal relationship between the child and his or her mother and father, if the adoption has this effect in the Contracting State where it was made.

(2) In the case of an adoption having the effect of terminating a pre-existing legal parent-child relationship, the child shall enjoy in the receiving State, and in any other Contracting State where the adoption is recognized, rights

equivalent to those resulting from adoptions having this effect in each such State.

(3) The preceding paragraphs shall not prejudice the application of any provision more favourable for the child, in force in the Contracting State which recognizes the adoption. . . .

CHAPTER VI—GENERAL PROVISIONS

Article 28: The Convention does not affect any law of a State of origin which requires that the adoption of a child habitually resident within that State take place in that State or which prohibits the child's placement in, or transfer to, the receiving State prior to adoption.

Article 29: There shall be no contact between the prospective adoptive parents and the child's parents or any other person who has care of the child until the requirements of Article 4, sub-paragraphs a) to c), and Article 5, sub-paragraph a), have been met, unless the adoption takes place within a family or unless the contact is in compliance with the conditions established by the competent authority of the State of origin.

Article 30:

(1) The competent authorities of a Contracting State shall ensure that information held by them concerning the child's origin, in particular information concerning the identity of his or her parents, as well as the medical history, is preserved.

(2) They shall ensure that the child or his or her representative has access to such information, under appropriate guidance, in so far as is permitted by the law of that State.

Article 31: Without prejudice to Article 30, personal data gathered or transmitted under the Convention, especially data referred to in Articles 15 and 16, shall be used only for the purposes for which they were gathered or transmitted.

Article 32:

(1) No one shall derive improper financial or other gain from an activity related to an intercountry adoption.

(2) Only costs and expenses, including reasonable professional fees of persons involved in the adoption, may be charged or paid.

(3) The directors, administrators and employees of bodies involved in an adoption shall not receive remuneration which is unreasonably high in relation to services rendered.

Article 33: A competent authority which finds that any provision of the Convention has not been respected or that there is a serious risk that it may not be respected, shall immediately inform the Central Authority of its

State. This Central Authority shall be responsible for ensuring that appropriate measures are taken.

Article 34: If the competent authority of the State of destination of a document so requests, a translation certified as being in conformity with the original must be furnished. Unless otherwise provided, the costs of such translation are to be borne by the prospective adoptive parents.

Article 35: The competent authorities of the Contracting States shall act expeditiously in the process of adoption.

Source: The Hague Conference on Private International Law, "Convention of 29 May 1993 on Protection of Children and Co-Operation in Respect of Intercountry Adoption," *Collection of Conventions, 1951–2003* (Antwerp, Belgium: Maklu Uitgevers N.V., 2003).

2. Excerpts from the U.S. Intercountry Adoption Act of 2000

The following Act was passed by the U.S. Congress and signed into law by President Clinton on October 6, 2000. It implements the Hague Convention on the Protection of Children, which was passed by the United Nations in 1993. Note the continued use of "the best interests of the child" which has been perhaps the defining phrase for modern adoption law since its beginnings in the nineteenth century.

An Act
To provide for implementation by the United States of the Hague Convention on the Protection of Children and Co-operation in Respect of Intercountry Adoption, and for other purposes.

Be it enacted by the Senate and House of Representatives of the United States of America in Congress assembled, . . .

FINDINGS AND PURPOSES.

(a) **Findings.**—Congress recognizes—

    (1) the international character of the Convention on Protection of Children and Co-operation in Respect of Intercountry Adoption (done at The Hague on May 29, 1993); and

    (2) the need for uniform interpretation and implementation of the Convention in the United States and abroad, and therefore finds that enactment of a Federal law governing adoptions and prospective adoptions subject to the Convention involving United States residents is essential.

(b) **Purposes.**—The purposes of this Act are—

(1) to provide for implementation by the United States of the Convention;

(2) to protect the rights of, and prevent abuses against, children, birth families, and adoptive parents involved in adoptions (or prospective adoptions) subject to the Convention, and to ensure that such adoptions are in the children's best interests; and

(3) to improve the ability of the Federal Government to assist United States citizens seeking to adopt children from abroad and residents of other countries party to the Convention seeking to adopt children from the United States.

SEC. 3. DEFINITIONS.

As used in this Act:

(1) **Accredited agency.**—The term "accredited agency" means an agency accredited under title II to provide adoption services in the United States in cases subject to the Convention.

(2) **Accrediting entity.**—The term "accrediting entity" means an entity designated under section 202(a) to accredit agencies and approve persons under title II.

(3) **Adoption service.**—The term "adoption service" means—

(A) identifying a child for adoption and arranging an adoption;

(B) securing necessary consent to termination of parental rights and to adoption;

(C) performing a background study on a child or a home study on a prospective adoptive parent, and reporting on such a study;

(D) making determinations of the best interests of a child and the appropriateness of adoptive placement for the child;

(E) post-placement monitoring of a case until final adoption; and

(F) where made necessary by disruption before final adoption, assuming custody and providing child care or any other social service pending an alternative placement.

The term "**providing**," with respect to an adoption service,

includes facilitating the provision of the service.

(4) **Agency.**—The term "agency" means any person other than an individual.

(5) **Approved person.**—The term "approved person" means a person approved under title II to provide adoption services in the United States in cases subject to the Convention. . . .

TITLE III—RECOGNITION OF CONVENTION ADOPTIONS IN THE UNITED STATES

Sec. 301. Adoptions of Children Immigrating to the United States.

(a) **Legal Effect of Certificates Issued by the Secretary of State.—**

    (1) **Issuance of certificates by the secretary of state.—**The Secretary of State shall, with respect to each Convention adoption, issue a certificate to the adoptive citizen parent domiciled in the United States that the adoption has been granted or, in the case of a prospective adoptive citizen parent, that legal custody of the child has been granted to the citizen parent for purposes of emigration and adoption, pursuant to the Convention and this Act, if the Secretary of State—

        (A) receives appropriate notification from the central authority of such child's country of origin; and

        (B) has verified that the requirements of the Convention and this Act have been met with respect to the adoption.

    (2) **Legal effect of certificates.—**If appended to an original adoption decree, the certificate described in paragraph (1) shall be treated by Federal and State agencies, courts, and other public and private persons and entities as conclusive evidence of the facts certified therein and shall constitute the certification required by section 204(d)(2) of the Immigration and Nationality Act, as amended by this Act.

(b) **Legal Effect of Convention Adoption Finalized in Another Convention Country.—**A final adoption in another Convention country, certified by the Secretary of State pursuant to subsection (a) of this section or section 303(c), shall be recognized as a final valid adoption for purposes of all Federal, State, and local laws of the United States.

(c) **Condition on Finalization of Convention Adoption by State Court.—** In the case of a child who has entered the United States from another Convention country for the purpose of adoption, an order declaring the adoption final shall not be entered unless the Secretary of State has issued the certificate provided for in subsection (a) with respect to the adoption. . . .

Sec. 303. Adoptions of Children Emigrating from the United States.

(a) **Duties of Accredited Agency or Approved Person.—**In the case of a Convention adoption involving the emigration of a child residing in the United States to a foreign country, the accredited agency or approved person providing adoption services, or the prospective adoptive parent or parents acting on their own behalf (if permitted by the laws of such other Convention country in which they reside and the laws of the State in which the child resides), shall do the following:

(1) Ensure that, in accordance with the Convention—

(A) a background study on the child is completed;

(B) the accredited agency or approved person—

(i) has made reasonable efforts to actively recruit and make a diligent search for prospective adoptive parents to adopt the child in the United States; and

(ii) despite such efforts, has not been able to place the child for adoption in the United States in a timely manner; and

(C) a determination is made that placement with the prospective adoptive parent or parents is in the best interests of the child.

(2) Furnish to the State court with jurisdiction over the case—

(A) documentation of the matters described in paragraph (1);

(B) a background report (home study) on the prospective adoptive parent or parents (including a criminal background check) prepared in accordance with the laws of the receiving country; and

(C) a declaration by the central authority (or other competent authority) of such other Convention country—

(i) that the child will be permitted to enter and reside permanently, or on the same basis as the adopting parent, in the receiving country; and

(ii) that the central authority (or other competent authority) of such other Convention country consents to the adoption, if such consent is necessary under the laws of such country for the adoption to become final. . . .

(b) **Conditions on State Court Orders.**—An order declaring an adoption to be final or granting custody for the purpose of adoption in a case described in subsection (a) shall not be entered unless the court—

(1) has received and verified to the extent the court may find necessary—

(A) the material described in subsection (a)(2); and

(B) satisfactory evidence that the requirements of Articles 4 and 15 through 21 of the Convention have been met; and

(2) has determined that the adoptive placement is in the best interests of the child. . . .

Source: Public Law 106-279. U.S. Code, 2000.

12 Orphans in Literature for American Children

T he orphan is a recurring character in literature all around the world, in stories directed to people of all ages. Folk stories and "fairy tales" in many cultures frequently center on the experiences of orphaned or abandoned children struggling to make their way in the world (see, for example, the Seneca tale at the beginning of Chapter 7). Often there are differences in gender expectations—with orphaned boys being expected to develop independence and self-reliance while abandoned girls must model patience and honesty. The following stories, essays, poem, and memoir illustrate several ways that orphaned characters have served to entertain, educate, and provide a variety of moral values to generations of American children.

1. Edmund Morris, from *Farming for Boys*

Focusing on an orphaned boy named "John Hancock" who is working as a peddler, this story sends a moral lesson to a character in the novel named Tony—himself a foster child living with "Uncle Benny"—and, more importantly, to its audience of middle-class children. The orphan here offers a positive model of how to succeed despite adversity. The answer, for boys: hard work.

While this conversation was going on, the boys had noticed some traveler winding his slow and muddy way up the road toward where they were standing. As he came nearer, they discovered him to be a small boy, not so large as either Joe or Tony; and just as Uncle Benny had finished his elucidation of the fence against fortune, the traveler reached the spot where the group were conversing, and with instinctive good sense stepped up out of the mud upon the pile of rails which had served as standing-ground for the others. He was a short, thick-set fellow, warmly clad, of quick movement, keen, intelligent look, and a piercing black eye, having in it all the business fire of a juvenile Shylock. Bidding good afternoon to the group, and scraping from his thick boots as much of the mud as he could, he proceeded to business without further loss of time. Lifting the cover from a basket on his arm, he displayed its flashing contents before the eyes of Joe and Tony, asking them if they didn't want a knife, a comb, a tooth-brush, a burning-glass, a cake of pomatum, or something else of an almost endless list of articles, which he ran over with a volubility exceeding anything they had ever experienced.

The little fellow was a pedler. He plied his vocation with a glibness and pertinacity that confounded the two modest farmer's boys he was addressing. Long intercourse with the great public had given him a perfect self-possession, from which the boys fairly shrunk back with girlish timidity. There was nothing impudent or obtrusive in his manner, but a quiet, persevering self-reliance that could not fail to command attention from any audience, and which, to the rustics he was addressing, was particularly imposing. To Uncle Benny the scene was quite a study. He looked and listened in silence. He was struck with the cool, independent manner of the young pedler, his excessive volubility, and the tact with which he held up to Joe and Tony the particular articles most likely to attract their attention. He seemed to know intuitively what each boy coveted the most. Tony's great longing had been for a pocket-knife, and Joe's for a jack-knife. The boy very soon discovered this, and, having both in his basket, crowded the articles on his customers with an urgency that nothing but the low condition of their funds could resist. After declining a dozen times to purchase, Tony was forced to exclaim, "But we have no money. I never had a shilling in my life."

The pedler-boy seemed struck with conviction of the truth of Tony's declaration, and that he was only wasting time in endeavoring to sell where there was no money to pay with. He accordingly replaced the articles in his basket, shut down the lid, and with unaltered civility was bidding the company good bye, when Uncle Benny broke silence for the first time.

"What is your name, my lad?" he inquired.

"John Hancock, sir," was the reply.

"I have heard that name before," rejoined Uncle Benny. "You were not at the signing of the Declaration of Independence?"

"No, sir," replied the courageous little fellow, "I wish I had been,—but my name was there."

This was succeeded by quite a colloquy between them, ending with Uncle Benny's purchasing, at a dollar apiece, the coveted knives, and presenting them to the delighted boys. Then, again addressing the pedler, he inquired, "Why do you follow this business of peddling?"

"Because I make money by it," he quickly replied.

"But have you no friends to help you, and give you employment at home?" continued the old man.

"Got no friends, sir," he responded. "Father and mother both dead, and I had to help myself; so I turned newsboy in the city, and then made money enough to set up in peddling, and now I am making more."

Uncle Benny was convinced that he was talking with a future millionaire. But while admiring the boy's bravery, his heart overflowed with pity for his loneliness and destitution, and with a yearning anxiety for his welfare. Laying his hand on his shoulder, he said: "God bless you and preserve you, my boy! Be industrious as you have been, be sober, honest, and truthful. Fear God above all things, keep his commandments, and, though you have no earthly parent, he will be to you a heavenly one."

The friendless little fellow looked up into the old man's benevolent face with an expression of surprise and sadness,—surprise at the winning kindness of his manner, as if he had seldom met with it from others, and sadness, as if the soft voices of parental love had been recalled to his yet living memory. Then, thanking him with great warmth, he bid the company good bye, and, with his basket under his arm, continued his tiresome journey over the muddy highway to the next farm-house.

"There!" said the old man, addressing Tony, "did you hear what he said? 'Father and mother both dead, and I had to help myself!' Why, it is yourself over again. Take a lesson from the story of that boy, Tony!"

Source: Serialized in *Our Young Folks*, 1865–1866, the installment from which this selection is taken appeared in April 1865 (pp. 238–40).

2. Hesba Stretton [Sarah Smith], "Jessica's Temptation"

In this story, readers are introduced to a girl who initially lives with her neglectful mother in a large city—before eventually being abandoned. Jess spends most days begging on the streets or earning money as an errand girl. Like most girl heroines, Jess demonstrates virtue not by hard work, as the peddler boy did in the previous story, but, first, by not begging for food, and second, by being honest. "Mr. Daniel" eventually adopts Jess, who also helps to redeem his hardened soul through her constancy and selflessness.

Jessica kept her part of the bargain faithfully; and though the solemn and silent man under the dark shadow of the bridge looked out for her every morning as he served his customers, he caught no glimpse of her wan face and thin little frame. But when the appointed time was finished, she presented herself at the stall, with her hungry eyes fastened again upon the piles of buns and bread and butter, which were fast disappearing before the demands of the buyers. The business was at its height, and the famished child stood quietly on one side watching for the throng to melt away. But as soon as the nearest church clock had chimed eight, she drew a little nearer to the stall, and at a signal from its owner she slipped between the trestles of his stand, and took up her former position on the empty basket. To his eyes she seemed even a little thinner, and certainly more ragged, than before; and he laid a whole bun, a stale one which was left from yesterday's stock, upon her lap, as she lifted the cup of coffee to her lips with both her benumbed hands.

"What's your name?" she asked, looking up to him with her keen eyes.

"Why?" he answered, hesitatingly, as if he was reluctant to tell so much of himself; "my christened name is Daniel."

"And where do you live, Mr. Dan'el?" she enquired.

"Oh, come now!" he exclaimed, "if you're going to be impudent, you'd better march off. What business is it of yours where I live? I don't want to know where you live, I can tell you."

"I didn't mean no offence," said Jess, humbly; "only I thought I'd like to know where a good man like you lived. You're a very good man, aren't you, Mr. Dan'el?"

"I don't know," he answered, uneasily; "I'm afraid I'm not."

"Oh, but you are, you know," continued Jess. "You make good coffee; prime! And buns too! And I've been watching you hundreds of times afore you saw me, and the police leaves you alone, and never tells you to move on. Oh, yes! you must be a very good man."

Daniel sighed, and fidgeted about his crockery with a grave and occupied air, as if he were pondering over the child's notion of goodness. He made good coffee, and the police left him alone! It was quite true; yet still as he counted up the store of pence which had accumulated in his strong canvas bag, he sighed again still more heavily. He purposely let one of his pennies fall upon the muddy pavement, and went on counting the rest busily, while he furtively watched the little girl sitting at his feet. Without a shade of change upon her small face, she covered the penny with her foot, and drew it in carefully towards her, while she continued to chatter fluently to him. For a moment a feeling of pain shot a pang through Daniel's heart; and then he congratulated himself on having entrapped the young thief. It was time to be leaving now; but before he went he would make her move her bare foot, and disclose the penny concealed beneath it, and then he would warn her never to venture near his stall again. This was her gratitude, he thought; he had given her two breakfasts and more kindness than he had shown to any fellow-creature for many a long year; and, at the first chance, the young jade turned upon him, and robbed him! He was brooding over it painfully in his mind, when Jessica's uplifted face changed suddenly, and a dark flush crept over her pale cheeks, and the tears started to her eyes. She stooped down, and picking up the coin from amongst the mud, she rubbed it bright and clean upon her rags, and laid it upon the stall close to his hand, but without speaking a word. Daniel looked down upon her solemnly and searchingly.

"What's this ?" he asked.

"Please, Mr. Daniel," she answered, "it dropped, and you didn't hear it."

"Jess," he said, sternly, "tell me all about it."

"Oh, please," she sobbed, "I never had a penny of my very own but once; and it rolled close to my foot; and you didn't see it; and I hid it up sharp; and then I thought how kind you'd been, and how good the coffee and buns are, and how you let me warm myself at your fire; and please, I couldn't keep the penny any longer. You'll never let me come again, I guess."

Daniel turned away for a minute, busying himself with putting his cups and saucers into the basket, while Jessica stood by trembling, with the large tears rolling slowly down her cheeks. The snug, dark corner, with its warm fire of charcoal, and its fragrant smell of coffee, had been a paradise to her for these two brief spans of time; but she had been guilty of the sin which would drive her from it. All beyond the railway arch the streets stretched away, cold and dreary, with no friendly faces to meet hers, and no warm cups of coffee to refresh her; yet she was only lingering sorrowfully to hear the words spoken which should forbid her to return to this pleasant spot. Mr. Daniel turned round at last, and met her tearful gaze, with a look of strange emotion upon his own solemn face.

"Jess," he said, "I could never have done it myself. But you may come here every Wednesday morning, as this is a Wednesday, and there'll always be a cup of coffee for you."

She thought he meant that he could not have hidden the penny under his foot, and she went away a little saddened and subdued, notwithstanding her great delight in the expectation of such a treat every week; while Daniel, pondering over the struggle that must have passed through her childish mind, went on his way, from time to time shaking his head, and muttering to himself, "I couldn't have done it myself: I never could have done it myself."

Source: Chapter 2 of *Jessica's First Prayer* (London, 1867) is available online at http://www3.shropshire-cc.gov.uk/etexts/E000286.htm.

3. Fanny Barrow, "Tessa, the Little Orange-Girl"

A warm-hearted American woman's adoption of an orphaned Italian girl from an imprisoning slum affirms the ideology that supported the "orphan train" programs (see Chapter 2, especially)—an ideology that shapes many modern stories of international adoption.

All that sunny afternoon, little Tessa sat on the steps of the great church in the beautiful city of Naples, selling oranges. Her sweet Italian words of entreaty dropped like a little song from her lips, which sometimes trembled with tearful earnestness, for her mother was very ill at home, and the money received from the sale of the fruit, perhaps, would be enough to bring the doctor and help.

Only a few oranges were left in Tessa's basket, when a lovely looking American lady came out of the church. In her hand was a great bunch of violets of Parma. Their delicious odor filled the atmosphere around her; but not sweeter were they than the lady's beautiful face, and violet eyes, which rested, full of compassion, upon the child, the moment her ear caught the pleading Italian words, which in English, would be: "Sweet lady! dear lady! buy my oranges of Sicily! and let me go home to my mother, and the good God will bless you forever!"

"You poor little thing!" said the lady, in Italian, which she spoke perfectly; "here is money for your oranges—give them all to me. And now tell me, why are you in such haste to go home? See, the sun is still shining on the great dome of the church. It is yet early. But, come; I will go with you."

The child's large eyes were lifted up in astonishment to the lady's face. A smile of gratitude, that seemed almost breaking into a sob, parted her lips. The joy of thus suddenly finding a friend, and the grief for her mother, struggled for mastery in her little bosom. She started up, crying, "*Gracias signora carissima!*" and quickly followed the lady down the steps of the church, her little, bare feet making a soft pit-a-pat, like far-away echoes to the other's steps, as they soon turned into a very narrow and silent street. Then Tessa told her pitiful story; how her father was lost in the cruel sea, when out in his fishing-boat; during a wild storm; how her mother made and mended nets for their support, and the little girl never wanted bread— and sometimes, on festa days, had a bunch of grapes—until a week ago, when her mother was stricken down by a cruel fever, and could work no more. Then her Uncle Cola, who himself was very poor, had bought some oranges, and given them to her to sell. With the money they brought, Tessa got more oranges; "and sometimes, *Signora mia,*" she said, pitifully, "I sell enough to give us bread. But yesterday I was so hungry! oh, so hungry! and my poor mother grew so white.—so white—"

Great tears started to Tessa's eyes. With tender compassion the lady stooped down, and kissed her, saying, "Don't cry, little one; you shall never be hungry again, if I can help it."

It was now sunset—the glorious Italian sunset. Tessa and her new friend hurried on, and were soon in a very narrow, mean street, which ran down to the bay of Naples. One of the miserable homes stood a little back, and into this one Tessa and her new friend entered. The next moment they stood at the bed-side of the dying mother.

Yes, dying! Her fading eyes, which were fixed with pathetic yearning upon the door brightened for a moment as Tessa flew into the feeble arms stretched out to her. A prayer of thanksgiving fell from her mother's lips, as the child, in a few rapid words, explained why the Signora was there. Then some tearful, broken sentences passed between the mother and Tessa's friend—piteous words of farewell on one side, earnest, loving, promises on the other. But what peace and comfort those earnest, loving assurances brought to the mother's heart! for her little one was to be taken by the Signora to that far-off, glorious, free America, where plenty ever reigned! She was to be loved and cared for as if she was Signora's own child. In the mother's dying moments was this promise given and received. And not a moment too soon, for a little while after, with a grateful look, and feeble pressure of the lady's hand, the Italian mother went into everlasting rest.

Little broken-hearted Tessa! She had to be taken by force from her dead mother's side: and for many days she refused to be comforted. *"Oh! madre mia! madre mia!"* was her incessant wail. But God is very merciful. He softens grief as time goes on; and by and by little Tessa began to smile, and put her soft arms around the neck of her new mamma,—and soon she could say "mother," and "I love you," and many other English words.

And this is the story, so far, of little Tessa, whose picture you have here. Who knows but some day you may meet the pretty little Italian girl with her adopted American mother?

Source: *St. Nicholas Magazine* 8 (September 1881): 869–70.

4. "Doesn't Anybody Want a Little Boy?"

This story from early in the twentieth century portrays boys living in orphanages as "branded" with the scars of institutionalization, reflecting the increasing discomfort with orphanages as the dominant solution for displaced children, and teaches that adults—especially unmarried women, interestingly—ought to adopt them.

There was a curious shuffling sound outside the open windows. The noise of the surface cars failed to drown it, and the beat of horses' hoofs on the asphalt only seemed to measure the undertone of swish, swish.

Fifty boys, at least, and evidently returning from a day's outing, for the street along which they shuffled their homeward way led from one of the Coney Island landings.

Back from Coney Island, and not a smile on a single face! Behind the gentle-faced nun who led the procession came the rest of the boys two by two and hand in hand, and fluttering along, like benevolent black-winged doves, four or five other sisters guided the flock.

On each and every countenance was the brand of the institution. Not a cruel brand, perhaps—none of the boys had actually suffered in the marking, but it was there for those who looked to recognize—the brand of the impersonal, the unindividual. There was no eagerness, no skipping, no gabbling, and not a single, single smile.

But, then, how could a little boy be expected to have a first-class time at Coney Island, with no mother to tell about the breathless ride down the chutes, and how he wasn't afraid, not a bit—well, perhaps a mite 'way up at the top. And how could any boy enjoy Bostock's animals to the very limit who couldn't the next day reproduce the den of lions for the benefit of his little sister, and excite in her some of the terror that had gripped his very soul at the roaring of the very biggest lion of all?

The institution has many arms and a great big heart of some kind. It must have, to have clothed all these boys so neatly, to have given them good shoes and stockings,—new hats, too.

But they were all alike, you see, and it seemed pretty certain that not one boy there knew the bliss of owning a ragged, disreputable cap that he could drag down over his eyes or wear just as he pleased. Not one could run an errand for mother and earn a penny to buy gum that he'd keep stuck under the bed at night. And maybe not one of them knew the smell of cookies baking, or had ever had a present of a little pie baked all for himself by a good-natured cook.

For they were all, all alike, you see. The suits were all alike, the shoes too, except as to size, and the new blue straw hats, stretching in two shining rows, and the little boys themselves—all, all alike—and that was the pity of it.

It didn't seem as if Charley and John and Billy Peters and Jim Sanderson had all been to Coney Island and had had a bully time. It was just fifty, and each one lost among the others.

Some of them very likely had never known their mothers. Perhaps the institution had mothered and fathered them from their babyhood, but still even these, sometimes, at night, say, may have vague, uneasy fears that there's something they're missing—something they're never going to have.

It's better, far better, to be fed and clothed and taught; better to have the kind, gentle sisters watching over them; better to walk hand in hand and two by two and to wear shiny blue hats bought by the hundred—much better than to be left to grow up as best you can, to sell newspapers and half starve, to use the language of the gutter, and smoke picked-up cigarette-ends when you're only eight years old—far, far better!

But there must be homes here and there, where the little boy has gone on a long, long journey—homes where it's going to be a good many years before mother will start to find him. And if there were only a little corner in a home like that where a little boy could creep in and find out that he really was somebody, after all! He wouldn't be *the* little boy, and mother couldn't love him in just the same way; but perhaps, after a time, he'd deserve some love on his own account—after he got acquainted and began to feel real "homey."

And there must be women who haven't any boys and never will have any boys—women who haven't married, but just lived along, and now they're wondering if they too aren't missing something.

It seems as if a woman like that could get just a mine of comfort and enjoyment out of one of those blue-hatted, neatly-shod, well-clothed and well-fed little creatures that came back from Coney without a smile on one serious child face.

Of course it's no one's duty—no woman really ought to—but oh, if some one only *wanted* to!

Doesn't *anybody* want a little boy?

Source: *The Delineator* 71, no. 3 (March 1908): 424.

5. George Birdseye, "A Matter of Selection"

In this poem, we see an early version of the "chosen child" explanation (see Chapter 3) which became a dominant narrative model for telling adopted children of their status throughout much of the twentieth century.

> Said a vulgar little girl, who was sneering at another
>   In accents that were very far from mild,
> "You ain't got no father, you ain't got no mother—
>   You ain't nothin' but a horrid 'dopted child!"
> "I'm quite as good as you," came the answer from the other.
>   "I was carefully selected from a lot.
> But only look at you—your father and your mother
>   Had to keep you if they wanted to or not!"

Source: Originally published in the *Boston Globe*, date unknown. Reprinted in *Charities* 9, no. 23 (December 6, 1902): 584.

6. Helen Grigsby Doss, "All God's Children"

Helen Doss and her husband adopted twelve children from a variety of nationalities and ethnicities in the middle of the twentieth century—a time when international adoption was quite rare. The family first gained national attention when The Reader's Digest *and* Life *magazines published stories and pictures of them in 1949 and 1951, respectively, referring to them as the "One-Family United Nations." Doss's own 1954 memoir of her family's life together—from which the following passage is excerpted—makes a compelling argument for integration and racial harmony. It was published four months before the landmark Supreme Court case,* Brown v. Board of Education, *which mandated the integration of public schools.*

Our children never thought of themselves as looking particularly different from each other. One day, when Donny was eight and Alex a year old, Donny crouched on the floor to encourage his little brother to walk. Alex reached out both hands, took a hesitating step, and tumbled into Donny's arms. The high-pitched giggle interlaced with the hearty boy-sized chuckle, then Donny looked up at me, blue eyes wide and sincere under his thatch of blond hair. "Mama," he said, glancing fondly at the Oriental ivory face beside him, at the black appleseed eyes that crinkle into slits when Alex laughs, "if he was seven years older, and if I had black hair, everybody would think that him and me was twins!"

They felt that much alike, our children, and often they took it for granted that this alikeness would show. Naturally they could see that there were minor and inconsequential variations, that Rita had "the blackest, shiniest hair," that Teddy could toast browner in the sun than the rest, but persons bearing such unearned distinctions were polite enough not to gloat. There are only two times I can remember when differences within our family seemed to be of any concern, and then, each time, it was only because a small child developed a sudden fear that a minor dissimilarity might be a physical handicap to the bearer. Once Teddy looked into the mirror at his own brown eyes and then studied Donny, solicitude puckering his face like a walnut.

"Donny?" he asked, "how can you see out of blue eyes?"

Also there was the early-winter day when Timmy watched Carl trim brown spots from apples with the point of a knife.

"Why do you do that, Daddy?" he asked.

"Bad spots," Carl said.

Later I noticed Timmy staring at me, his usually frolicking brown eyes now worried.

"Daddy gonna cut pieces out of you?"

"Heavens, no," I laughed. "What made you say that?"

His fingers slid gently over the freckles on my arm. "Bad spots," he said.

It is the outsiders who imagine that our family is made up of incompatible opposites. Those who have never ventured beyond the white bars of their self-imposed social cages too often take for granted that a different color skin on the outside makes for a different kind of being, not of necessity completely human, on the inside. . . .

Some of the skeptical find it hard to believe that people of all races are born with the same kind of vocal chords for speech, the same kind of taste buds in the tongue, the same type of digestive apparatus capable of assimilating a wide variety of foods. Differences between national or racial groups are mostly just differences in culture. It is not heredity but a cultural pattern that makes the British love their royalty, the Chinese reverence their scholars, and the Eskimos relish partially decomposed and frozen raw fish. Cultural mores, not genes, determine the language we speak, our notions as to the wearing of a sarong, a kilt, or a stuffy business suit, and whether or not we think it polite to belch after a meal.

We try to explain these things, whenever we think the backs of the mis-informed are strong enough to bear the truth; but the boners go march-ing on. One afternoon a businessman was talking to Carl at our front door. Rita whizzed down the driveway sloping from the church to the road, made too sharp a turn and flew off her trike, landing square on her nose.

"Wow," Carl said, poised to take off at the first wail from down below. "My daughter took quite a spill."

But there was no wail. Teddy was beside her in an instant, helping Rita brush herself off. They giggled as both hopped back on their tricycles and sped off around the circle drive again. Carl relaxed and smiled. "I thought she was going to yell her head off from that bump. She's a tough little kid, though, and a good sport."

The man shrugged. "Actually, coming from such a primitive stock, she couldn't possibly have felt it the way a *Caucasian* would have. I doubt if her nerve endings are very highly developed."

Primitive nerve endings! Our children don't need the studious anthro-pologists and ethnologists to tell them that such fantastic notions are hog-wash, because they already know that people are more alike than different; nor do they need the proof of microscopes and IQ tests and statistics cov-ering years of careful research, to believe that modern science finds no race superior to any other.

These scientific ideas are not new. Nearly two thousand years ago, the same thing was said in a different language, "God hath made of one blood all nations of men, for to dwell on the face of the earth." East may be East and West may be West, but the twain *can* meet and get along with each other, when each looks the other in the face and admits the truth we find in the Bible: God is the Father of all mankind; we are all God's children, and all men are brothers.

Why do people refuse to believe this, singling out certain portions of their fellow men to hate, to discriminate against, even to persecute?

First, prejudice is a contagious disease, as easily caught as measles, the babe from his parents, the school child from his playmates, the adult from his fellow workers and neighbors. To compound the social tragedy, preju-dice once caught is hard to cure, since it unwittingly serves a number of morbid purposes. When a man is picked on by his boss, he can slam home and take it out on his family, and frequently does; however, a more socially approved outlet is to turn around and release the feelings of hate and anger on those of a minority racial group. If denied certain yearned-for oppor-tunities and privileges, there is a devilish quirk within man which gives him perverse satisfaction in seeing that at least one segment of the population enjoys even less opportunities and privileges than he. . . . Worse yet, he will try to keep minority groups in a deprived and subjugated position, to prove what his ego wants to believe. . . .

War has always been a socially glorified outlet for pent-up angers and frustrations of whole peoples. In America, our Negroes have provided another scapegoat, and so we have race riots, Jim Crowism, and the Ku Klux Klan. On the West Coast, first the Chinese, then the Japanese, provided another handy outlet for our inner tensions, and we have had discrimination in jobs and housing, an Orientals Exclusion Act, and the "relocation centers" of World War II.

What can we do about it? There is no easy answer, no quick solution. Civil-rights legislation, while no cure, can alleviate some situations, like a clean slash of a surgeon's knife to cut away festering flesh. Education, through books, magazines, newspapers, and the public schools will help. But, in the long run, we can never eliminate race-discrimination until a controlling number of the world's population is composed of more emotionally healthy and mature individuals.

Source: *The Family Nobody Wanted* (Boston: Little, Brown, & Co., 1954; reprint, Boston: Northeastern University Press, 2001), 164–65, 166–70.

III Bibliography

13 General Adoption and Child Welfare History References and Online Resources

GENERAL ADOPTION HISTORY

Benet, Mary Kathleen. 1976. *The Politics of Adoption.* New York: Free Press.

Berebitsky, Julie. 2000. *Like Our Very Own: Adoption and the Changing Culture of Motherhood, 1851–1950.* Lawrence: University of Kansas Press.

Cahn, Naomi R. 2003. "Perfect Substitutes or the Real Thing?" *Duke Law Journal* 52 (April): 1077–1166.

Cahn, Naomi R., and Joan Heifetz Hollinger, eds. 2004. *Families by Law: An Adoption Reader.* New York: New York University Press.

Carp, E. Wayne. 1998. *Family Matters: Secrecy and Disclosure in the History of Adoption.* Cambridge, MA: Harvard University Press.

———. 1998b. "Orphanages vs. Adoption: The Triumph of Biological Kinship, 1800–1933." In *With Us Always: A History of Private Charity and Public Welfare,* ed. Donald T. Critchlow and Charles H. Parker, 123–44. Lanham, MD: Rowman and Littlefield.

Carp, E. Wayne, ed. 2002. *Adoption in America: Historical Perspectives.* Ann Arbor: University of Michigan Press.

Kawashima, Yasuhide. 1981–1982. "Adoption in Early America." *Journal of Family Law* 20: 677–96.

Melosh, Barbara. 2002. *Strangers and Kin: The American Way of Adoption.* Cambridge, MA: Harvard University Press.

Modell, Judith Schachter. 1994. *Kinship with Strangers: Adoption and Interpretations of Kinship in American Culture.* Berkeley: University of California Press.

———. 2002. *A Sealed and Secret Kinship: Policies and Practices in American Adoption.* Providence, RI: Berghahn Press.

Sokoloff, Burton Z. 1993. "Antecedents of American Adoption." *The Future of Children* 3, no. 1: 17–25.

Wegar, Katarina. 1997. *Adoption, Identity, and Kinship: The Debate over Sealed Birth Records*. New Haven, CT: Yale University Press.

GENERAL HISTORY OF CHILD WELFARE: KINSHIP CARE, FOSTER CARE, ORPHANAGES, AND NEGLECT AND ABUSE

Ashby, LeRoy. 1997. *Endangered Children: Dependence, Neglect, and Abuse in American History*. New York: Twayne.

Bartholet, Elizabeth. 1999. *Nobody's Children: Abuse and Neglect, Foster Drift, and the Adoption Alternative*. Boston: Beacon Press.

Berrick, Jill Duerr. 1998. "When Children Cannot Remain Home: Foster Family Care and Kinship Care." *Future of Children: Protecting Children from Abuse and Neglect* 8, no. 1: 72–87.

Billingsley, Andrew, and Jeanne M. Giovannoni. 1972. *Children of the Storm: Black Children and American Child Welfare*. New York: Harcourt Brace Jovanovich.

Bremner, Robert et al., eds. 1974. *Children and Youth in America: A Documentary History*. 6 vols. Cambridge, MA: Harvard University Press.

Broad, Bob. 2001. "Kinship Care: Supporting Children in Extended Family and Friends Placement." *Adoption and Fostering* 25, no. 2: 36–52.

Cauthen, Nancy K., and Edwin Amenta. 1996. "Not for Widows Only: Institutional Politics and the Formative Years of Aid to Dependent Children." *American Sociological Review* 61, no. 3: 427–48.

Costin, Lela, Howard Jacob Kargar, and David Stoesz. 1996. *The Politics of Child Abuse in America*. New York: Oxford University Press.

English, P. C. 1984. "Pediatrics and the Unwanted Child in History." *Pediatrics* 73 (May): 699–715.

Folks, Homer. 1902/1978. *The Care of Destitute, Neglected and Delinquent Children*. NASW Classics Series. Washington, DC: National Association of Social Workers.

Gordon, Linda. 1988. *Heroes of Their Own Lives: The Politics and History of Family Violence: Boston, 1880–1960*. New York: Viking.

Hacsi, Timothy A. 1995. "From Indenture to Family Foster Care: A Brief History of Child Placing." *Child Welfare* 74, no. 1: 162–80.

————. 1997. *Second Home: Orphan Asylums and Poor Families in America*. Cambridge, MA: Harvard University Press.

Hegar, Rebecca, and Maria Scannapieco. 1995. "From Family Duty to Family Policy: The Evolution of Kinship Care." *Child Welfare* 74, no. 1: 200–216.

Hegar, Rebecca L., and Maria Scannapieco, eds. 1999. *Kinship Foster Care: Policy, Practice, and Research*. New York: Oxford University Press.

Lindsey, Duncan. 1994. *The Welfare of Children*. New York: Oxford University Press.

Mason, Mary Ann. 1994. *From Father's Property to Children's Rights: The History of Child Custody in America*. New York: Columbia University Press.

Pleck, Elizabeth Hafkin. 1987. *Domestic Tyranny: The Making of Social Policy Against Family Violence from Colonial Times to the Present*. New York: Oxford University Press.

Roberts, Dorothy. 2002. *Shattered Bonds: The Color of Child Welfare*. New York: Basic Books.

Sealander, Judith. 2003. *The Failed Century of the Child: Governing America's Young in the Twentieth Century*. Cambridge: Cambridge University Press.

Smith, Eve P., and Lisa A. Merkel-Holguin, eds. 1996. *A History of Child Welfare*. New Brunswick, NJ: Transaction Publishers.

Youcha, Geraldine. 1995. *Minding the Children: Child Care in America from Colonial Times to the Present*. New York: Scribner.

Zelizer, Viviana A. Rotman. 1985. *Pricing the Priceless Child: The Changing Social Value of Children*. New York: Basic Books.

HISTORY OF U.S. DOMESTIC ADOPTION AND CUSTODY LAW

Ben-Or, Joseph. 1976. "The Law of Adoption in the United States: Its Massachusetts Origins and the Statute of 1851." *New England Historical and Genealogical Register* 130 (October): 259–70.

Brosnan, John F. 1922. "The Law of Adoption." *Columbia Law Review* 22, no. 4: 332–42.

Buell, Carol. 2001. "Legal Issues Affecting Alternative Families: A Therapist's Primer." In *Gay and Lesbian Parenting*, ed. Deborah F. Glazer and Jack Drescher, 7–30. New York: Haworth Medical Press.

Cahn, Naomi R., and Joan Heifetz Hollinger, eds. 2004. *Families by Law: An Adoption Reader*. New York: New York University Press.

Carp, E. Wayne. 2004. *Adoption Politics: Bastard Nation and Ballot Initiative 58*. Lawrence: University Press of Kansas.

Grossberg, Michael. 1985. *Governing the Hearth: Law and the Family in Nineteenth-Century America*. Chapel Hill: University of North Carolina Press.

———. 1993. "Children's Legal Rights? A Historical Look at a Legal Paradox." In *Children at Risk in America: History, Concepts, and Public Policy*, ed. Roberta Wollons, 111–40. Albany: State University of New York Press.

Hawes, Joseph M. 1991. *The Children's Rights Movement: A History of Advocacy and Protection*. Boston: Twayne Publishers.

Hoyt, Edward A., and Michael Sherman. 1996. "Adoption and the Law in Vermont, 1804–1863: An Introductory Essay." *Vermont History* 64 (Summer): 159–73.

Minow, Martha, ed. 1993. *Family Matters: Readings on Family Lives and the Law*. New York: The New Press.

Presser, Stephen B. 1971. "The Historical Background of the American Law of Adoption." *Journal of Family Law* 11: 443–516.

Rentoul, Gervais. 1927. "The State and the Adoption of Children." *Contemporary Review* 131: 59–65.

Zainaldin, Jamil Shaheen. 1976. "The Origins of Modern Legal Adoption: Child Exchange in Boston, 1851–93." Ph.D. diss., University of Chicago.

———. 1979. "The Emergence of a Modern American Family Law: Child Custody, Adoption, and the Courts, 1796–1851." *Northwestern University Law Review* 73, no. 6: 1038–89.

ADOPTION STATISTICS

Bachrach, Christine A. 1986. "Adoption Plans, Adopted Children, and Adoptive Mothers." *Journal of Marriage and the Family* 48, no. 2: 243–53.

Bachrach, Christine A., Katherine Louden, and Penelope Maza. 1991. "On the Path to Adoption: Adoption Seeking in the United States." *Journal of Marriage and the Family* 53, no. 3: 705–18.

Bonham, Gordon Scott. 1977. "Who Adopts? The Relationship of Adoption and Social Demographic Characteristics of Women." *Journal of Marriage and the Family* 39, no. 2: 295–306.

Carp, E. Wayne, and Anna Leon-Guerrero. 2002. "When in Doubt, Count: World War II as a Watershed in the History of Adoption." In *Adoption in America: Historical Perspectives*, ed. E. Wayne Carp, 181–217. Ann Arbor: University of Michigan Press.

Chandra, Anjani et al. 1999. "Adoption, Adoption Seeking, and Relinquishment for Adoption in the United States." *Advance Data from Vital and Health Statistics of the Centers for Disease Control and Prevention/National Center for Health Statistics* 306 (May 11): 1–15.

Evan B. Donaldson Adoption Institute. 1997. *Benchmark Adoption Survey: Report on the Findings*. New York: Evan B. Donaldson Insitute.

Herman, Ellen. 2005. "Adoption Statistics." *Adoption History Project*. http://darkwing.uoregon.edu/~adoption/topics/adoptionstatistics.htm.

Maza, Penelope. 1984. "Adoption Trends: 1944–1975." *Child Welfare Research Notes* 9 (August): 1–4.

Placek, Paul J. 1999. "National Adoption Data." In *Adoption Factbook*. Vol. 3. Collected for National Council for Adoption. Waite Park, MN: Park Press.

Stolley, Kathy S. 1993. "Statistics on Adoption in the United States." *The Future of Children* 3, no. 1: 26–42.

U.S. State Department. 2005. "Immigrant Visas Issued to Orphans Coming to the U.S. 2002–2004." http://travel.state.gov/family/adoption/stats/stats_451.html.

FOSTER CARE STATISTICS

Child Welfare League of America. 2004. "The Health of Children in Out of Home Care." *Child and Family Development: Health Care: Facts and Figures*. http://www.cwla.org/programs/health/healthcarecwfact.htm.

———. 2004b. "Quick Facts About Foster Care." *Child Welfare: Family Foster Care*. http://www.cwla.org/programs/fostercare/factsheet.htm.

Children's Bureau. 2004. "National Adoption and Foster Care Statistics, 1999–2003." *Adoption and Foster Care Analysis and Reporting System (AFCARS)*. August. http://www.acf.hhs.gov/programs/cb/dis/afcars/publications/afcars.htm.

Evan B. Donaldson Adoption Institute. 2002. "Foster Care Facts." *Facts About Adoption*. http://www.adoptioninstitute.org/FactOverview/foster.html.

U.S. Department of Health and Human Services. Administration for Children and Families. 2002. "AFCARS Report." http://www.acf.hhs.gov/programs/cb/publications/afcars/report9.htm.

————. 2002b. "National Adoption and Foster Care Statistics." http://www.acf.hhs.gov/programs/cb/dis/afcars/publications/afcars.htm.

GENERAL ADOPTION REFERENCE BOOKS AND ONLINE RESOURCES

Adamec, Christine A., and William L. Pierce, eds. 1991. *The Encyclopedia of Adoption.* New York: Facts on File. http://encyclopedia.adoption.com/.

Children's Bureau, United States Department of Health and Human Resources. *National Adoption Information Clearinghouse.* http://naic.acf.hhs.gov/.

Evan B. Donaldson Adoption Institute. *Research Resources.* http://www.adoptioninstitute.org/research/intro.html.

Gilman, Lois. 1998. *The Adoption Resource Book.* 4th ed. New York: HarperCollins.

Herman, Ellen. 2003. *The Adoption History Project.* http://darkwing.uoregon.edu/~adoption/.

Miles, Susan Goodrich. 1991. *Adoption Literature for Children and Young Adults: An Annotated Bibliography.* Westport, CT: Greenwood Press.

National Center for Adoption Law and Policy. 2005. Adoption LawSite. http://www.adoptionlawsite.org/main_cur.asp.

Niles, Reg. 1981. *Adoption Agencies, Orphanages, and Maternity Homes: An Historical Directory.* Garden City, NY: Phileas Deigh Corp.

ADOPTION INFORMATION/RESEARCH ORGANIZATIONS

Adopt US Kids. United States Children's Bureau. http://www.adoptuskids.org/.

Adoption Media LLC. Adoption.Com: Adoption Community. 459 N. Gilbert Rd., Suite C-100, Gilbert, AZ 85234. http://www.adoption.com/ and http://www.adoption.org.

Evan B. Donaldson Adoption Institute. 525 Broadway, 6th floor, New York, NY 10012. http://www.adoptioninstitute.org/.

North American Council on Adoptable Children. 970 Raymond Avenue, Suite 106, St. Paul, MN 55114. http://www.nacac.org.

NATIONAL PRO- AND ANTI-ADOPTION ADVOCACY GROUPS

The Alma Society: Adoptees' Liberty Movement Society. P.O. Box 85, Denville, NJ 07834. http://almasociety.org/.

American Adoption Congress: Families Rooted in Truth. 1000 Connecticut Ave., NW, Suite 9, Washington, DC 20036. http://www.americanadoptioncongress.org/.

Bastard Nation: The Adoptee Rights Organization. P.O. Box 271672, Houston, TX 77277-1672. http://www.bastards.org/.

Concerned United Birthparents. P.O. Box 503475, San Diego, CA 92150. http://www.cubirthparents.org/.

National Council for Adoption. 225 N. Washington St., Alexandria, VA 22314-2561. http://www.adoptioncouncil.org/.

Transracial Abductees. http://www.transracialabductees.org/index.html.

CHILD WELFARE ORGANIZATIONS (RESEARCH AND/OR ADVOCACY, ESPECIALLY RELEVANT TO FOSTER AND KINSHIP CARE)

ABA Center on Children and the Law. 740 15th Street, NW, Washington, DC 20005. http://www.abanet.org/child/.

The Annie E. Casey Foundation (and the AECF "Kids Count" Project). 701 St. Paul St., Baltimore, MD 21202. http://www.aecf.org/.

Chapin Hall Center for Children. University of Chicago, 1313 East 60th Street, Chicago, IL 60637. http://www.chapinhall.org/home_new.asp.

Child Welfare League of America. 440 First St. NW, Third Floor, Washington, DC 20001-2085. http://www.cwla.org/.

Child Welfare Research Institute. Duncan Lindsey, Professor of Social Work, UCLA, Los Angeles, CA. http://www.childwelfare.com/.

Children Now: Child Advocacy Home Page. 1212 Broadway, 5th Floor, Oakland, CA 94612. http://www.childrennow.org/.

Children's Defense Fund. 25 E Street NW, Washington, DC 20001. http://www.childrensdefense.org/.

Families USA. 1334 G Street NW, Washington, DC 20005. http://www.familiesusa.org/.

Fostering Results. Children & Family Research Center. 2 N. LaSalle, Suite 1700, Chicago, IL 60602. http://www.fosteringresults.org/.

Future of Children. The Woodrow Wilson School of Public and International Affairs. Princeton University and The Brookings Institute. http://www.futureofchildren.org/.

Generations United, National Center on Grandparents and Other Relatives Raising Children. 1333 H Street, NW, Suite 500 W, Washington, DC 20005. http://www.gu.org/projg&o.asp.

National Association of Black Social Workers. 1220 11th Street, NW, Washington, DC 20001. http://www.nabsw.org/.

National Center for Children in Poverty. Columbia University, Mailman School of Public Health. 215 W. 125th Street, 3rd Floor, New York, NY 10027. http://www.nccp.org/.

National Child Welfare Resource Center on Legal and Judicial Issues. (A Service of the Children's Bureau.) http://www.abanet.org/child/rclji/.

National Clearinghouse on Child Abuse & Neglect Information. Administration for Children and Families, U.S. Deparment of Health and Human Services. http://nccanch.acf.hhs.gov/index.cfm.

National Indian Child Welfare Association. 5100 SW Macadam Avenue, Suite 300, Portland, OR 97239. http://www.nicwa.org/index.asp.

Pew Charitable Trusts. 2005 Market Street, Suite 1700, Philadelphia, PA 19103-7077. http://www.pewtrusts.com/.

Pew Commission on Children in Foster Care. 2233 Wisconsin Avenue, NW, Suite 535, Washington, DC 20007. http://pewfostercare.org/.

Urban Institute. "Child Welfare Research." 2100 M Street, NW, Washington, DC 20037. http://www.urban.org/content/IssuesInFocus/childwelfareresearch /childwelfare.htm.

14 Orphans, Orphanages, and Orphan Stories: Early Forms of Adoption and Fostering in Multicultural and Interdisciplinary Perspectives

ORPHANS AND ADOPTION: ANTHROPOLOGICAL PERSPECTIVES

Brady, Ivan, ed. 1976. *Transactions in Kinship: Adoption and Fosterage in Oceania.* Honolulu: University of Hawaii Press.

Goody, Jack. 1969. "Adoption in Cross-Cultural Perspective." *Comparative Studies in Society and History* 11, no. 1: 55–78.

———. 1983. *The Development of Family and Marriage in Europe.* Cambridge: Cambridge University Press.

Luomala, Katharine. 1987. "Reality and Fantasy: The Foster Child in Hawaiian Myths and Customs." *Pacific Studies* 10, no. 2: 1–45.

Modell, Judith. 1994. *Kinship with Strangers: Adoption and Interpretations of Kinship in American Culture.* Berkeley: University of California Press.

———. 2002. *A Sealed and Secret Kinship: Policies and Practices in American Adoption.* Providence, RI: Berghahn Press.

Terrell, John E., and Judith Modell. 1994. "Anthropology and Adoption." *American Anthropologist* 96, no. 1: 155–61.

NORTH AMERICAN INDIAN FAMILY STRUCTURES AND ADOPTION

Bentz, Marilyn G. 1996. "Child Rearing." In *Encyclopedia of North American Indians,* ed. Frederick E. Hoxie, 115–18. Boston: Houghton Mifflin. Full-text at: college.hmco.com/history/readerscomp/naind/html/na_007000_childrearing.htm.

Gutiérrez, Ramón. 1991. *When Jesus Came the Corn Mothers Went Away: Marriage, Sexuality and Power in New Mexico, 1500–1846.* Palo Alto, CA: Stanford University Press.

Hirschfelder, Arlene, ed. 1995. *Native Heritage: Personal Accounts by American Indians, 1790 to the Present.* New York: Macmillan.

Kan, Sergie, ed. 2001. *Strangers to Relatives: The Adoption and Naming of Anthropologists in Native North America.* Lincoln: University of Nebraska Press.

Lismer, Marjorie. 1974. "Adoption Practices of the Blood Indians of Alberta, Canada." *Plains Anthropologist* 19, no. 3: 25–33.

McGoun, William E. 1984. "Adoption of Whites by 18th Century Cherokees." *Journal of Cherokee Studies* 9, no. 1: 37–41.

Miller, Jay. 1996. "Families." In *Encyclopedia of North American Indians*, ed. Frederick E. Hoxie, 192–97. Boston: Houghton Mifflin. Full-text at: college.hmco. com/history/readerscomp/naind/html/na_011700_families.htm.

———. 2004. "Kinship, Family Kindreds, and Community." In *A Companion to American Indian History*, ed. Phillip J. Deloria and Neal Salisbury, 139–53. Malden, MA: Blackwell.

Moulin, Sylvie. 1991. "Nobody Is an Orphan." *Studies in American Indian Literatures: The Journal of the Association for the Study of American Indian Literatures* 3, no. 3: 14–18.

Perdue, Theda. 1979. *Slavery and the Evolution of the Cherokee Society, 1540–1866.* Knoxville: University of Tennessee Press.

Petershoare, Lillian. 1985. "Tlingit Adoption Practices, Past and Present." *American Indian Culture and Research Journal* 9, no. 2: 1–32.

Strong, Pauline Turner. 1999. *Captive Selves, Captivating Others: The Politics and Poetics of Colonial American Captivity Narratives.* Boulder, CO: Westview/Perseus.

———. 2002. "Transforming Outsiders: Captivity, Adoption, and Slavery Reconsidered." In *A Companion to American Indian History*, ed. Phillip J. Deloria and Neal Salisbury, 339–56. Malden, MA: Blackwell.

Szasz, Margaret Connell. 1988. *Indian Education in the American Colonies, 1607–1783.* Albuquerque: University of New Mexico Press.

ROOTS: FROM WEST AFRICAN FOSTERING TRADITIONS TO EARLY AFRICAN AMERICAN FLEXIBLE FAMILY STRUCTURES

Billingsley, Andrew. 1968. *Black Families in White America.* Englewood Cliffs, NJ: Prentice-Hall.

———. 1992. *Climbing Jacob's Ladder: The Enduring Legacy of Afro-American Families.* New York: Simon & Schuster.

Bledsoe, Caroline. 1993. "The Politics of Polygyny in Mende Education and Child Fosterage Transactions." In *Sex and Gender Hierarchies*, ed. Barbara D. Miller, 170–92. Cambridge: Cambridge University Press.

Bledsoe, Caroline, and Uche C. Isiugo-Abhanihe. 1989. "Strategies of Child Fosterage Among Mende 'Grannies.' " In *African Reproduction and Social Organi-*

zation in Sub-Saharan Africa, ed. Ron Lesthaegue, 442–75. Berkeley: University of California Press.

Dill, Bonnie Thornton. 1998. "Fictive Kin, Paper Sons, and *Commpadrazgo*: Women of Color and the Struggle for Family Survival." In *Families in the U.S.: Kinship and Domestic Politics*, ed. Karen V. Hansen and Anita Ilta Garey, 431–45. Philadelphia: Temple University Press.

Du Bois, W.E.B. 1909/1970. *The Negro American Family*. Cambridge, MA: MIT Press.

Goody, Esther N. 1982. *Parenthood and Social Reproduction: Fostering and Occupational Roles in West Africa*. Cambridge: Cambridge University Press.

Hill, Robert B. 1977. *Informal Adoptions Among Black Families*. Washington, DC: National Urban League.

———. 1999. *The Strengths of African American Families: Twenty-Five Years Later*. Rev. ed. Lanham, MD: University Press of America.

Holmes, Gilbert A. 1995. "The Extended Family System in the Black Community: A Child-Centered Model for Adoption Policy." *Temple Law Review* 68: 1649–85. Excerpted in *Families by Law: An Adoption Reader*, ed. Naomi R. Cahn and Joan Heifetz Hollinger, 119–22. New York: New York University Press.

Penningroth, Dylan C. 2003. *The Claims of Kinfolk: African American Property and Community in the Deep South*. Chapel Hill: University of North Carolina Press.

Stack, Carol. 1974. *All Our Kin: Strategies for Survival in a Black Community*. New York: Harper and Row.

Sudarkasa, Niara. 1980. "African and Afro-American Family Structure: A Comparison." *Black Scholar* 11, no. 1: 37–60.

———. 1998. "Interpreting the African Heritage in Afro-American Family Organizaiton." In *Families in the U.S.: Kinship and Domestic Politics*, ed. Karen V. Hansen and Anita Ilta Garey, 91–104. Philadelphia: Temple University Press.

EUROPEAN MODELS: INDENTURESHIPS, APPRENTICESHIPS, AND INFORMAL ADOPTION

Ashby, LeRoy. 1997. *Endangered Children: Dependency, Neglect, and Abuse in American History*. New York: Twayne.

Behlmer, George. 2002. "What's Love Got to Do with It? 'Adoption' in Victorian and Edwardian England." In *Adoption in America: Historical Perspectives*, ed. E. Wayne Carp, 82–100. Ann Arbor: University of Michigan Press.

Bremner, Robert et al., eds. 1974. *Children and Youth in America: A Documentary History*. 6 vols. Cambridge, MA: Harvard University Press.

Brundage, Anthony. 1998. "Private Charity and the 1834 Poor Law." In *With Us Always: A History of Private Charity and Public Welfare*, ed. Donald T. Critchlow and Charles H. Parker, 99–119. Lanham, MD: Rowman and Littlefield.

Goody, Jack. 1983. *The Development of Family and Marriage in Europe*. Cambridge: Cambridge University Press.

Jernegan, Marcus W. 1931. *Laboring and Dependent Classes in Colonial America, 1607–1783*. Chicago: University of Chicago Press.

Mason, Mary Ann. 1994. *From Father's Property to Children's Rights: The History of Child Custody in America*. New York: Columbia University Press.

Sokoloff, Burton Z. 1993. "Antecedents of American Adoption." *The Future of Children* 3, no. 1: 17–25.

Towner, Lawrence W. 1962. "The Indentures of Boston's Poor Apprentices, 1734–1805." *Proceedings of the Colonial Society of Massachusetts* 43: 417–34.

Youcha, Geraldine. 1995. *Minding the Children: Child Care in America from Colonial Times to the Present*. New York: Scribner.

CHILD-SAVING: PLACING-OUT, ORPHAN TRAINS, AND EARLY FORMS OF FOSTER CARE

Bellingham, Bruce. 1983. "The 'Unspeakable Blessing': Street Children, Reform Rhetoric, and Misery in Early Industrial Capitalism." *Politics and Society* 12, no. 3: 303–30.

———. 1984. " 'Little Wanderers': A Socio-Historical Study of the Nineteenth-Century Origins of Child Fostering and Adoption Reforms, Based on Early Records of the New York Children's Aid Society." Ph.D. diss., University of Pennsylvania.

———. 1986. "Institution and Family: An Alternative View of Nineteenth-Century Child Saving." *Social Problems* 33, no. 6: S33–57.

———. 1990. "Waifs and Strays: Child Abandonment, Foster Care, and Families in Mid-Nineteenth Century New York." In *The Uses of Charity: The Poor on Relief in the Mid-Nineteenth Century Metropolis*, ed. Peter Mandler, 123–60. Philadelphia: University of Pennsylvania Press.

Brophy, A. Blake. 1972. *Foundlings on the Frontier: Racial and Religious Conflict in Arizona Territory, 1904–1905*. Tucson: University of Arizona Press.

Cook, Jeanne F. 1995. "A History of Placing-Out: The Orphan Trains." *Child Welfare* 74, no. 1: 181–93.

Crenson, Matthew A. 1998. *Building the Invisible Orphanage: The Prehistory of the American Welfare System*. Cambridge, MA: Harvard University Press.

Hacsi, Tim. 1995. "From Indenture to Family Foster Care: A Brief History of Child Placing." *Child Welfare* 74, no. 1: 162–80.

Holloran, Peter C. 1989. *Boston's Wayward Children: Social Services for Homeless Children, 1830–1930*. Rutherford, NJ: Fairleigh Dickinson University Press.

Holt, Marilyn Irvin. 1992. *The Orphan Trains: Placing Out in America*. Lincoln: University of Nebraska Press.

Jones, Sondra. 1999. " 'Redeeming' the Indian: The Enslavement of Indian Children in New Mexico and Utah." *Utah Historical Quarterly* 67, no. 3: 220–41.

Kidder, Clark. 2001. *Orphan Trains and Their Precious Cargo: The Life's Work of Rev. H. D. Clarke*. Bowie, MD: Heritage Books.

Morton, Marian J. 2000. "Institutionalizing Inequalities: Black Children and Child Welfare in Cleveland, 1859–1998." *Journal of Social History* 34, no. 1: 141–62.

O'Connor, Stephen. 2001. *Orphan Trains: The Story of Charles Loring Brace and the Children He Saved and Failed.* Boston: Houghton Mifflin.

Vogt, Martha Nelson, and Christina Vogt. 1983. *Searching for Home: Three Families from the Orphan Trains.* Grand Rapids, MI: Triumph Press.

ORPHANAGES (INCLUDING CATHOLIC AND JEWISH CHILD SERVICES)

Abrams, Jeanne. 1989–1990. "For a Child's Sake: The Denver Sheltering Home for Jewish Children in the Progressive Era." *American Jewish History* 79, no. 2: 181–202.

Bellingham, Bruce. 1986. "Institution and Family: An Alternative View of Nineteenth-Century Child Saving." *Social Problems* 33, no. 6: S33–S53.

Bellows, Barbara. 1993. *Benevolence Among Slaveholders: Assisting the Poor in Charleston, 1670–1860.* Baton Rouge: Louisiana State University Press.

Bogan, Hyman. 1992. *The Luckiest Orphans: A History of the Hebrew Orphan Asylum of New York.* Urbana: University of Illinois Press.

Brown, Dorothy M., and Elizabeth McKeown. 1997. *The Poor Belong to Us: Catholic Charities and American Welfare.* Cambridge, MA: Harvard University Press.

Carp, E. Wayne. 1998. "Orphanages vs. Adoption: The Triumph of Biological Kinship, 1800–1933." In *With Us Always: A History of Private Charity and Public Welfare*, ed. Donald T. Critchlow and Charles H. Parker, 123–44. Lanham, MD: Rowman and Littlefield.

Clement, Priscilla Ferguson. 1986. "Children and Charity: Orphanages in New Orleans, 1817–1914." *Louisiana History* 27, no. 4: 337–51.

Cmiel, Kenneth. 1995. *A Home of Another Kind: One Chicago Orphanage and the Tangle of Child Welfare.* Chicago: University of Chicago Press.

Downs, Susan Whitelaw, and Michael Sherraden. 1983. "The Orphan Asylum in the Nineteenth Century." *Social Service Review* 57 (June): 272–90.

Dulberger, Judith A. 1996. *"Mother Donit Fore the Best": Correspondence of a Nineteenth-Century Orphan Asylum.* Syracuse, NY: Syracuse University Press.

Fink, Arthur E. 1971. "Changing Philosophies and Practices in North Carolina Orphanages." *North Carolina Historical Review* 48 (October): 333–58.

Frey, Cecile P. 1981. "The House of Refuge for Colored Children." *The Journal of Negro History* 66, no. 1: 10–25.

Friedman, Reena Sigman. 1994. *These Are Our Children: Jewish Orphanages in the United States, 1880–1925.* Hanover, NH: Brandeis University Press.

Hasci, Timothy A. 1997. *Second Home: Orphan Asylums and Poor Families in America.* Cambridge, MA: Harvard University Press.

Holt, Marilyn Irvin. 2001. *Indian Orphanages.* Lawrence: University Press of Kansas.

Jones, Marshall B. 1989. "Crisis of the American Orphanage, 1931–1940." *Social Service Review* 63 (December): 613–29.

Katz, Michael. 1986. *In the Shadow of the Poorhouse: A Social History of Welfare in America.* New York: Basic Books.

Morton, Marian J. 2000b. "Surviving the Great Depression: Orphanages and Orphans in Cleveland." *Journal of Urban History* 26, no. 4: 438–55.

Pfeffer, Paula F. 2002. "A Historical Comparison of Catholic and Jewish Adoption Practices in Chicago, 1833–1933." In *Adoption in America: Historical Perspectives,* ed. E. Wayne Carp, 101–23. Ann Arbor: University of Michigan Press.

Polster, Gary Edward. 1990. *Inside Looking Out: The Cleveland Jewish Orphan Asylum, 1868–1924.* Kent, OH: Kent State University Press.

Porter, Susan L. 2002. "A Good Home: Indenture and Adoption in Nineteenth-Century Orphanages." In *Adoption in America: Historical Perspectives,* ed. E. Wayne Carp, 27–50. Ann Arbor: University of Michigan Press.

Rothman, David. 1971. *The Discovery of the Asylum: Social Order and Disorder in the New Republic.* Boston: Little, Brown.

Witmer, Nancy J. "The Mennonite Children's Home, 1909–1972." *Pennsylvania Mennonite Heritage* 8, no. 4: 2–12.

Zmora, Nurith. 1994. *Orphanages Reconsidered: Child Care Institutions in Progressive Era Baltimore.* Philadelphia: Temple University Press.

THE PROGRESSIVE ERA "DISCOVERY" OF CHILD ABUSE AND THE BEGINNINGS OF CHILD WELFARE PROFESSIONALIZATION, 1890s–1940s

Anderson, Paul Gerard. 1989. "The Origin, Emergence, and Professional Recognition of Child Protection." *Social Service Review* 63, no. 2: 222–44.

Ashby, LeRoy. 1984. *Saving the Waifs: Reformers and Dependent Children, 1890–1917.* Philadelphia: Temple University Press.

Balcom, Karen. 2002. "The Traffic in Babies: Cross-Border Adoption, Baby-Selling, and the Development of Child Welfare Systems in the United States and Canada, 1930–1960." Ph.D. diss., Rutgers University.

Billingsley, Andrew, and Jeanne M. Giovannoni. 1972. *Children of the Storm: Black Children and American Child Welfare.* New York: Harcourt, Brace, Jovanovich.

Bremner, Robert H., ed. 1974. *Care of Dependent Children in the Late Nineteenth and Early Twentieth Century.* New York: Arno Press.

Broder, Sherri. 2002. *Tramps, Unfit Mothers, and Neglected Children: Negotiating the Family in Nineteenth-Century Philadelphia.* Philadelphia: University of Pennsylvania Press.

Costin, Lela B. 1991. "Unraveling the Mary Ellen Legend: Origins of the 'Cruelty' Movement." *Social Service Review* 65, no. 2: 203–24.

Costin, Lela B., Howard Jacob Karger, and David Stoesz. 1996. *The Politics of Child Abuse in America, Child Welfare.* New York: Oxford University Press.

Cravens, Hamilton. "Child Saving in Modern America, 1870s–1990s." In *Children at Risk in America: History, Concepts, Public Policy,* ed. Roberta Wollons, 3–31. Albany: State University of New York Press.

Gittens, Joan. 1994. *Poor Relations: The Children of the State in Illinois, 1818–1990*. Urbana: University of Illinois Press.

Gordon, Linda. 1988. *Heroes of Their Own Lives: The Politics and History of Family Violence: Boston, 1880–1960*. New York: Viking.

Herman, Ellen. 2005. "Baby Farming." *The Adoption History Project*. http://darkwing.uoregon.edu/~adoption/topics/babyfarming.html.

Ladd-Taylor, Molly. 1994. *Mother-Work: Women, Child Welfare, and the State, 1890–1930*. Urbana: University of Illinois Press.

Lindenmeyer, Kriste. 1997. *"A Right to Childhood": The U.S. Children's Bureau and Child Welfare*. Urbana: University of Illinois Press.

Muncy, Robin. 1991. *Creating a Female Dominion in American Reform, 1890–1935*. New York: Oxford University Press.

O'Donnell, Sandra M. 1994. "The Care of Dependent African American Children in Chicago: The Struggle Between Black Self-Help and Professionalism." *Journal of Social History* 27, no. 4: 763–76.

Pleck, Elizabeth Hafkin. 1987. *Domestic Tyranny: The Making of Social Policy Against Family Violence from Colonial Times to the Present*. New York: Oxford University Press.

Stehno, Sandra M. 1985. "Foster Care for Dependent Black Children in Chicago, 1899–1934." Ph.D. diss., University of Chicago.

Tiffin, Susan. 1982. *In Whose Best Interest? Child Welfare Reform in the Progressive Era*. Westport, CT: Greenwood Press.

Walker, George. 1918. *The Traffic in Babies: An Analysis of the Conditions Discovered During an Investigation Conducted in the Year 1914*. Baltimore, MD: The Norman, Remington Co.

Zelizer, Viviana A. 1988. "From Baby Farms to Baby M." *Society* 25 (March/April): 23–28.

ORPHAN STORIES: NARRATIVES, ANTHOLOGIES, AND LITERARY STUDIES OF ADOPTION, FOSTER CARE, AND DEPENDENT CHILDREN

Adoption Narratives

General Anthologies of Narratives by Adoptees, Birth Parents, and Adoptive Parents

Casey, Fills, and Marisa Catalina Casey. 2004. *Born in Our Hearts: Stories of Adoption*. Deerfield Beach, FL: Health Communications.

Horner, Susan E. 2002. *Loved by Choice: True Stories that Celebrate Adoption*. Grand Rapids, MI: Fleming H. Revell.

Kltazkin, Amy, ed. 1999. *A Passage to the Heart: Writings from Families with Children from China*. St. Paul, MN: Yeoung & Yeoung Book Company.

Wadia-Ells, Susan, ed. 1995. *The Adoption Reader: Birth Mothers, Adoptive Mothers and Adopted Daughters Tell Their Stories*. Seattle: Seal Press, 1995.

Adoptees: Selected Narratives and Anthologies

Ehrlich, Henry. 1977. *A Time to Search: The Moving and Dramatic Stories of Adoptees in Search of Their Parents.* New York: Paddington.

Eldridge, Sherrie. 1999. *Twenty Things Adopted Kids Wish Their Adoptive Parents Knew.* New York: Random House.

Fisher, Florence. 1973. *The Search for Anna Fisher.* New York: Arthur Fields Books.

John, Jaiya. 2002. *Black Baby, White Hands: A View from the Crib.* Silver Springs, MD: Soul Water Publishers.

Krementz, Jill, ed. 1982. *How It Feels to Be Adopted.* New York: Knopf.

Lifton, Betty Jean. 1975. *Twice Born: Memoirs of an Adopted Daughter.* New York: McGraw-Hill.

MacLeod, Jean. 2003. *At Home in This World: A China Adoption Story.* Warren, NJ: EMK Press.

Mah, Adeline Yen. 1997. *Falling Leaves: The Memoir of an Unwanted Chinese Daughter.* New York: Michael Joseph/Penguin.

Paton, Jean. 1954. *The Adopted Break Silence: The Experiences and Views of Forty Adults Who Were Adopted as Children.* Philadelphia: Life History Study Center.

——— (Ruthena Hill Kittson). 1968. *Orphan Voyage.* New York: Vantage.

Saffian, Sarah. 1998. *Ithaka: A Daughter's Memoir of Being Found.* New York: Basic Books.

Silber, Kathleen, and Phyllis Speedlin. 1991. *Dear Birthmother.* San Antonio, TX: Corona Publishing.

Simon, Rita James. 2000. *In Their Own Voices: Transracial Adoptees Tell Their Stories.* New York: Columbia University Press.

Trenka, Jane-Jeong. 2003. *The Language of Blood: A Memoir.* St. Paul, MN: Borealis Books.

Wilkinson, Sook, and Nancy Fox, eds. 2002. *After the Morning Calm: Reflections of Korean Adoptees.* Detroit: Sunrise Ventures.

Birth Parents: Selected Narratives and Anthologies

Dorris, Michael. 1990. *The Broken Cord.* New York: HarperCollins.

Dusky, Lorraine. 1979. *The Birthmark.* New York: M. Evans and Co.

Jones, Merry Bloch. 1993. *Birthmothers: Women Who Relinquish Babies for Adoption Tell Their Stories.* Chicago: Chicago Review Press.

Kane, Beth J. 1999. *Thank You, Son, for Finding Me: A Birthmother's Story.* Fairfield, CT: Aslan Publishers.

Loux, Ann Kimble. 1997. *The Limits of Hope: An Adoptive Mother's Story.* Charlottesville: University Press of Virginia.

Mason, Mary Martin. 1995. *Out of the Shadows: Birthfathers' Stories.* Edina, MN: O. J. Howard.

Schaefer, Carol. 1991. *The Other Mother: A Woman's Love for the Child She Gave Up for Adoption.* New York: Soho Press.

Townsend, Rita, and Ann Perkins, eds. 1991. *Bitter Fruit: Women's Experiences of Un-
    planned Pregnancy, Abortion, and Adoption.* Alameda, CA: Hunter House.

Adoptive Parents

Bates, J. Douglas. 1993. *Gift Children: A Story of Race, Family, and Adoption in a Di-
    vided America.* New York: Ticknor & Fields.

Champnella, Cindy. 2003. *The Waiting Child: How the Faith and Love of One Orphan
    Saved Another.* New York: St. Martin's Press.

Evans, Karin. 2000. *The Lost Daughters of China: Abandoned Girls, Their Journey to Amer-
    ica, and the Search for a Missing Past.* New York: Jeremy P. Tarcher/Penguin.

Garlock, Terry L. 2001. *Melanie and Me: A Chinese Daughter Transforms Her Adoptive
    Dad.* New York: Xlibris.

Green, Jesse. 1999. *The Velveteen Father: An Unexpected Journey to Parenthood.* New York:
    Random/Ballantine.

Rush, Sharon E. 2000. *Loving Across the Color Line: A White Adoptive Mother Learns
    About Race.* Lanham, MD: Rowman and Littlefield.

Savage, Dan. 1999. *The Kid: What Happened After My Boyfriend and I Decided to Go Get
    Pregnant: An Adoption Story.* New York: Dutton.

Winter, Marjorie. 1956. *For the Love of Martha.* New York: Julian Messner.

Wolff, Jana. 1999. *Secret Thoughts of an Adoptive Mother.* Kansas City, MO: Andrews
    and McMeel.

Woodard, Sarah L. 2002. *Daughter from Afar: A Family's International Adoption Story.*
    New York: Writer's Club Press.

Twentieth-Century Foster Care/Orphanage Narratives and Anthologies

Buchwald, Art. 1992. *Leaving Home: A Memoir.* New York: Penguin.

Burch, Jennings Michael. 1984. *They Cage the Animals at Night: The True Story of a
    Child Who Learned to Survive.* New York: Penguin/Signet.

Desetta, Al, ed. 1996. *The Heart Knows Something Different: Teenage Voices from the Fos-
    ter Care System.* By "Youth Communication." New York: Persea Books.

Harrison, Kathryn. 2003. *Another Place at the Table: A Story of Shattered Childhoods Re-
    deemed by Love.* New York: Jeremy P. Tarcher/Putnam.

McKenzie, Richard. 1996. *The Home: A Memoir of Growing Up in an Orphanage.* New
    York: Basic Books.

McLain, Paula. 2003. *Like Family: Growing Up in Other People's Houses: A Memoir.*
    Boston: Little, Brown.

Parent, Marc. 1998. *Turning Stones: My Days and Nights with Children at Risk: A Case-
    worker's Story.* New York: Ballantine Books.

Pelzer, Dave. 1995. *A Child Called "It": One Child's Courage to Survive.* Deerfield
    Beach, FL: Health Communications.

Selected Scholarship on Adoption, Foster Care, and Displaced Children in American Literature

Amiran, Minda Rae. 1992. " 'She Was Wildly Clad': Orphan Girls in Earlier Children's Literature." *The Mid-Atlantic Almanac* 1: 85–92

Askeland, Lori. 1998. " 'The Means of Draining the City of These Children': Domesticity and Romantic Individualism in Charles Loring Brace's Emigration Plan, 1853–1861." *American Transcendental Quarterly* 12, no. 2: 145–62.

———. 2003. " 'Has a Mother a Right to Her Children?': Fanny Fern's Urban Sketches and the 'Birth' of Foster Care and Legalized Adoption in Mid-Nineteenth Century America." *a/b: auto/biography studies* 18, no. 2: 171–95.

Baym, Nina. 1978. *Woman's Fiction: A Guide to Novels by and about Women in America, 1820–1870.* Ithaca, NY: Cornell University Press.

Berebitsky, Julie. 2000. *Like Our Very Own: Adoption and the Changing Culture of Motherhood, 1851–1950.* Lawrence: University Press of Kansas.

———. 2001. "Redefining 'Real' Motherhood: Representations of Adoptive Mothers, 1900–1950." In *Imagining Adoption: Essays on Literature and Culture,* ed. Marianne Novy, 83–96. Ann Arbor: University of Michigan Press.

———. 2002. "Rescue a Child and Save the Nation: The Social Construction of Adoption in *The Delineator,* 1907–1911." In *Adoption in America: Historical Perspectives,* ed. E. Wayne Carp, 124–39. Ann Arbor: University of Michigan Press.

Castaneda, Claudia. 2001. "Incorporating the Transnational Adoptee." In *Imagining Adoption: Essays on Literature and Culture,* ed. Marianne Novy, 277–301. Ann Arbor: University of Michigan Press.

———. 2002. "Available Childhood: Race, Culture, and the Transitional Adoptee." In *Figurations: Child, Bodies, Worlds.* Durham, NC: Duke University Press.

Craft, Linda J. 1995. "International Adoption as a Fictional Construct: Francisco Goldman's *The Long Night of the White Chickens.*" *RLA: Romance Languages Annual* 7: 430–35.

Deans, Jill R. 1999. "Albee's Substitute Children: Reading Adoption as a Performance." *Journal of Dramatic Theory and Criticism* 13, no. 2: 57–79.

———. 2000. "Horton's Irony: Reading the Culture of Embryo Adoption." *Interdisciplinary Literary Studies: A Journal of Criticism and Theory* 2, no. 1: 1–20.

———. 2001. "Performing the Search in Adoption Autobiography: *Finding Christa* and *Reno Finds Her Mom.*" *Biography: An Interdisciplinary Quarterly* 24, no. 1: 85–98.

———. 2003. "The Birth of Contemporary Adoption Autobiography: Florence Fisher and Betty Jean Lifton." *a/b: auto/biography studies* 18, no. 2: 239–58.

Hipchen, Emily, and Jill R. Dean, eds. 2003. Introduction. Special Issue: "Adoption Life Writing: Origins and Other Ghosts." *a/b: auto/biography studies* 18, no. 2: 163–70.

Kraus, Barbara. 2003. "Bastard Logic and the Epics of Female Illegitimacy." *a/b: auto/biography studies* 18, no. 2: 196–218.

Melosh, Barbara. 2002. "Adoption Stories: Autobiographical Narrative and the Politics of Identity." In *Adoption in America: Historical Perspectives,* ed. E. Wayne Carp, 218–45. Ann Arbor: University of Michigan Press.

Miles, Susan G., ed. 1991. *Adoption Literature for Children and Young Adults: An Annotated Bibliography.* Westport, CT: Greenwood Press.

Modell, Judith. 2001. "Natural Bonds, Legal Boundaries: Modes of Persuasion in Adoption Rhetoric." In *Imagining Adoption: Essays on Literature and Culture,* ed. Marianne Novy, 207–30. Ann Arbor: University of Michigan Press.

Moulin, Sylvie. 1991. "Nobody Is an Orphan." *Studies in American Indian Literatures: The Journal of the Association for the Study of American Indian Literatures* 3, no. 3: 14–18.

Nelson, Claudia. 2001. "Drying the Orphan's Tear: Changing Representations of the Dependent Child in America, 1870–1930." *Children's Literature: Annual of The Modern Language Association Division on Children's Literature and The Children's Literature Association* 29: 52–70.

———. 2001b. "Nontraditional Adoption in Progressive-Era Orphan Narratives." *Mosaic: A Journal for the Interdisciplinary Study of Literature* 34, no. 2: 181–97.

———. 2003. *Little Strangers: Portrayals of Adoption and Foster Care in America, 1850–1929.* Bloomington: Indiana University Press.

Novy, Marianne, ed. 2001. *Imagining Adoption: Essays on Literature and Culture.* Ann Arbor: University of Michigan Press.

———. 2005. *Reading Adoption: Family and Difference in Fiction and Drama.* Ann Arbor: University of Michigan Press.

Park, Shelley. 2005. "Real (M)othering: The Metaphysics of Maternity in Children's Literature." In *Adoption Matters: Philosophical and Feminist Essays,* ed. Sally Haslanger and Charlotte Witt, 171–94. Ithaca, NY: Cornell University Press.

Patton, Sandra. 1996. "Race/Identity/Culture/Kin: Constructions of African American Identity in Transracial Adoption." In *Getting a Life: Everyday Uses of Autobiography,* ed. Sidonie Smith and Julia Watson, 271–96. Minneapolis: University of Minnesota Press.

———. 2000. *Birth Marks: Transracial Adoption in Contemporary America.* New York: New York University Press.

Singley, Carol J. 2002. "Building a Nation, Building a Family: Adoption in Nineteenth Century American Children's Literature." In *Adoption in America: Historical Perspectives,* ed. E. Wayne Carp, 51–81. Ann Arbor: University of Michigan Press.

Treacher, Amal, and Ilan Katz. 2001. "Narrative and Fantasy in Adoption." *Adoption and Fostering* 25, no. 3: 20–28.

Wirth-Nesher, Hana. 1986. "The Literary Orphan as National Hero: Huck and Pip." *Dickens Studies Annual: Essays on Victorian Fiction* 15: 259–73.

Wong, Hertha. 1991. "Adoptive Mothers and Thrown-Away Children in the Novels of Louise Erdrich." In *Narrating Mothers: Theorizing Maternal Subjectivities,* ed. Brenda O. Daly and Maureen T. Reddy, 176–92. Knoxville: University of Tennessee Press.

15 Secrecy and Adoption: Infertility, Illegitimacy, Parental "Fitness" Standards, and the Move to Openness in the Twentieth Century

THE PROFESSIONALIZATION OF ADOPTION IN THE EARLY TWENTIETH CENTURY: "MATCHING" POLICIES, FITNESS TESTS, AND MINIMUM STANDARDS

Austin, Linda Tollett. 1993. *Babies for Sale: The Tennessee Children's Home Adoption Scandal.* Westport, CT: Praeger.

Bartholet, Elizabeth. 2004. "Adoption and the Parental Screening System." In *Families by Law: An Adoption Reader*, ed. Naomi R. Cahn and Joan Heifetz Hollinger, 72–74. New York: New York University Press.

Berebitsky, Julie. 2000. *Like Our Very Own: Adoption and the Changing Culture of Motherhood, 1851–1950.* Lawrence: University of Kansas Press.

Bernstein, Nina. 2001. *The Lost Children of Wilder: The Epic Struggle to Change Foster Care.* New York: Pantheon Books.

Gill, Brian Paul. 2002. "Adoption Agencies and the Search for the Ideal Family, 1918–1965." In *Adoption in America: Historical Perspectives*, ed. E. Wayne Carp, 160–80. Ann Arbor: University of Michigan Press.

Gordon, Linda. 1999. *The Great Arizona Orphan Abduction.* Cambridge, MA: Harvard University Press.

Herman, Ellen. 2000. "The Difference Difference Makes: Justine Wise Polier and Religious Matching in Twentieth-Century Child Adoption." *Religion and American Culture* 10 (Winter): 57–98.

———. 2001. "Families Made by Science: Arthur Gesell and the Technologies of Modern Child Adoption." *Isis* 92, no. 3: 684–715.

———. 2002. "The Paradoxical Rationalization of Modern Adoption." *Journal of Social History* 36, no. 2: 339–85.

Hough, Mazie. 2001. " 'To Conserve the Best of the Old': The Impact of Professionalization on Adoption in Maine." *Maine History* 40, no. 3: 190–218.

May, Elaine Tyler. 1995. *Barren in the Promised Land: Childless Americans and the Pursuit of Happiness.* New York: Basic Books.

Melosh, Barbara. 2002. "Families by Design: 'Fitness' and 'Fit' in the Creation of Kin." In *Strangers and Kin: The American Way of Adoption.* Cambridge, MA: Harvard University Press.

Modell, Judith, and Naomi Dambacher. 1997. "Making a 'Real' Family: Matching and Cultural Biologism in American Adoption." *Adoption Quarterly* 1, no. 2: 3–33.

Stern, Alexandra Minna, and Howard Markel, eds. 2002. *Formative Years: Children's Health in the United States, 1880–2000.* Ann Arbor: University of Michigan Press.

SELECTED SOURCES ON THE HISTORY OF SECRECY IN ADOPTION

Baer, Janine M. 2004. *Growing in the Dark: Adoption Secrecy and Its Consequences.* Philadelphia: Xlibris.

Benet, Mary Kathleen. 1976. *The Politics of Adoption.* New York: Free Press.

Carp, E. Wayne. 1998. *Family Matters: Secrecy and Disclosure in the History of Adoption.* Cambridge, MA: Harvard University Press.

Cole, E., and Kay Donley. 1990. "History, Values, and Placement Policy Issues in Adoption." In *The Psychology of Adoption,* ed. David Brodzinsky and Marshall Schechter, 273–90. New York: Oxford University Press.

Modell, Judith. 2002. *A Sealed and Secret Kinship: Policies and Practices in American Adoption.* Providence, RI: Berghahn Press.

Wegar, Katarina. 1997. *Adoption, Identity, and Kinship: The Debate over Sealed Birth Records.* New Haven, CT: Yale University Press.

THE SEARCH MOVEMENT/ADOPTEE RIGHTS MOVEMENT AND THE CONTROVERSY SURROUNDING THE OPENING OF CLOSED RECORDS

Allen, Leslie. 1980. "Confirming the Constitutionality of Sealing Adoption Records." *Brooklyn Law Review* 46 (Summer): 717–45.

Baran, Annette, Reuben Pannor, and Arthur D. Sorosky. 1974. "Adoptive Parents and the Sealed Record Controversy." *Social Casework* 55 (November): 531–36.

Cahn, Naomi, and Jana Singer. 1999. "Adoption, Identity, and the Constitution: The Case for Opening Closed Records." *University of Pennsylvania Journal of Constitutional Law* 2 (December): 150–95.

Carp, E. Wayne. 2004. *Adoption Politics: Bastard Nation and Ballot Initiative 58.* Lawrence: University Press of Kansas.

Fisher, Florence. 1973. *The Search for Anna Fisher.* New York: Fawcett Crest.

Herman, Ellen. 2004. "We Have a Long Way to Go: Attitudes Toward Adoption." In *Families by Law: An Adoption Reader,* ed. Naomi R. Cahn and Joan Heifetz Hollinger, 134–35. New York: New York University Press.

Leighton, Kimberly. 2005. "Being Adopted and Being a Philosopher: Exploring Identity and the 'Desire to Know' Differently." In *Adoption Matters: Philosophical and Feminist Essays*, ed. Sally Haslanger and Charlotte Witt, 146–70. Ithaca, NY: Cornell University Press.

Lifton, Betty Jean. 1979. *Lost and Found: The Adoption Experience*. New York: Dial Press.

———. 1994. *Journey of the Adopted Self: A Quest for Wholeness*. New York: Basic Books.

Paton, Jean. 1954. *The Adopted Break Silence: The Experiences and Views of Forty Adults Who Were Adopted as Children*. Philadelphia: Life History Study Center.

——— (Ruthena Hill Kittson). 1968. *Orphan Voyage*. New York: Vantage.

Samuels, Elizabeth J. 2001. "The Idea of Adoption: An Inquiry into the History of Adult Adoptee Access to Birth Records." *Rutgers Law Review* 53 (Winter): 367–405.

Sorosky, Arthur D., Annette Baran, and Reuben Pannor. 1978. *The Adoption Triangle: Sealed or Opened Records: How They Affect Adoptees, Birth Parents, and Adoptive Parents*. San Antonio, TX: Corona Publishing.

Teller, Delores. 1998. "Open Records: The People Decide." *Adoptive Families* 31, no. 5: 26–27.

INFERTILITY, UNWANTED PREGNANCY, AND ILLEGITIMACY, PRE-1973

Brumberg, Joan Jacobs. 1984. " 'Ruined Girls': Changing Community Response to Illegitimacy in Upstate New York, 1890–1920." *Journal of Social History* 18, no. 2: 247–72.

Carp, E. Wayne. 1994. "Professional Social Workers, Adoption, and the Problem of Illegitimacy, 1915–1945." *Journal of Policy History* 6, no. 3: 161–84.

Gordon, Linda. 1994. *Pitied but Not Entitled: Single Mothers and the History of Welfare, 1890–1935*. New York: The Free Press.

Kunzel, Regina G. 1993. *Fallen Women, Problem Girls: Unmarried Mothers and the Professionalization of Benevolence, 1890–1945*. New Haven, CT: Yale University Press.

Ladd-Taylor, Molly, and Lauri Umansky, eds. 1998. *"Bad" Mothers: The Politics of Blame in Twentieth-Century America*. New York: New York University Press.

Marsh, Margaret, and Wanda Ronner. 1996. *The Empty Cradle: Infertility in America from Colonial Times to the Present*. Baltimore, MD: Johns Hopkins University Press.

May, Elaine Tyler. 1995. *Barren in the Promised Land: Childless Americans and the Pursuit of Happiness*. New York: Basic Books.

Morton, Marian J. 1993. *And Sin No More: Social Policy and Unwed Mothers in Cleveland, 1855–1990*. Columbus: Ohio State University Press.

Reagan, Leslie. 1997. *When Abortion Was a Crime: Women, Medicine, and Law in the United States, 1867–1973*. Berkeley: University of California Press.

Reilly, Philip. 1991. *The Surgical Solution: A History of Involuntary Sterilization in the United States*. Baltimore, MD: Johns Hopkins University Press.

Solinger, Rickie. 1992. *Wake Up Little Susie: Single Pregnancy and Race Before* Roe v. Wade. New York: Routledge.

Townsend, Rita, and Ann Perkins, eds. 1991. *Bitter Fruit: Women's Experiences of Unplanned Pregnancy, Abortion, and Adoption.* Alameda, CA: Hunter House.

Young, Leontine. 1954. *Out of Wedlock: A Study of the Problems of the Unmarried Mother and Her Child.* New York: McGraw-Hill.

INFERTILITY, TEEN PREGNANCY, AND NEW REPRODUCTIVE TECHNOLOGIES SINCE 1973

Bartholet, Elizabeth. 1999. *Family Bonds: Adoption, Infertility and the New World of Child Production.* Boston: Beacon Press.

Campbell, Courtney S., ed. 1992. *What Price Parenthood? Ethics and Assisted Reproduction.* Brookfield, VT: Ashgate Publishing Company.

Cornell, Drucilla. 2005. "Adoption and Its Progeny: Rethinking Family Law, Gender, and Sexual Difference." In *Adoption Matters: Philosophical and Feminist Essays*, ed. Sally Haslanger and Charlotte Witt, 19–46. Ithaca, NY: Cornell University Press.

Deans, Jill R. 2000. "Horton's Irony: Reading the Culture of Embryo Adoption." *Interdisciplinary Literary Studies: A Journal of Criticism and Theory* 2, no. 1: 1–20.

Dickenson, Donna L., ed. 2002. *Ethical Issues in Maternal-Fetal Medicine.* New York: Cambridge University Press.

Dooley, Delores. 2003. *Ethics of New Reproductive Technologies: Cases and Questions.* New York: Berghahn Books.

Field, Martha. 1993. "New Reproductive Technologies: Do New Reproductive Techniques Threaten the Family?" In *Family Matters: Readings on Family Lives and the Law*, ed. Martha Minow, 96–103. New York: New Press/W. W. Norton.

Ince, Susan. 1993. "Inside the Surrogate Industry." In *Family Matters: Readings on Family Lives and the Law*, ed. Martha Minow, 104–14. New York: New Press/W. W. Norton.

Inhorn, Marcia C., and Frank van Balen, eds. 2002. *Infertility Around the Globe: New Thinking on Childlessness, Gender, and Reproductive Technologies.* Berkeley: University of California Press.

James, David N. 1999. "Adoption and Restrictions on Abortion." In *Encyclopedia of Reproductive Technologies*, ed. Annette Burfoot, 125–27. Boulder, CO: Westview Press.

Lacey, Linda J. 1998. " 'O Wind Remind Him That I Have No Child': Infertility and Feminist Jurisprudence." *University of Michigan Journal of Gender and Law* 5, no. 1: 163–204.

Layne, Linda L. 2003. *Motherhood Lost: A Feminist Account of Pregnancy Loss in America.* New York: Routledge.

McElroy, Wendy. 2002. "Breeder Reactionaries: The 'Feminist' War on New Reproductive Technologies." In *Liberty for Women: Freedom and Feminism in the Twenty-First Century*, ed. Wendy McElroy, 267–78. Chicago: Ivan R. Dee/Independent Institute.

Meyers, Diana Tietjens, Kenneth Kipnis, and Cornelius F. Murphy, Jr., eds. *Kindred Matters: Rethinking the Philosophy of the Family.* Ithaca, NY: Cornell University Press.

Michie, Helena, and Naomi R. Cahn. 1997. *Confinements: Fertility and Infertility in Contemporary Culture.* New Brunswick, NJ: Rutgers University Press.

Nussbaum, Martha C. 2002. "Whether from Reason or Prejudice: Taking Money for Bodily Services." In *Liberty for Women: Freedom and Feminism in the Twenty-First Century,* ed. Wendy McElroy, 88–120. Chicago: Ivan R. Dee/Independent Institute.

Roberts, Dorothy. 1995. "The Genetic Tie." *University of Chicago Law Review* 62 (Winter): 209–73.

Shanley, Mary Lyndon. 2002. "Collaboration and Commodification in Assisted Procreation: Reflections on an Open Market and Anonymous Donation in Human Sperm and Eggs." *University of Massachusetts Law and Society Review* 36, no. 2: 257–85.

Shapiro, Vivian B., Janet R. Shapiro, and Isabel H. Paret. 2001. *Complex Adoption and Assisted Reproductive Technology: A Developmental Approach to Clinical Practice.* New York: The Guilford Press.

Skolnick, Arlene. 1998. "Solomon's Children: The New Biologism, Psychological Parenthood, Attachment Theory, and the Best Interests Standard." In *All Our Families: New Policies for a New Century,* ed. Mary Ann Mason, Arlene Skolnick, and Stephen D. Sugarman, 236–55. New York: Oxford University Press.

Sollinger, Rickie. 2002. *Beggars and Choosers: How the Politics of Choice Shapes Adoption, Abortion, and Welfare in the United States.* New York: Hill & Wang.

Stevens, Jacqueline. 2005. "Methods of Adoption: Eliminating the Genetic Privilege." In *Adoption Matters: Philosophical and Feminist Essays,* ed. Sally Haslanger and Charlotte Witt, 68–95. Ithaca, NY: Cornell University Press.

Wegar, Katarina. 1997. "In Search of Bad Mothers: Social Constructions of Birth and Adoptive Motherhood." *Women's Studies International Forum* 20, no. 1: 77–86.

Williams, Constance Willard. 1995. "Teenage Motherhood." In *Mental Health, Racism, and Sexism,* ed. Charles V. Willie et al., 199–216. Pittsburgh: University of Pittsburgh Press.

Woliver, Laura R. 2002. *The Political Geographies of Pregnancy.* Urbana: University of Illinois Press.

ADOPTION WITH CONTACT, OPEN, OR COOPERATIVE ADOPTION: HISTORY, PSYCHOLOGY, AND LAW

Allen, Anita L. 2005. "Open Adoption Is Not for Everyone." In *Adoption Matters: Philosophical and Feminist Essays,* ed. Sally Haslanger and Charlotte Witt, 47–67. Ithaca, NY: Cornell University Press.

Appell, Annette R. 1995. "Blending Families Through Adoption: Implications for Collaborative Adoption Law and Practice." *Boston University Law Review* 75 (September): 997–1061.

————. 1998. "Increasing Options to Improve Permanency: Considerations in Drafting an Adoption with Contact Statute." *Children's Legal Rights Journal* 18, no. 4: 24–51.

Baran, Annette, and Reuben Pannor. 1990. "Open Adoption." In *The Psychology of Adoption*, ed. David Brodzinsky and Marshall Schechter, 316–22. New York: Oxford University Press.

Baran, Annette, Reuben Pannor, and Arthur D. Sorosky. 1976. "Open Adoption." *Social Work* 21, no. 2: 97–101.

Brooks, Susan L. 2001. "The Case for Adoption Alternatives." *Family Court Review* 39, no. 1: 43–53.

Cahn, Naomi. 2002. "Birthing Relationships." *Wisconsin Women's Law Journal* 17 (Spring): 163–204.

Caplan, Lincoln. 1990. *An Open Adoption*. New York: Farrar, Straus & Giroux.

Chapman, Cathy, Patricia Dorner, Kathleen Silber, and Terry Winterberg. 1986. "Meeting the Needs of the Adoption Triangle Through Open Adoption: The Birthmother." *Child and Adolescent Social Work* 3 (Winter): 203–13.

————. 1987. "Meeting the Needs of the Adoption Triangle Through Open Adoption: The Adoptive Parent." *Child and Adolescent Social Work* 4 (Spring): 3–13.

————. 1987b. "Meeting the Needs of the Adoption Triangle Through Open Adoption: The Adoptee." *Child and Adolescent Social Work* 4 (Summer): 78–91.

Child Welfare League of America. 2004. "Post-Adoption Contact: CWLA 2000 Standards." In *Families by Law: An Adoption Reader*, ed. Naomi R. Cahn and Joan Heifetz Hollinger, 174–75. New York: New York University Press.

Gritter, James. 1997. *The Spirit of Open Adoption*. Washington, DC: CWLA Press.

Gross, Harriet E. 1997. "Variants of Open Adoptions: The Early Years." *Marriage and Family Review* 25, no. 1: 19–42.

Hollinger, Joan H. 1988/2004. "Appendix 13-B: Open Adoption or Post-Adoption Agreements." In *Adoption Law and Practice*, ed. Joan H. Hollinger et al. New York: Matthew Bender.

McGough, L. S., and A. Peltier-Falahahwazi. 1999. "Secrets and Lies: A Model Statute for Cooperative Adoption." *Louisiana Law Review* 60 (Fall): 13–32.

Modell, Judith S. 2001. "Open Adoption: Extending Families, Exchanging Facts." In *New Directions in Anthropological Kinship*, ed. Linda Stone, 246–63. Lanham, MD: Rowman and Littlefield.

National Adoption Information Clearinghouse. 2004. "Cooperative Adoption: Contact Between Adoption Families and Birth Families After Finalization." Reprinted in *Adoption Library. Adoption.com*. http://library.adoption.com/ Birth-Parents-After-Adoption/Cooperative-Adoptions-Contact-Between-Adoptive-Families-and-Birth-Families-After-Finalization/article/94/1.html.

Pavao, Joyce Maguire. 1998. *The Family of Adoption*. Boston: Beacon Press.

Rappaport, Bruce M. 1992. *The Open Adoption Book*. New York: Macmillan.

Ruskai, Melina Lois, and Sharon Kaplan Roszia. 1993. *The Open Adoption Experience*. New York: HarperCollins.

Savage, Dan. 1999. *The Kid: What Happened After My Boyfriend and I Decided to Go Get Pregnant: An Adoption Story.* New York: Dutton.

Silber, Kathleen, and Patricia M. Dorner. 1990. *Children of Open Adoption and Their Families.* Dallas, TX: Corona Publishing.

Silverberg, A. 1996. "Open Adoption: Is It Legally Enforceable? Should It Be?" *Adoptive Families* 29, no. 6: 14–16.

Young, Alison H. 1998. "Reconceiving the Family: Challenging the Paradigm of the Exclusive Family." *The American University Journal of Gender and Law* 6, no. 3: 505–56.

16 Crossing Boundaries: Issues and Controversies in Contemporary Foster Care and Adoption

SELECTED RESOURCES ON DEPENDENT CHILDREN AND FOSTER CARE, POST-1945

Abramovitz, Mimi. 1988. "Aid to Families with Dependent Children: Single Mothers in the Twentieth Century." In *Regulating the Lives of Women: Social Welfare Policy from Colonial Times to the Present*, 313–42. Boston: South End Press.

Bartholet, Elizabeth. 2000. *Nobody's Children: Abuse and Neglect, Foster Drift, and the Adoption Alternative*. Boston: Beacon Press.

———. 2004. "The Challenge of Children's Rights Advocacy: Problems and Progress in the Area of Child Abuse and Neglect." *Whittier Journal of Child and Family Advocacy* 3 (Spring): 215–30.

Bell, Winifred. 1965. *Aid to Dependent Children*. New York: Columbia University Press.

Bernstein, Nina. 2002. *The Lost Children of Wilder: The Epic Struggle to Change Foster Care*. New York: Vintage Books.

Billingsley, Andrew, and Jeanne M. Giovannoni. 1972. *Children of the Storm: Black Children and American Child Welfare*. New York: Harcourt, Brace, Jovanovich.

Cahn, Naomi R. 1999. "Children's Interest in a Familial Context: Poverty, Foster Care, and Adoption." *Ohio State University Law Journal* 60, no. 6: 1189–90.

Cauthen, Nancy K., and Edwin Amenta. 1996. "Not for Widows Only: Institutional Politics and the Formative Years of Aid to Dependent Children." *American Sociological Review* 61, no. 3: 427–48.

Dill, Bonnie Thornton et al. 1999. "Race, Family Values, and Welfare Reform." In *A New Introduction to Poverty: The Role of Race, Power, and Politics*, ed. Louis Kushnick and James Jennings, 263–86. New York: New York University Press.

Edin, Kathryn, and Laura Lein. 1997. *Making Ends Meet: How Welfare Mothers Survive Welfare and Low-Wage Work*. New York: Russell Sage Foundation.

Geiser, Robert L. 1995. "The Shuffled Child and Foster Care." In *Child Abuse: A Multidisciplinary Survey: Protecting Abused Children: Protective Services and Proceedings, Foster Care, Termination of Parental Rights*, ed. Byrgen Finkelman, 37–42. New York: Garland Publishing.

Gelles, Richard J. 1996. *The Book of David: How Preserving Families Can Cost Children's Lives*. New York: Basic Books.

Gittens, Joan. 1994. *Poor Relations: The Children of the State of Illinois, 1818–1990*. Urbana: University of Illinois Press.

Goldberg, Gertrude Schaffner, and Sheila D. Collins. 2001. *Washington's New Poor Law: Welfare Reform and the Roads Not Taken, 1935 to the Present*. New York: Apex Press.

Guggenheim, Martin. 1999. "The Foster Care Dilemma and What to Do About It: Is the Problem That Too Many Children Are Not Being Adopted Out of Foster Care or That Too Many Children Are Entering Foster Care?" *University of Pennsylvania Journal of Constitutional Law* 2, no. 1: 141–49.

Hegar, Rebecca L., and Maria Scannapieco, eds. 1999. *Kinship Foster Care: Policy, Practice, and Research*. New York: Oxford University Press.

Jackson, Sondra, and Sheryl Brisset-Chapman. 1999. *Serving African American Children: Child Welfare Perspectives*. New Brunswick, NJ: Transaction Publishers.

Jimenez, Mary Ann. 1990. "Permanency Planning and the Child Abuse Prevention and Treatment Act: The Paradox of Child Welfare Policy." *Journal of Sociology and Social Welfare* 17, no. 3: 54–70.

Johnson, Elizabeth I., and Jane Waldfogel. 2002. "Parental Incarceration: Recent Trends and Implications for Child Welfare." *Social Service Review* 76, no. 3: 460–79.

Kelly, Greg, and Robbie Gilligan, eds. 1999. *Issues in Foster Care: Policy Practice and Research*. London: Jessica Kingsley Publishers.

Levy, Denise Urias, and Sonya Michel. 2002. "More Can Be Less: Child Care and Welfare Reform in the United States." In *Child Care Policy at the Crossroads: Gender and Welfare State Restructuring*, ed. Sonya Michel and Rianne Mahon, 239–66. New York: Routledge.

Lindsey, Duncan. 1994. *The Welfare of Children*. New York: Oxford University Press.

Morton, Marian J. 2000. "Institutionalizing Inequalities: Black Children and Child Welfare in Cleveland, 1859–1998." *Journal of Social History* 34, no. 1: 141–62.

Mushlin, Michael. 1994. "Unsafe Havens: The Case for Constitutional Protection of Foster Children from Abuse and Neglect." In *Child, Parent and State: Law and Policy Reader*, ed. S. Randall Humm et al., 186–223. Philadelphia: Temple University Press.

Patterson, James T. 1981. *America's Struggle Against Poverty, 1900–1980*. Cambridge, MA: Harvard Univesity Press.

Pelton, Leroy H. 1989. *For Reasons of Poverty: A Critical Analysis of the Public Child Welfare System of the United States*. New York: Praeger.

Piven, Frances Fox, and Richard A. Cloward. 1971. *Regulating the Poor: The Functions of Public Welfare*. New York: Random House.

Power, Martha Bauman, and Brenda Krause Eheart. 2000. "From Foster Care to Fostering Care: The Need for Community." *Sociological Quarterly* 41, no. 1: 85–102.

Roberts, Dorothy. 2003. *Shattered Bonds: The Color of Child Welfare*. New York: Basic Books.

Rosner, David, and Gerald Markowitz. 1993. "Race in Foster Care." *Dissent* 40, no. 2: 233–37.

Schorr, Nanette. 1993. "Foster Care and the Politics of Compassion." In *Family Matters: Readings on Family Lives and the Law*, ed. Martha Minow, 117–24. New York: New Press/W. W. Norton.

Shirk, Martha, and Gary Stangler. 2004. *On Their Own: What Happens to Kids When They Age Out of the Foster Care System*. Boulder, CO: Westview Books.

Taylor, Delores, and Philip Starr. 1995. "Foster Parenting: An Integrative Review of the Literature." In *Child Abuse: A Multidisciplinary Survey: Protecting Abused Children: Protective Services and Proceedings, Foster Care, Termination of Parental Rights*, ed. Byrgen Finkelman, 1–16. New York: Garland Publishing.

Toth, Jennifer. 1998. *Orphans of the Living: Stories of America's Children in Foster Care*. New York: Free Press.

SELECTED SOURCES ON THE "RE-DISCOVERY" OF CHILD ABUSE IN THE LATE TWENTIETH CENTURY

Carp, E. Wayne. 1991. "Family History, Family Violence: A Review Essay." *Journal of Policy History* 3, no. 2: 203–23.

Costin, Lela B., Howard Jacob Karger, and David Sotesz. 1996. *The Politics of Child Abuse in America*. New York: Oxford University Press.

Crewdson, John. 1988. *By Silence Betrayed: Sexual Abuse of Children in America*. Boston: Little, Brown.

Demos, John. 1986. "Child Abuse in Context: An Historian's Perspective." In *Past, Present, and Personal: The Family and Life Course in America*, ed. John Demos, 68–91. New York: Oxford University Press.

Dorne, Clifford K. 2002. *An Introduction to Child Maltreatment in the United States: History, Public Policy, and Research*. 3rd ed. Monsey, NY: Willow Tree Press.

Evans, Hughes. 2002. "The Discovery of Child Sexual Abuse in America." In *Formative Years: Children's Health in the United States, 1880–2000*, ed. Alexandra Minna Stern and Howard Markel, 233–59. Ann Arbor: University of Michigan Press.

Finkelman, Byrgen, ed. 1995. *Child Abuse: A Multidisciplinary Survey: Protecting Abused Children: Protective Services and Proceedings, Foster Care, Termination of Parental Rights*. New York: Garland Publishing.

Pleck, Elizabeth. 1987. *Domestic Tyranny: The Making of Social Policy Against Family Violence from Colonial Times to the Present*. New York: Oxford University Press.

Wexler, Robert. 1990. *Wounded Innocents: The Real Victims of the War Against Child Abuse*. Buffalo, NY: Prometheus Books.

ADOPTION AND FOSTER CARE BY SINGLE, GAY, AND LESBIAN PARENTS

Benkov, Laura. 1994. *Reinventing the Family: The Emerging Story of Lesbian and Gay Parents.* New York: Crown.

Bozett, Frederick W. 1987. *Gay and Lesbian Parents.* New York: Praeger.

Brill, Stephanie A. 2001. *The Queer Parent's Primer: A Lesbian and Gay Families' Guide to Navigating the Straight World.* Oakland, CA: New Harbinger.

Buell, Carol. 2001. "Legal Issues Affecting Alternative Families: A Therapist's Primer." In *Gay and Lesbian Parenting*, ed. Deborah F. Glazer and Jack Drescher, 7–30. New York: Haworth Medical Press.

Burns, Kate, ed. 2005. *Gay and Lesbian Families.* Detroit: Greenhaven Press.

Crespi, Lee. 2001. "And Baby Makes Three: A Dynamic Look at Development and Conflict in Lesbian Families." In *Gay and Lesbian Parenting*, ed. Deborah F. Glazer and Jack Drescher, 7–30. New York: Haworth Medical Press.

Dowd, Nancy E. "Single Parent Adoption." In *Families by Law: An Adoption Reader*, ed. Naomi R. Cahn and Joan Heifetz Hollinger, 252–56. New York: New York University Press.

Evan B. Donaldson Adoption Institute. 2005. "Adoption by Lesbians and Gays: A National Survey of Adoption Agency Policies, Practices, and Attitudes." http://www.adoptioninstitute.org. Reprinted as "Gay Adoption is Commonly Accepted," in *Gay And Lesbian Families*, ed. Kate Burns, 46–54. Detroit: Greenhaven Press.

Ferrero, Eric, Joshua Freker, and Travis Foster. 2005. *Too High a Price: The Case Against Restricting Gay Parenting.* New York: ACLU Lesbian and Gay Rights Project.

Green, George D., and Frederick W. Bozett. 1991. "Lesbian Mothers and Gay Fathers." In *Homosexuality: Research Implications for Public Policy*, ed. John C. Gonsiorek and James D. Weinrich, 197–214. Thousand Oaks, CA: Sage.

Green, Jesse. 1999. *The Velveteen Father: An Unexpected Journey to Parenthood.* New York: Villard.

Hollinger, Joan Heifetz. 2004. "Second Parent Adoptions Protect Children with Two Mothers or Two Fathers." In *Families by Law: An Adoption Reader*, ed. Naomi R. Cahn and Joan Heifetz Hollinger, 235–38. New York: New York University Press.

Mallon, Gerald P. 1999. *Let's Get This Straight: A Gay and Lesbian-Affirming Approach to Child Welfare.* New York: Columbia University Press.

———. 2000. "Gay Men and Lesbians as Adoptive Parents." *Journal of Gay and Lesbian Social Services* 11, no. 4: 1–21.

———. 2004. *Gay Men Choosing Adoption.* New York: Columbia University Press.

Martin, April. 1993. "Adoption." In *The Lesbian and Gay Parenting Handbook: Creating and Raising Our Families*, 117–56. New York: HarperPerennial.

National Adoption Information Clearinghouse. April 2000. *Gay and Lesbian Adoptive Parents: Resources for Professionals and Parents.* http://www.calib.com/naic/pubs/f_gay.cfm.

Patterson, Charlotte J. 1994. "Lesbian and Gay Couples Considering Parenthood: An Agenda for Research, Service, and Advocacy." In *Social Services for Gay and Lesbian Couples*, ed. L. A. Kurdek, 33–56. New York: Harrington Park Press.

———. 1997. "Gay Fathers." In *The Role of the Father in Child Development*, ed. Michael E. Lamb, 245–60. New York: John Wiley.

Ricketts, Wendell. 1991. *Lesbians and Gay Men as Foster Parents*. Portland, ME: National Child Welfare Resource Center/Center for Child and Family Policy, Edmund S. Muskie Institute of Public Affairs/University of Southern Maine.

Stacey, Judith, and Timothy J. Biblarz. 2001. "(How) Does the Sexual Orientation of Parents Matter?" *American Sociological Review* 66, no. 2: 159–83.

Stanton, Glenn T., and Bill Maier. 2004. *Marriage on Trial: The Case Against Same-Sex Marriage and Parenting*. Downers Grove, IL: InterVarsity Press.

"State Appeals Court Rulings That Deny or Approve Second Parent Adoption by Same-Sex Couples." In *Families by Law: An Adoption Reader*, ed. Naomi R. Cahn and Joan Heifetz Hollinger, 239–47. New York: New York University Press.

Tobias, Sarah. 2005. "Several Steps Behind: Gay and Lesbian Adoption." In *Adoption Matters: Philosophical and Feminist Essays*, ed. Sally Haslanger and Charlotte Witt, 95–111. Ithaca, NY: Cornell University Press.

SOURCES FOCUSING ON BOTH TRANSRACIAL AND INTERNATIONAL ADOPTION

Bartholet, Elizabeth. 1993. *Family Bonds: Adoption and the Politics of Parenting*. Boston: Houghton Mifflin.

Bergquist, Kathleen Ja Sook. 2004. "International Asian Adoption: In the Best Interest of the Child?" *Texas Wesleyan Law Review* 10 (Spring): 343–50.

Briggs, Laura. 2003. "Mother, Child, Race, and Nation: The Visual Iconography of Rescue and the Politics of Transnational and Transracial Adoption." *Gender and History* 15, no. 2: 179–200.

Feigelman, William, and Arnold R. Silverman. 1984. "The Long-Term Effects of Transracial Adoption." *Social Service Review* 58, no. 4: 588–602.

Freundlich, Madelyn. 2000. *Adoption and Ethics: The Role of Race, Culture, and National Origin*. Washington, DC: CWLA.

Perry, Twila. 1998/2004. "Transracial and International Adoption: Mothers, Hierarchy, Race, and Feminist Legal Theory." *Yale Journal of Law and Feminism* 10, no. 1: 101–45. Excerpted in *Families by Law: An Adoption Reader*, ed. Naomi R. Cahn and Joan Heifetz Hollinger, 265–69. New York: New York University Press.

Simon, Rita J., and Howard Alstein. 2000. *Adoption Across Borders: Serving the Children in Transracial and Intercountry Adoption*. Lanham, MD: Rowman and Littlefield.

SELECTED TRANSRACIAL ADOPTION SOURCES

Banks, R. Richard. 1998/2004. "The Color of Desire: Fulfilling Adoptive Parents' Racial Preferences Through Disciminatory State Action." *Yale Law Journal* 107 (January): 875–964. Excerpted in *Families by Law: An Adoption Reader*, ed. Naomi R. Cahn and Joan Heifetz Hollinger, 200–205. New York: New York University Press.

Bartholet, Elizabeth. 1991/2003. "Where Do Black Children Belong: The Politics of Race Matching in Adoption." *University of Pennsylvania Law Review* 163 (May): 1163–1256. Excerpted in *Mixed Race America and the Law*, ed. Kevin J. Johnson, 353–63. New York: New York University Press.

Colker, Ruth. 1995/2001. "Bi: Race, Sexual Orientation, Gender and Disability." *Ohio State University Law Journal* 56, no. 1: 1–67. Excerpted in *Mixed Race America and the Law*, ed. Kevin J. Johnson, 375–78. New York: New York University Press.

Collmeyer, Patricia M. 1995. "From 'Operation Brown Baby' to 'Opportunity': The Placement of Children of Color at the Boys and Girls Aid Society of Oregon." *Child Welfare* 74 (January/February): 242–63.

Day, Dawn. 1979. *The Adoption of Black Children: Counteracting Institutional Discrimination.* Lexington, MA: Lexington Books.

Dobie, Kathy. 1989. "Nobody's Child: The Battle over Interracial Adoption." *Village Voice* 8 (August): 18–.

Fenton, Zanita E. 1993/2003. "In a World Not Their Own: The Adoption of Black Children." *Harvard Blackletter Journal* 10: 39–66. Excerpted in *Mixed Race America and the Law*, ed. Kevin J. Johnson, 368–74. New York: New York University Press.

Fogg-Davis, Hawley. 2002. *The Ethics of Transracial Adoption.* Ithaca, NY: Cornell University Press.

————. 2003. "Racial Intimacy and Racial Politics: Adoption in the U.S. and Brazil." *National Political Science Review* 9, no. 1: 76–86.

Gaber, Ivor, and Jane Aldridge. 1994. *In the Best Interest of the Child: Culture, Identity and Transracial Adoption.* London: Free Association Books.

Haslanger, Sally. 2005. "You Mixed? Racial Identity Without Racial Biology." In *Adoption Matters: Philosophical and Feminist Essays*, ed. Sally Haslanger and Charlotte Witt, 265–90. Ithaca, NY: Cornell University Press.

Holmes, Gilbert A. 1995. "The Extended Family System in the Black Community: A Child-Centered Model for Adoption Policy." *Temple Law Review* 68 (Winter): 1649–85. Excerpted in *Families by Law: An Adoption Reader*, ed. Naomi R. Cahn and Joan Heifetz Hollinger, 119–22. New York: New York University Press.

Howe, Ruth-Arlene W. 1997. "Transracial Adoption (TRA): Old Prejudices and Discrimination Float under a New Halo." *Boston University Public Interest Law Journal* 6 (Winter): 409–72.

Kennedy, Randall. 1984. "Orphans of Separatism: The Painful Politics of Transracial Adoption." *The American Prospect* 17 (Spring): 40–42.

———. 2003. *Interracial Intimacies: Sex, Marriage, Identity, and Adoption.* New York: Pantheon.

Kupenda, Angela Mae et al. 1998/1999. "Law, Life and Literature: Using Literature and Life to Expose Transracial Adoption Laws as Adoption on a One-Way Street." *Buffalo Public Interest Law Journal* 17: 43–69.

Ladner, Joyce A. 1977. *Mixed Families: Adopting Across Racial Boundaries.* Garden City, NY: Anchor Press/Doubleday.

Ladner, Joyce A., and Ruby M. Gourdine. 1995. "Transracial Adoptions." In *Mental Health, Racism, and Sexism,* ed. Charles V. Willie et al., 171–90. Pittsburgh: University of Pittsburgh Press.

Macaulay, Jacqueline, and Stewart Macaulay. 1995. "Adoption for Black Children: A Case Study of Expert Discretion." In *Child, Family and State,* ed. Robert H. Mnookin and D. Kelly Weisberg, 790–810. Boston: Little, Brown.

Maillard, Kevin Noble. 2003/2004. "Parental Ratification: Legal Manifestations of Cultural Authenticity in Cross-Racial Adoption." *American Indian Law Review* 28, no. 1: 107–40.

McRoy, Ruth G., and Zena Oglesby et al. 1997. "Achieving Same-Race Adoptive Placements for African American Children: Culturally Sensitive Practice Approaches." *Child Welfare* 76, no. 1: 85–105.

McRoy, Ruth G., and Louis A. Zurcher Jr. 1983. *Transracial and Inracial Adoptees: The Adolescent Years.* Sprinfield, IL: Charles Thomas.

Patton, Sandra. 2000. *Birth Marks: Transracial Adoption in Contemporary America.* New York: New York University Press.

Perry, Twila L. 1993/2003. "The Transracial Adoption Controversy: An Analysis of Discourse and Subordination." *New York University Review of Law and Social Change* 21, no. 1: 33–108. Excerpted in *Mixed Race America and the Law,* ed. Kevin J. Johnson, 364–67. New York: New York University Press.

Roberts, Dorothy. 2005. "Feminism, Race, and Adoption Policy." In *Adoption Matters: Philosophical and Feminist Essays,* ed. Sally Haslanger and Charlotte Witt, 234–46. Ithaca, NY: Cornell University Press.

Rush, Sharon E. 2000. *Loving Across the Color Line: A White Adoptive Mother Learns About Race.* Lanham, MD: Rowman and Littlefield.

Satz, Martha. 2001. "Should Whites Adopt African American Children? One Family's Phenomenological Response." In *Imagining Adoption: Essays on Literature and Culture,* ed. Marianne Novy, 267–76. Ann Arbor: University of Michigan.

Simon, Rita J., and Howard Altstein. 2002. *Adoption, Race, and Identity: From Infancy to Young Adulthood.* New Brunswick, NJ: Transaction Publishers.

Williams, Patricia J. 1994. "Spare Parts, Family Values, Old Children, Cheap." *New England Law Review* 28 (Summer): 913–27.

Woodhouse, Barbara Bennett. 1995/2004. "Are You My Mother? Conceptualizing Children's Identity Rights in Transracial Adoption." *Duke Journal of Gender Law and Policy* 2: 107–29. Excerpted in *Families by Law: An Adoption Reader,* ed. Naomi R. Cahn and Joan Heifetz Hollinger, 194–99. New York: New York University Press.

THE HISTORY OF ADOPTION/ABDUCTION OF NATIVE AMERICAN CHILDREN AND THE INDIAN CHILD WELFARE ACT OF 1978

Fanschel, David. 1972. *Far from the Reservation: The Transracial Adoption of Indian Children.* Metuchen, NJ: Scarecrow Press.

Flood, Renee Sansom. 1995. *Lost Bird of Wounded Knee: Spirit of the Lakota.* New York: Scribner's.

Garner, Suzanne. 1993. "The Indian Child Welfare Act: A Review." *Wicazo Sa Review* 9, no. 1: 47–51.

Graham, Lorie M. 2001. " 'The Past Never Vanishes': A Contextual Critique of Existing Indian Family Doctrine." *American Indian Law Review* 23, no. 1: 1–54. Excerpted in *Mixed Race America and the Law*, ed. Kevin J. Johnson, 385–92. New York: New York University Press.

Hawkins-Leon, Cynthia G. 1997–1998. "The Indian Child Welfare Act and the African American Tribe: Facing the Adoption Crisis." *Brandeis Journal of Family Law* 36 (Spring): 201–18.

Hollinger, Joan Heifetz. 2004. "Who Are Indian Children within the Scope of the Federal Indian Child Welfare Act (ICWA)?" In *Families by Law: An Adoption Reader*, ed. Naomi R. Cahn and Joan Heifetz Hollinger, 221–27. New York: New York University Press.

Johnson, Troy R. 1999. "The State and the American Indian: Who Gets the Indian Child?" *Wicazo Sa Review* 14, no. 1: 197–214.

Jones, Sondra. 1999. " 'Redeeming' the Indian: The Enslavement of Indian Children in New Mexico and Utah." *Utah Historical Quarterly* 67, no. 3: 220–41.

Kennedy, Randall. 2003. "Race, Children, and Custody Battles: The Special Status of Native Americans." In *Interracial Intimacies: Sex, Marriage, Identities and Adoption*, 480–518. New York: Pantheon.

MacEachron, Ann E., Nora S. Gustavsson, Suzanne Cross, and Allison Lewis. 1996. "The Effectiveness of the Indian Child Welfare Act of 1978." *Social Service Review* 70, no. 3: 451–63.

Metteer, Christine. 1996/2003. "*Pigs in Heaven*: A Parable of Native American Adoption under the Indian Child Welfare Act." *Arizona State Law Journal* 28 (Summer): 589. Excerpted in *Families by Law: An Adoption Reader*, ed. Naomi R. Cahn and Joan Heifetz Hollinger, 228–32. New York: New York University Press.

Strong, Paula Turner. 2001. "To Forget Their Tongue, Their Name, Their Whole Relation: Extra-Tribal Adoption, the Indian Child Welfare Act, and the Trope of Captivity." In *Relative Values: Reconfiguring Kinship Studies*, ed. Sarah Franklin and Susan McKinnon, 468–94. Durham, NC: Duke University Press.

SELECTED INTERNATIONAL ADOPTION RESOURCES

Alstein, Howard, and Rita James Simon, eds. 1990. *Intercountry Adoption: A Multinational Perspective.* New York: Praeger.

Bartholet, Elizabeth. 1988–. "International Adoption: Overview." In *Adoption Law and Practice*, ed. Joan H. Hollinger et al., 1–43. New York: Matthew Bender.

Castaneda, Claudia. 2001. "Incorporating the Transnational Adoptee." In *Imagining Adoption: Essays on Literature and Culture*, ed. Marianne Novy, 277–300. Ann Arbor: University of Michigan Press.

Hermann, Kenneth J., Jr., and Barbara Kaspar. 1992. "International Adoption: The Exploitation of Women and Children." *Afflia* 7 (Spring): 45–58.

Hoksbergen, Rene. 2002. "Experiences of Dutch Families Who Parent an Adopted Romanian Child." *Journal of Development and Behavioral Pediatrics* 6 (December): 403–9.

Hollinger, Joan Heiftetz. 2004. "Intercountry Adoption: A Frontier without Borders." In *Families by Law: An Adoption Reader*, ed. Naomi R. Cahn and Joan Heifetz Hollinger, 215–18. New York: New York University Press.

Hollingsworth, Leslie Doty. 2003. "International Adoption Among Families in the United States: Considerations of Social Justice." *Social Work* 48, no. 2: 209–18.

Judge, Sharon Lesar. 1999. "Eastern European Adoptions: Current Status and Implications for Intervention." *Topics in Early Childhood Special Education* 19 (Winter): 244–52.

Lemke Muniz de Faria, Yara-Colette. 2003. " 'Germany's "Brown Babies" Must Be Helped! Will You?' U.S. Adoption Plans for Afro-German Children, 1950–1955." *Callaloo* 26, no. 2: 342–62.

Lovelock, Kirsten. 2000. "Intercountry Adoption as a Migratory Practice: A Comparative Analysis of Intercountry Adoption and Immigration Policy and Practice in the United States, Canada, and New Zealand in the Post–WWII Period." *International Migration Review* 34, no. 3: 907–49.

Maguire, Moira J. 2002. "Foreign Adoptions and the Evolution of Irish Adoption Policy, 1945–52." *Journal of Social History* 36, no. 2: 387–404.

Park, Soon Ho. 1994. "Forced Child Migration: Korea-Born Intercountry Adoptees in the United States." Ph.D. diss., University of Hawaii.

Register, Cheri. 1990. *Are Those Kids Yours? American Families with Children Adopted from Other Countries*. New York: Free Press.

Van Leeuwen, Michelle. 1999. "The Politics of Adoptions Across Borders: Whose Interests Are Served? A Look at the Emerging Markets of Infants from China." *Pacific Rim Law and Policy Journal* 8 (January): 189–218.

Index

About the Editor
and Contributors

LORI ASKELAND is associate professor of English at Wittenberg University, where she also teaches courses in Women's Studies and Africana Studies. She has published numerous scholarly articles and book reviews on family creation in nineteenth-century American literature and culture, and has contributed articles to several specialized encyclopedias on topics related to the history of adoption, foster care, and the American family. She is currently at work on a memoir of her experiences adopting her nieces from foster care, entitled *Grafting: A Love Story*.

ELIZABETH BARTHOLET is the Morris Wasserstein Public Interest Professor of Law at Harvard Law School, where she teaches civil rights and family law, specializing in child welfare, adoption, and reproductive technology. Before joining the Harvard faculty, she was engaged in civil rights and public interest work, first with the NAACP Legal Defense Fund, and later as founder and director of the Legal Action Center, a nonprofit organization in New York City focused on criminal justice and substance-abuse issues. Professor Bartholet's publications include *Nobody's Children: Abuse and Neglect, Foster Drift, and the Adoption Alternative* (1999) and *Family Bonds: Adoption, Infertility, and the New World of Child Production* (1999), along with many articles and legal reviews. Professor Bartholet has won several awards for her writing and her related advocacy work in the area of adoption and child welfare.

DIANNE CREAGH is a graduate student at Stony Brook University in New York. Her dissertation focuses on the history of Catholic and Jewish adoption and foster care in New York City. She has presented her work at national meetings of the Organization of American Historians and the Berkshire Conference on the History of Women, and she has taught many courses in U.S. social and cultural history, women's history, and feminist studies.

MARILYN IRVIN HOLT has been an adjunct professor at the University of Kansas and Emporia State University. She has written for a number of academic journals, and served as a research consultant for the PBS American Experience documentaries. Her book publications include *Orphan Trains: Placing Out in America* (1992) and *Indian Orphanages* (2001).

CLAUDIA NELSON is associate professor of English at Texas A&M University. She is the author of *Boys Will Be Girls: The Feminine Ethic and British Children's Fiction, 1857–1917* (1991), *Invisible Men: Fatherhood in Victorian Periodicals, 1850–1910* (1995), and *Little Strangers: Portrayals of Adoption and Foster Care in America, 1850–1929* (2003). She has also coedited three volumes of critical essays, most recently *Sexual Pedagogies: Sex Education in Britain, Australia, and America, 1878–2000* (2004), and is the general editor of the book series Studies in Childhood from 1700 to the Present.

MARTHA SATZ, assistant professor of English at Southern Methodist University, has exploited her dual academic background in philosophy and literature to publish essays on such diverse topics as Jane Austen, Richard Wright, the Holocaust, issues of gender and race in children's readings, and disability studies. The adoptive mother of two biracial children, she has published several essays on transracial adoption. She is currently at work on a book focused on adoption, race, and literature.